W9-DCJ-191

Work-Family Challenges for Low-Income Parents and Their Children

Edited by

Ann C. Crouter
Alan Booth
The Pennsylvania State University

LAWRENCE ERLBAUM ASSOCIATES, PUBLISHERS
2004   Mahwah, New Jersey   London

Editor:	Bill Webber
Editorial Assistant:	Kristin Duch
Cover Design:	Sean Trane Sciarrone
Textbook Production Manager:	Paul Smolenski
Text and Cover Printer:	Victor Graphics, Inc.

Camera ready copy for this book was provided by the editors.

Copyright © 2004 by Lawrence Erlbaum Associates, Inc.
All rights reserved. No part of this book may be reproduced in any form, by photostat, microform, retrieval system, or any other means, without prior written permission of the publisher.

Lawrence Erlbaum Associates, Inc., Publishers
10 Industrial Avenue
Mahwah, New Jersey 07430
www.erlbaum.com

Library of Congress Cataloging-in-Publication Data

Work-family challenges for low-income parents and their children / edited by Alan Booth, Ann C. Crouter.
    p. cm.
    Includes bibliographical references and index.
ISBN 0-8058-4600-X (cloth : alk. paper)
ISBN 0-8058-5077-5 (pbk. : alk. paper)
1. Work and family—United States. 2. Working poor—United States.
   3. Working poor—Government policy—United States. 4. Poor children—Services for—United States. I. Booth, Alan, 1935–
  II. Crouter, Ann C.
HD4904.25.W725   2004
362.85'0973—dc22
                                2003049525
                                     CIP

Books published by Lawrence Erlbaum Associates are printed on acid-free paper, and their bindings are chosen for strength and durability.

Printed in the United States of America
10 9 8 7 6 5 4 3 2 1

Andrew London

Work-Family Challenges for Low-Income Parents and Their Children

Contents

CONTENTS vii

Preface

The recent welfare legislation that has pushed many single mothers into the paid labor force has sparked renewed interest in and debate about the plight of low-income and working poor families in the United States today. Much of the extant research on work and family issues has focused on middle-class and professional families, often families with two breadwinners. Much less is known about how low-income and working poor families, many of whom are single-parent families, navigate work and family and manage these often-conflicting roles and responsibilities. The challenges are particularly daunting for the parents of young children. Often young themselves and lacking in job-related skills and job seniority, these mothers and fathers must not only find jobs that support their families, but also must make affordable child care arrangements.

As the chapters in this book attest, existing policies and programs are not always designed to meet the needs of low-income and working poor families. A careful examination of these issues also reveals some important trade-offs that merit closer attention by policy makers. For example, welfare regulations that increase mothers' human and social capital may have hidden costs for children, especially adolescents, who may find themselves caring for younger siblings and having to forego after-school activities. Another trade-off is that longer work hours may make it difficult for mothers to enroll their children in Head Start, the subsidized child care program that has emphasized quality of care and sought to enhance children's health, development, and school readiness. Head Start, as presently configured, is often offered as a partial day and/or partial year program, scheduling that does not dovetail with the schedules of many working parents. The chapters in this volume, written by a distinguished array of researchers representing multiple disciplines and at the top of their fields, explore these important and timely issues as well as others.

This volume is based on the presentations and discussions from a national symposium on "Work-Family Challenges for Low-Income Parents and their Children", held at the Pennsylvania State University on October 10–11, 2003, as the tenth in a series of annual interdisciplinary symposia focused on family issues. The book is divided into four sections, each dealing with a different aspect of the topic. Each section includes a chapter by the lead author(s), followed by shorter chapters by discussants.

In the first section of the volume, Jared Bernstein, an economist at the Economic Policy Institute, sets the stage for the entire volume by looking at the big economic picture. He analyzes how the availability, content, and stability of jobs for the working poor have changed in recent decades and discusses the implications of these changes for the widening inequality between haves and have-nots. In separate chapters, sociologist Paula England (Northwestern University) and demographers Lynne Casper and Rosalind King, both at the National Institute of Child Health and Human

Development, underscore the importance of considering gender and family structure in any analysis of work-family challenges. Demographers and rural sociologists Leif Jensen and Timothy Slack (Pennsylvania State University) contextualize Bernstein's portrait, focusing particularly on the phenomenon of underemployment.

One of the most dramatic changes in the workplace in recent years has been the shift to a "24/7" economy. This transition has meant that an increasing number of people, particularly employees in low-level jobs though not exclusively so, work a non-day shift. The second section of the volume begins with a lead chapter by Harriet Presser, a demographer at the University of Maryland. This chapter considers the implications of working afternoon, evening, and rotating shifts for families and children. The other chapters in this section expand upon the elements of the time and timing of work that may be particularly important. Maureen Perry-Jenkins, a developmental scholar at the University of Massachusetts, draws from her in-depth, longitudinal study of working-class couples making the transition to parenthood and back to work to consider how young couples experience shift work. David Almeida, an expert on midlife at the University of Arizona, takes advantage of daily diary data to examine how temporal features of work mesh with the ongoing flow of family life. Stepping back to look at the issue of family time in a theoretical context, Kerry Daly, a family scholar at the University of Guelph, outlines an important set of considerations for the next generation of research studies.

Aletha Huston, a developmental psychologist at the University of Texas-Austin, discusses how well the childcare needs of low-income families are being met in her lead chapter. In their chapters, Barrie Thorne, a sociologist at the University of California-Berkeley who brings a feminist lens to the area of work and family, Cybele Raver, a developmental psychologist at the University of Chicago, and Martha Zaslow, a developmental researcher at the non-profit consulting firm Child Trends, each elaborate on Huston's central points while weaving in findings from their own work. These contributions underscore the fact that childcare workers themselves are often low-income workers and that one way to improve the quality and availability of care is to make working in this line of work pay better.

In the final section of the volume, Susan Clampet-Lundquist (University of Pennsylvania), Kathryn Edin (Northwestern University), Andrew London (Syracuse University), Ellen K. Scott (University of Oregon), and Vicki Hunter (Kent State University), a team of sociologists who look at this question from an ethnographic point of view, portray in vivid detail the day-to-day difficulties single mothers experience in making the transition from welfare to work. For these mothers, the welfare office, and its rules, timetables, and expectations, becomes yet another challenge to manage. The other chapters in this section take different approaches to better understanding the implications of recent welfare reform. Benjamin Karney and Shauna Springer, researchers from the University of Florida who study marital dynamics, focus on whether the current push to encourage marriage in low-income populations is a good use of state and federal funds, given other challenges that these families face. Lynne A. Bond and Amy M. Carmola Hauf, both developmentally-oriented community psychologists at the University of Vermont, lay out a constructive approach to engaging communities, welfare agencies, workplaces, and families collaborations in developing support systems for low-income working parents. Finally, Andrew Cherlin (Johns Hopkins University) brings his sociological and demographic lenses, as well as his unique vantage point as director of the ambitious "Three Cities Project", to the task of scrutinizing the difficulties families face in complying with the welfare regulations.

The final chapter is an integrative commentary by Dan Hawkins and Shawn Whiteman, both of Pennsylvania State University. This interdisciplinary team summarizes the themes woven throughout the volume and suggests next steps for research.

ACKNOWLEDGMENTS

The editors are grateful to the many organizations at Penn State that sponsor the annual symposium and book series, including the Population Research Institute, the Social Science Research Institute, the Children, Youth, and Families Consortium, the Prevention Research Center, the Center for Human Development and Family Research in Diverse Contexts, the Child Studies Center, the Center for Work and Family Research, and the Departments of Economics, Human Development and Family Studies, Labor and Industrial Relations, Psychology, and Sociology, and the Crime Law and Justice Program and the Women's Studies Program. The editors also gratefully acknowledge core financial support in the form of a five-year grant funded by the National Institute of Child Health and Human Development (NICHD), as well as ongoing, substantive guidance and advice from Christine Bachrach and Lynne Casper of NICHD. In addition, we acknowledge the ongoing support and commitment of Lawrence Erlbaum Associates, especially Bill Webber, to publish the volumes in this growing series. The support of all of these partners, year after year, has enabled us to attract the excellent scholars from a range of backgrounds and disciplines, on whom the quality and integrity of the series depends.

A lively, interdisciplinary group of scholars from across the Penn State community meets with us annually to generate symposia topics and plans and is available throughout the year for brainstorming and problem solving. We appreciate their enthusiasm, intellectual support, and creative ideas. We are especially grateful to Mark Hayward, Jeanette "Jan" Cleveland, Karen Bierman, and Stacy Rogers for presiding over symposium sessions and for steering discussion in productive directions. The many details that go into planning a symposium and producing a volume are always under-estimated by the organizers. In this regard, we are especially grateful for the strong cooperation and constructive spirit of our administrative staff, including Tara Murray, William Harnish, Diane Mattern, Kim Zimmerman, and Sherry Yocum. Finally, we could not have accomplished this work without the incredible organizational skills, work ethic, and commitment of Ann Morris and Barbara King—conference organizers, diplomats, and manuscript movers par excellence!

—Ann C. Crouter
—Alan Booth

Work-Family Challenges for Low-Income Parents and Their Children

I

How Has the Availability, Content, and Stability of the Jobs Available for the Working Poor Changed in Recent Decades?

1

THE LOW-WAGE LABOR MARKET: TRENDS AND POLICY IMPLICATIONS

Jared Bernstein
Economic Policy Institute

Introduction

This chapter attempts to do two things. First, there is an empirical examination of the low-wage labor market, past, present, and future, using a set of descriptive tables and figures. Second, I ruminate about the role of low-wage work in our economy, arguing that for both political and economic reasons it plays an integral role in our society. For this reason, through booms and busts, low-wage employment, along with working poverty, will continue to play a significant role in our labor market, a view supported by recent Bureau of Labor Statistics occupational projections through 2010. The conclusion introduces some policy recommendations targeted at the gap between the earnings of low-wage workers and the economic/social needs of their families.

The empirical part of the chapter needs little introduction. It includes a fairly extensive set of tabulations designed to shed some light on the characteristics of low-wage workers and their jobs. Data permitting, I introduce some historical perspective, particularly regarding the extent of low-wage work, wages, and, to a lesser extent, compensation. To gain some insights about future trends in low-wage work, the Bureau of Labor Statistics' (BLS) occupational projections of job growth over the next decade are presented and discussed.

The less empirical part of the chapter is a broad discussion of the role of low-wage work in our economy and our society. The goal is partially to gain a better understanding of the context of low-wage work in America. But beyond that, a better understanding of context will hopefully lead to a more appropriate set of policies designed to address the problem of working poverty.

The line of reasoning regarding these issues is as follows. Relative to most other industrialized economies, we create a large share of low-wage jobs that provide little protection from the vicissitudes of the market. This has always been the case here, but is more so now, post-welfare reform, when historically large numbers of working parents are more dependent on earnings than at any time in the past 30–40 years. A particularly dramatic finding in this regard is that twenty years ago, the income of low-income mother-only families was comprised of about 40% earnings and 40% public assistance. In 2000, those shares were 10% cash

3

assistance (including the value of food stamps) and 73% earnings (including the value of the Earned Income Tax Credit).

At the same time, we pride ourselves on the number of jobs we create and our low unemployment and inflation rates relative to other industrialized (e.g., European) economies. We also, as a society, tend to be very suspicious of market interventions that block the path of the "invisible hand." In addition, we're very cost conscious—when a program is introduced to raise the quality (i.e., stability, compensation, etc.) of low-wage jobs, its potential impact on prices is often a major political stumbling block.

These realizations lead us to the following contention: our large and growing low-wage labor market is an integral part of our macroeconomy and our lives. More than any other country, we depend on low-wage, low-productivity services to sustain our life styles. The impact of this reality, to put it in a somewhat reductionist manner, is that an inequality-generating structure has evolved in our economy/labor market of which low-wage service employment is an integral component. These jobs serve to reduce unemployment and raise employment rates, hold down prices, and serve an increasingly bifurcated (by income/class) society.

What are the implications and consequences of this? First, we should be clear that the low-wage labor market is alive and growing and is embedded in our economic lives. Despite popular rhetoric to the contrary, this is not a nation of computer analysts. At the same time, there is no reason why the living standards of low-wage workers should not rise as the economy grows. As shown below, the full-employment economy of the latter 1990s had a very significant and positive impact on the wages, compensation, and incomes of low-income working families. Even in this context, however, the incomes of many low-income families fell below a level that would reliably enable them to meet their basic consumption needs. Even in the best of times, we still need to be certain that a coherent and accessible set of work-related supports is in place to close the gap between earnings in this sector and the consumption needs of families who work there.

Part I: The Low-Wage Labor Market, Past, Present, and Future

There are, of course, numerous ways to define the low-wage labor market. A few decades ago, a theoretical framework for viewing the low-wage labor market was articulated by political economists. Their discussions of "segmented labor markets" still provide a useful framework through which to view the problem (see Bernstein & Hartmann, 1999). This research, associated with Harrison, David Gordon, Piore, and others, argues that jobs are "organized into two institutionally and technologically disparate segments, with the property that labor mobility tends to be greater within than between segments" (Harrison & Sum, 1979, p. 88). Core jobs, those in the primary segment, pay higher wages and are more likely to provide fringe benefits (such as health insurance and paid vacations). Jobs in this segment also have ladders upward (often within the firm, called "internal labor markets"), whereby workers can improve their earnings and living standards over time.[1]

Conversely, jobs in the secondary segment tend to lack upward mobility. They pay lower wages, offer fewer benefits, tend to be non-union, and generally offer worse working conditions than primary-sector jobs. They are also less stable than core jobs, leading to higher levels of job turnover and churning in this sector. Race and gender based discrimination are more common here than in the primary segment.

Today's literature is much less theoretical and tends to draw on large microdata sets to examine the employment, earnings, and characteristics of those earning low wages. An important distinction here is in regard to the sample of interest: are we interested in all low-wage workers regardless of family income or are we only interested in the low earnings of workers in low-income families? Examining the overall sample of low-wage workers is the best way to learn about the structure of low-wage labor: what types of jobs are there, what do they pay, both in terms of wages and fringes, who holds them, what determines their growth or diminution? The other group, a sub-sample of the first, is conditioned on income and focuses more on the living standards of low-income working families, a group that has much currency in discussions of welfare reform and working poverty.

The distinctions are useful from a policy perspective. Policies such as the Earned Income Tax Credit, a wage subsidy targeted at low-income working families, are wholly focused on the subset conditioned on income. Such policies do not aim to lift the living standards of low-wage workers in higher-income families. On the other hand, policies such as the minimum wage are universal (not income-tested) and aim to set labor standards in the low-wage sector regardless of income level.

How much low-wage work is there in our economy? To operationalize the concept, we need a measure of low-wage work. A common and accessible measure used by numerous analysts is the "poverty level wage". Figure 1.1 shows the share of low-wage workers with low-wage defined as the share of workers earnings less than the poverty line for a family of four divided by full-time, full-year work, or 2,080 hours, 1973–2000. Thus, this is the wage—$8.70 in 2001—that would lift a family of four with one year-round worker to the poverty line.

Note that this choice of wage level is largely arbitrary, though it has been used in other work of this type (note also that while the level is derived from the poverty threshold for a family of four, the data in the figure reflect no consideration of either income or family size).[2] The point is simply to choose an hourly wage

---

[1] Piore (1975) argued that upper and lower tiers exist within primary jobs. Upper-tier jobs, available to those with the highest levels of education, are less routinized and involve more independent work. Lower-tier jobs in the primary sector tend to be blue-collar, relatively high paying, and unionized.

[2] See, for example, Acs and Danziger (1993).

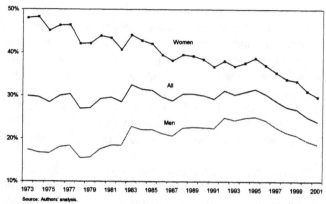

Figure 1.1.   Share of workers earning poverty-level wages, by gender, 1973-2001.

representative of pay in the low-wage sector, hold it constant through time, and observe what share of the workforce earns at or below that level. This answers the question of the prevalence of low-wage jobs generated by the economy over time.

Figure 1.1 reveals that while the share of low-wage work in the economy has trended down recently, it hovered about 30% for most of the period, ending at 24% in 2001.[3] This share represents about 27 million workers in that year. Prior to 1995, note the very different trends by gender, as low-wage work trended up for men and down for women. The differences are mostly to the fact that female workers over this period made relative (to men) gains in occupations, education, and experience. Men were also more negatively affected by the long-term decline in manufacturing employment and union density over this period. (These issues are explored below.) Still, the persistent gender gap is evident throughout the 28-year period.

Figure 1.2 plots the same variable by race for white, black, and Hispanic workers. The racial gaps are evident in the figure; in 1989, whites' rate of low-wage work was more than 10 percentage points below blacks and Hispanics. By the mid-1990s, about half of the Hispanic workforce earned low wages. The latter 1990s boom disproportionately lifted the real earnings of minorities and helped narrow the racial wage gap. This theme—the importance of tight labor markets in raising low wages—is one that we will emphasize throughout this chapter.

What are the characteristics of those who hold these jobs? Table 1.1 uses the same poverty-level wage definition as above, and examines shares for various characteristics. The first column is for all low-wage workers, while the second restricts the sample to those in families with less than $25,000. The third column provides data on all workers, so we can see where low-wage earners are over- and under-represented.

---

[3] The data in the figure are from the Current Population Survey, Outgoing Rotation Group files; the sample includes wage and salary workers, 18–64. Hourly wage values reflect only the wage value, i.e., they do not include the value of any fringes. See Mishel, Bernstein, and Boushey (2002), Appendix B, for a greater explanation.

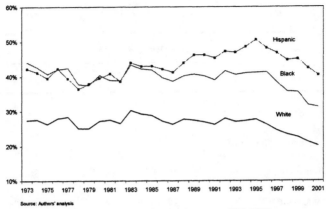

Source: Authors' analysis

Figure 1.2. Share of workers earning poverty-level wages, 1973-2001.

Table 1.1
Characteristics of Low-Wage Workers, *2001

	Low-wage workers		All workers
	All	In low-income	
Number of workers (in millions)	30,281,000	13,884,000	120,155,000
Percent of workforce	25.2%	11.6%	100.0%
Gender			
Male	41.3%	41.9%	52.0%
Female	58.7%	58.1%	48.1%
Race / ethnicity			
White	62.0%	53.7%	72.2%
Black	15.1%	19.4%	11.7%
Hispanic	18.6%	22.5%	11.4%
Age			
16-19	18.1%	12.2%	5.6%
20-30	31.4%	33.5%	24.3%
31 and older	50.5%	54.4%	70.1%

Table 1.1 cont'd.

	Low-wage workers		
	All	In low-income	All workers
Education			
Less than high school	30.1%	33.1%	12.5%
High school graduate	35.3%	37.8%	30.9%
Some college	27.0%	23.3%	29.4%
Bachelor degree or highe	7.6%	5.9%	27.3%
Work hours			
1-19 hours	13.8%	10.4%	5.6%
20-34 hours	25.6%	24.3%	12.4%
Full-time (35+ hrs.)	60.6%	65.3%	82.1%
Industry			
Retail trade	34.4%	33.5%	17.1%
Manufacturing	9.7%	10.8%	15.1%
Occupation			
Sales	17.6%	16.2%	11.3%
Service	13.2%	15.6%	6.4%
Food Preparation	13.2%	13.9%	5.2%
Union coverage			
Covered	6.4%	5.6%	14.8%
Not covered	93.6%	94.4%	85.2%

* See text for definition.
Source: CPS ORG.

Relative to the overall workforce, low-wage workers are disproportionately female, minority, younger, less highly educated, and less likely to work full time.[4] Still, three fifths work full-time, and when we control for low income, the full-time share increases to just below two thirds, compared to four fifths of the overall workforce. Note also that the 46% of workers who are both low-income and low-wage tend to be older and are more likely to be of minority status. Predictably, low-wage workers are over-represented in low-end industries and occupations, and under-represented in manufacturing (though about 10% of low-wage jobs are in low-end manufacturing such as apparel and food products). For example, while 17% of the overall workforce are employed in retail trade, for low-wage workers, that share is doubled. Relative to the overall workforce, a small share of low-wage workers are either union members or covered by collective bargaining agreements.

Sticking with our definition of low-wage work, Table 1.2 shows how low-wage workers are distributed by occupation and industry, 1979–2000. The values in the table refer to the percent of low-wage workers in each year—each column sums to 100%. The final column shows how low-wage shares have changed over time.

Table 1.2
Low-Wage Workers as Share of Low-Wage Workforce
by Industries and Occupations, 1979-2000

Industries	1979	1989	2000	Percentage Point Change 1979-2000
Agriculture	3.4%	3.2%	3.4%	0.0
Business Services	3.8%	6.1%	6.5%	2.7
Education and Social Services	10.9%	9.7%	10.8%	0.0
Finance	5.4%	4.9%	3.7%	-1.7
Medical Services	8.2%	7.0%	7.6%	-0.6
Personal Services and Entertainment	8.7%	8.8%	8.9%	0.2
Professional Services	2.6%	2.3%	2.3%	-0.2
Retail Trade	28.4%	31.4%	32.8%	4.4
Wholesale Trade	2.6%	3.0%	2.9%	0.3
Manufacturing	17.3%	14.4%	11.3%	-6.0
Mining and Construction	2.9%	3.5%	3.9%	1.0
Transportation and Utilities	3.3%	3.7%	3.9%	0.6
Public Admin	2.7%	2.0%	1.9%	-0.8

[4] The share of low-income workers in this table, 25.2%, differs slightly from the 2001 share in Figure 1.1 because the age sample in the table includes all workers aged 16 and older, while the figure limits the sample to those aged 18–64.

Table 1.2 cont'd.

				Percentage Point Change
Occupations	1979	1989	2000	1979-2000
White Collar	41.8%	42.2%	40.7%	-1.1
Managerial	3.5%	3.7%	3.7%	0.2
Professional	4.8%	4.6%	5.1%	0.3
Technical	0.8%	1.2%	1.3%	0.6
Clerical	24.6%	17.3%	14.5%	-10.1
Sales	8.2%	15.5%	16.1%	7.9
Services	24.8%	25.6%	29.1%	4.3
Protective Services	1.3%	1.7%	1.7%	0.4
Other Services	23.5%	24.0%	27.4%	3.9
Blue Collar	27.8%	26.7%	24.7%	-3.1
Craft	4.8%	6.0%	5.7%	0.9
Operatives	14.2%	9.6%	7.4%	-6.8
Transportation	2.9%	4.0%	3.7%	0.8
Laborers	5.9%	7.1%	7.9%	2.0
Other	5.6%	5.5%	5.4%	-0.1
Private Household Services	2.9%	1.9%	1.6%	-1.3
Farm	2.6%	3.5%	3.8%	1.1

Source: CPS ORG files. See text for definition of low-wage work.

Interestingly, with few exceptions shares have changed relatively little over time. A smaller share of low-wage workers are in manufacturing (there are also a smaller absolute number of such jobs), but this change is no larger than the overall decline in manufacturing employment as a share of total employment. Otherwise, the industry values show no large shifts. Similarly, a smaller share of low-wage workers are in clerical work; here again, however, the decline reflects the shrinking share of clerical jobs over time. Thus, low wages are less likely to be found in manufacturing and slightly more likely to be in service occupations.

These values on the distribution of low-wage workers by industry and occupation do not reveal any information about the impact of industry and occupational shifts on the probability of low-wage work. In decompositions shown in Bernstein and Hartmann (1999), we show that while such shifts are important, they are generally about one fifth of the increase in the likelihood of low-wage work for men (recall that the likelihood for women fell over this period). The important insight from this work is that while sectoral shifts mattered (industrial downgrading hurting males; occupational upgrading helping women), the larger factor driving the trend in low-wage work has been wage erosion within narrowly defined cells (by education, industry, occupation, etc.). We focus on wage trends in the next section.

Completing this descriptive section, Figure 1.3 tracks the share of working families with incomes less than twice the poverty line. In the literature on family budgets, this metric has been shown to be broadly similar to more comprehensive measures of how much income working families require to meet their basic consumption needs.[5] For a family of three (e.g., a mother with two children) two times poverty amounts to about $28,000 in 2000 (the last year of the 1990s recovery). The figure follows four different samples, though in each case they are families with positive labor earnings: (1) all working families, (2) all with children, (3) all with children plus a prime-age (25–54) head and at least 20 annual weeks of work (summing across the family), and (4) same as 3 but with at least 40 annual weeks of work.

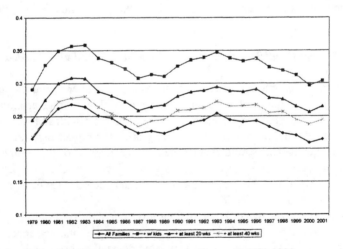

Figure 1.3.   Share of working families with income <2* poverty, 1979-2001.

For each series in the figure, two facts stand out. First, the series move in a cyclical fashion, increasing in the three downturns covered by the figure's time span (including 2001), and falling during recoveries. Second, none of the series end up significantly below where they begin (i.e., the share of working-poor and near-poor families remains at or above its level of over two decades ago).

Focusing on families with children significantly raises the levels of working poverty and near poverty, presumably because poverty thresholds rise for larger families. Selecting families based on their attachment to the labor force lowers the levels, particularly moving from all working families with children to those with a head who is in prime age (25–54) with at least 20 weeks at work (summing weeks worked across each family). Moving from 20 weeks at work to 40 lowers the level again, though somewhat surprisingly these families with the greatest connection to the labor force made the least progress over the 1990s, ending up in 2000 with working near-poverty rates of 23.8%, only 0.7 percentage points below their 1989 rate and two points higher than their 1979 rate. Apparently, larger gains accrued to working families who were formerly more marginally attached to the labor market.

Taken together, the prior figures and tables suggest that low-wage work is a non-trivial fixture of our labor market. Even among families with children whose parents are solidly connected to the labor market, the share with incomes below twice poverty remains at about the same level as two decades ago. While the tight labor market of the latter 1990s did reduce the share of the workforce with low earnings (regardless of family income), these shares too have not moved that much over time (the negative trend for women is an exception, though the gender gap persists).

Future Occupational Trends Relevant to the Low-Wage Labor Market

The Bureau of Labor Statistics projects the expected number of new jobs over the next ten years using models of and assumptions about future economic and demographic growth. Such predictions are notoriously difficult and must be taken with a grain of salt. For example, were immigration flows to change, labor supply would be altered. This would change the number of types of jobs in the future. Changes in future productivity trends—a very difficult trend to predict—would also make a big difference. Nevertheless, their track record is solid and much can be learned from their projections.

For our purposes, two relevant findings grow out of the projections. In support of a theme developed in the second part of the paper, we find no support for the widespread notion that large skill shifts in labor demand favoring highly educated workers are in our future. Second, of the ten occupations projected to add the most jobs over the next decade, seven are low-skill/low-wage, and only two are in IT (computer-related information technology). Also, the projections suggest a shift within low-wage employment towards occupations that pay lower average earnings.

One reason why the findings regarding the skill content of future jobs may surprise some readers is the fact that most citations from the projections focus on the occupations projected to grow the fastest over the next ten years, not those adding the most jobs. The difference is due to the fact that most of the fast-growing occupations are growing off of a low base compared to the occupations adding the most jobs. The fastest-growing occupation, according to the projections, is software engineers, which is expected to double, while the occupation adding the most jobs—food prep—is expected to grow by 31%. Yet the former is expected to add 380,000 jobs and the latter, 673,000 (see Table 1.3 for the top 10 occupations in both categories).

As shown in the top panel of Table 1.3, the occupations projected to grow most quickly tend to require relatively higher skills. While the table shows only the top 10 to conserve space, of the 30 occupations projected to grow most quickly, 10 (including the top 7) are in IT. Thirteen of these fast growers will require bachelor's degrees or greater and 13 will provide earnings in the top quartile of all jobs ($39,700 and over).[6]

It is of course instructive and important to learn about the occupations with fastest growth, but from our perspective the question of how the future labor market will differ from the present one depends more on the occupations adding the most jobs. As shown in the table, these occupations will comprise a larger share of employment than those growing quickly off a low base. If the Bureau's projections are accurate, these jobs will shape the landscape of the low-wage labor market in years to come.[7]

The Bureau also forecasts skill demands for the occupational projections. Here, the important difference is that while the fastest-growing jobs tend to require higher levels of education, the occupations expecting to add the most jobs require lower levels of skills. The skills required to become qualified for 16 of the top 30 can be acquired during short-term on-the-job-training (from a short demonstration of job duties up to one month of experience or instruction). Another three require moderate-term on-the-job training (one to twelve months of experience or informal training). These jobs also tend to pay less than the fastest-growing jobs, with 11 of the top 30 paying less than $18,490 and 18 paying less than $25,760 (the first and second annual earnings quartile in 2000).

---

[6] One job requiring a master's degree, mental health and substance abuse social workers, earns in the second highest quartile. Dental hygienists, a position that requires an associate degree, earn in the top quartile.

[7] The 30 fastest growing occupations made up about 3.9% of jobs in 2000 and are expected to make up 5.4% of all jobs in 2010. The 30 occupations that will add the greatest number of jobs made up about 29.6% of all jobs in 2000 and are expected to make up about 31.7% of jobs in 2010.

Table 1.3
BLS Occupational Projections:
Fastest Growing and Those Adding Most Jobs (numbers in thousands)

			Employment Shares	
Fastest Growing	2000	2010	2000	2010
Computer software engineers, applications	380	760	0.3%	0.5%
Computer support specialists	506	996	0.3%	0.6%
Computer software engineers, systems software	317	601	0.2%	0.4%
Network and computer systems administrators	229	416	0.2%	0.2%
Network systems and data communications analysts	119	211	0.1%	0.1%
Desktop publishers	38	63	0.0%	0.0%
Database administrators	106	176	0.1%	0.1%
Personal and home care aides	414	672	0.3%	0.4%
Computer systems analysts	431	689	0.3%	0.4%
Medical assistants	329	516	0.2%	0.3%
Total	2,869	5,100	2.0%	3.0%

			Employment Shares	
Adding Most Jobs	2000	2010	2000	2010
Combined food preparation and serving workers, including fast food	2,206	2,879	1.5%	1.7%
Customer service representatives	1,946	2,577	1.3%	1.5%
Registered nurses	2,194	2,755	1.5%	1.6%
Retail salespersons	4,109	4,619	2.8%	2.8%
Computer support specialists	506	996	0.3%	0.6%
Cashiers, except gaming	3,325	3,799	2.3%	2.3%
Office clerks, general	2,705	3,135	1.9%	1.9%
Security guards	1,106	1,497	0.8%	0.9%
Computer software engineers, applications	380	760	0.3%	0.5%
Waiters and waitresses	1,983	2,347	1.4%	1.4%
Total	20,460	25,364	14.1%	15.1%

Source: BLS Projections Web Page: http://www.bls.gov/emp/home.htm#tables

Despite the projection that many of the fastest-growing occupations will be in computer technology, on net the skill demands of the 2010 job market will not be much different than the skill demands of 2000, as shown in Table 1.4. The Bureau projects that 29.3% of net new jobs in the next ten years will require a bachelor's degree or greater, and low-skill jobs will continue to make up the lion's share of the U.S. job market. In 2000, 71.3% of all jobs required only work-related training. This share is projected to decline only slightly to 69.5%. Note also the lower average pay in the least skilled sector.

Table 1.4
Employment and Mean Earning by
Education and Training Category, 2000-2010

Education and training category	Percent of all jobs		2000 mean earnings
	2000	2010	
Total, all occupations	100.0%	100.0%	$33,089
Bachelor's or higher degree	20.7%	21.8%	56,553
Associate degree or postsecondary vocational award	8.1%	8.7%	35,701
Work-related training only, no postsecondary education	71.3%	69.5%	25,993

Source: Table 6 from Hecker, Occupational employment projections to 2010, *Monthly Labor Review*, Nov. 2001.

What does the 2010 job market look like for low-wage workers, most of whom do not have post-secondary education? While the share of all jobs that will require work-related training only is projected to remain steady, the distribution of these jobs appears to be shifting towards lower pay.

Unfortunately, the BLS doesn't provide projections for mean earnings by education/training level. However, as shown in Table 1.5, 28 of the 30 occupations with the greatest projected job losses require only work-related training. These 28 occupations pay higher wages on average than the 19 low-skilled occupations with the greatest projected job growth (the wage ranges represent quartiles of annual 2000 earnings). We compared the occupations with the greatest job decline with those with the greatest job growth, excluding those that require postsecondary education. Over half of the over one million jobs lost in the 28 occupations considered here had mean earnings in 2000 of greater than $25,760, or greater than half of all jobs. On the other hand, only 5.1% of the 6.7 million net new jobs in the 19 high-growth, low-skilled occupations considered here have earnings that high. Conversely, 11.6% of the jobs in declining low-skilled occupations pay less than $18,490 (or less than 75% of all jobs) in 2000, while 60.2% of the jobs in high-growth, low-skilled occupations have such low earnings. In other words, the projections suggest that jobs available for low-skilled workers will shift towards lower-paying occupations over the next decade.[8]

Table 1.5
Wage Distribution of Job Growth and Decline in Occupations Requiring Work-Related Training Only

	Percentage of jobs	
	28 occupations with largest job decline	19 occupations with largest job growth
$18,490 or less	11.6%	60.2%
$18,500-$25,760	35.1%	34.7%
$25,760-$39,660	53.3%	5.1%
$39,700 or more	0.0%	0.0%
Total number of jobs (in thousands)	1052	6726

Source: Compilation of Tables 4 and 5 from Hecker, Occupational employment projections to 2010, *Monthly Labor Review*, Nov. 2001.

The Quality of Low-Wage Jobs: Wages and Benefits

Job quality is understood by most labor economists to encompass wage level, fringes (such as health insurance and pension coverage), stability, mobility, and flexibility. We know by far the most about wage levels, our major focus in this section. We can also provide some information on benefits and mobility.

We begin by tracking the real 20th percentile wage of men and women in years 1973–2001 (Figure 1.4). This measure of low hourly wages fell quite steeply for men in the recession of the early 1980s and less so for women. From the mid-1980s through the mid-1990s, the series continued to decline for males and were fairly flat for women. The historically sharp increases driven by the tight labor market of the latter 1990s are clear at the end of the period. This increase (11% for men, 1995–2001 and 12% for women) brought men back to their 1981 level and women well above their previous peak.

---

[8] Of course, this simple analysis only accounts for the effect of shifting occupational shares. Wage trends within any occupation could grow due to supply, demand, and other determinants.

Still, even with these increases, the levels remain in the poverty-level range, particularly for women. The $7.50 that was the 20th percentile female wage in 2001 falls right in the range identified as the typical earnings of welfare leavers and other single-mothers who are ever-more dependent on low-wage earnings to meet their family's basic consumption needs. As we stress below, even with these gains and adding the value of the EITC and food stamps, earnings in the low-wage labor market are often inadequate given the costs faced by working parents.

Due to data limitations, we know less about the non-wage portion of the compensation package for low-wage workers. (Most of these data are available only for the average worker, and not therefore by wage level.) However, we can track the share of workers by wage fifth who receive health insurance and pensions through their employer, enabling us to glean important information about the quality of low-wage jobs over time. Table 1.6 provides these statistics (from the March CPS) for economic peak years 1979, 1989, and 2000. We include 1995 to show the impact of moving towards full employment in the latter 1990s.

Table 1.6

Change in Private Sector Employer-Provided
Health Insurance Coverage, 1979-00

	Percent with health insurance and pension coverage (%)								
					Percentage-point change				
Group*	1979	1989	1995	2000	1979-89	1989-00	1989-95	1995-00	1979-00
Health Insurance									
Wage fifth									
Lowest	40.7%	29.4%	27.7%	33.4%	-11.3%	4.1%	-1.7%	5.8%	-7.3%
Second	62.8%	54.7%	51.3%	57.7%	-8.1%	3.0%	-3.3%	6.3%	-5.1%
Middle	75.9%	69.4%	63.6%	68.3%	-6.5%	-1.1%	-5.8%	4.7%	-7.6%
Fourth	84.0%	78.6%	74.2%	77.0%	-5.5%	-1.6%	-4.4%	2.8%	-7.0%
Top	87.9%	83.7%	79.1%	81.2%	-4.2%	-2.5%	-4.6%	2.1%	-6.7%
Ratio of Top Fifth Share to Lowest									
Fifth Share	2.2	2.8	2.9	2.4					
Pension									
Wage fifth									
Lowest	19.5%	14.0%	14.1%	18.0%	-5.5%	4.0%	0.1%	3.9%	-1.5%
Second	38.0%	30.8%	33.1%	38.3%	-7.2%	7.5%	2.4%	5.2%	0.3%
Middle	53.3%	46.4%	47.6%	53.6%	-6.9%	7.3%	1.3%	6.0%	0.3%
Fourth	68.9%	60.2%	62.7%	65.7%	-8.7%	5.5%	2.4%	3.0%	-3.2%
Top	76.5%	70.2%	72.0%	73.0%	-6.3%	2.7%	1.8%	1.0%	-3.5%
Ratio of Top Fifth Share to Lowest									
Fifth Share	3.9	5.0	5.1	4.1					

* Private sector, wage and salary workers age 18-64, who worked at least 20 hours per week and 26 weeks per year.
Source: Mishel et al., 2002.

First, note that even after the high-pressure labor market of the latter 1990s, about one third of low-wage (bottom fifth) workers received employer-provided health insurance and less than one fifth received pension coverage. Second, and again despite the quantitatively significant gains over the 1995–2000 period, both pension and particularly health coverage were lower in 2000 than in 1979. Finally, while these declines in coverage were not isolated among the lowest earners, the last line of each panel shows that the basic inequality among health and pension provision was unaltered over the period. The highest paid workers were 2.2 times more likely to receive health coverage than the lowest paid workers in 1979, and 2.4 times more likely in 2000. Pension coverage results are similar.

Low-Wage Work and Welfare Reform

The passage of welfare reform in 1996 added a new and important dimension to the discussion of low-wage work in America. Far more so than any prior round of tinkering with our system of providing cash assistance to single parents (mostly mothers), the success of Temporary Assistance to Needy Families (TANF) was and is predicated on moving welfare recipients into the paid labor market, preferably in the private sector (i.e., into non-subsidized jobs).

A huge literature evaluates welfare reform, and is well beyond the scope of this paper. For our purposes, we would like to understand how welfare reform affects the context of low-wage work. That is, is there anything about this important policy change that could help us to understand the role of low-wage work in our economy and thus inform better policy?

First, welfare reform, in tandem with the strong economy of the latter 1990s, was responsible for an historically large increase in the share of single mothers entering the paid labor market. Data cited in Mishel, Bernstein, and Boushey (2000) show that after edging up slowly throughout the 1980s, employment rates of unmarried mothers increased sharply over the mid- to latter 1990s, the period when TANF was introduced. For never-married mothers, the increase was 20 percentage points in six years, from 46% to 66% from 1994–2000.

We would expect that this increase in paid employment would shift the income components of low-income, single-mother families toward earnings and away from public assistance. However, the magnitude of this shift turns out to be quite extraordinary. The values in Figure 1.5 represent the earnings (actual earnings plus the value of the EITC for a family with two children) and public assistance (means-tested cash benefits, including welfare and the reported value of food stamps) shares of family income for low-income, single-mother families. (We define low income as the average of the bottom half of the mother-only family income distribution.) From 1979 through the late 1980s, incomes of these families came fairly evenly from earnings and public assistance, wherein each contributed about 35–45% of income (the rest, a consistent share of about 20%, came from various other sources, including other cash benefits, child support, alimony, and interpersonal transfers).

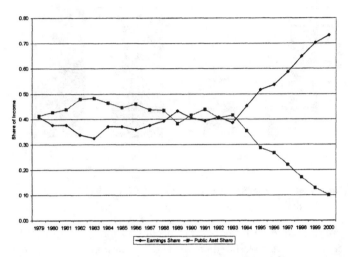

Figure 1.5.   Income components, low-income single mothers, 1979-2000.

Beginning around 1994, a gap began to open and as the decade progressed the gap grew very quickly, with a dramatic shift from public assistance to earnings. By 2000, the average public assistance share was about 10%, while the earnings share was 73%. Surveys like the one used for this figure tend to suffer from underreporting of welfare income, and this problem may have grown over the period of welfare reform. But the divergence of these two income shares is so large that correcting the picture by the assessing the degree of underreporting could not possibly change the conclusion that the shift towards earnings and away from benefits has been unprecedented. If a goal of welfare reform is to induce this type of shift, that goal has been realized.

The problem, however, is that while these families have more income on average they are still poor, or with EITC benefits, very near poor. Also, all of this work means work-related expenses. When we net these out, the economic conditions of these low-income families, while significantly improved, are still precarious. Figure 1.6 shows the real average income levels of single-mother families with incomes below the median for that group. Each bar shows the income components noted above: earnings, ETIC, cash assistance, the market value of food stamps, and EITC. We have added two other income sources: the value of the EITC that would accompany the average family's earnings for that year (assuming two children), and the market value of food stamps. The set of bars labeled "net" extracts work expenses from earnings, including childcare, using the method and values described in Short (2001).

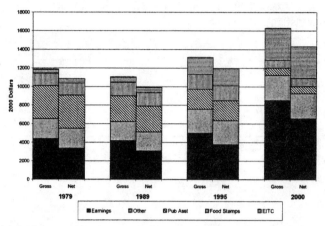

Figure. 1.6. Income of low-income single mother families, gross and net of work expenses, 1979-2000.

Average income for these families declined slightly over the 1980s, mostly due to declines in cash welfare benefits and real earnings that were not made up for by a higher value for food stamps and a slightly higher EITC. Welfare income continued to fall through 1995, but earnings grew. Importantly, the EITC was much expanded, growing from $590 to $1,800 (year 2000 dollars) for two-child families with these earnings levels.

As the previous figure showed, this trend towards less welfare and more earnings grew extremely quickly from 1995–1999. Gross earnings among these low-income single-mother families grew by $3,500 and EITC benefits, which are tied to earnings, grew by $1,600. Due to the increasing work expenses that accompany more time spent in the paid labor market, net earnings grew by $750 less than gross earnings. Over the same period, cash welfare benefits fell by about $1,400 and the market value of food stamps by $760. The average family thus ended up with income of $16,300 gross, about $2,400 above the poverty line but still below the level needed to make ends meet, especially considering that this represents the income of a working single parent with more than one child (the EITC is assigned based on this assumption). Netting out work expenses leaves an income level of about $14,300.

In other work (not shown here) we find similar, though less dramatic, increases in the importance of work and earnings for all low-income families, not simply those affected by welfare reform (Mishel et al., 2002). The message for us from these data is that low-wage work is very much a part, and probably a growing part, of the lives of millions of American families.

For those of us concerned about the living standards of families who depend on their earnings from this sector, or the well-being of the children in such families, or the extent of working poverty generated by our economy, this reality is unsettling.

We are compelled to think about what public policies are needed to address this reality and to make sure that those families who are making a good faith effort to "play by the rules of the game" earn enough income to meet their basic needs and perhaps even invest in their children's future. The rest of this chapter is devoted to these issues.

Part II: The Context of Low-Wage Work and Policies Designed to Help

Why have the trends evolved as shown above, particularly in Figures 1.1 and 1.2? Why does such a rich and technically advanced economy generate so much low-wage work? Why are seven of the ten occupations expected to add the most jobs over the next decade low-wage/low-skill occupations? Is this a desirable state of affairs? What, if anything, is the role of public policy in addressing working poverty? One could easily fill a volume answering these questions. The intention here is to offer a set of answers based less on rigorous proofs than on general analysis of the role and evolution of low-wage labor markets in our economy.

If we want to know what to do about working poverty, it makes sense to examine what factors might be behind the trends presented above. In the 1980s, when wage and income inequality were growing quickly and low wages were falling both in real and relative (to higher earners) terms, there was a lot of discussion about the increase in skill premiums. This shift, exemplified by the fast growth of the pay differential between college and high-school workers, was thought to have been driven by a shift in demand away from those with fewer skills/less education and toward those with more skill (in this literature, wage is a proxy for skill). Later papers argued that the shift in relative skill demands was driven by technology-induced demand for those with IT-related skills.

Upon closer examination, many aspects of this interpretation of the 1980s do not hold up very well. Without reviewing a large and complicated literature, the problem with the conventional view is that little systematic evidence was offered to clarify whether low wages were falling because of demand shifts against low-wage workers or whether the decline in the wages of such workers was more a function of a broad set of economic and social factors shifted against them, lowering the quality of their jobs, and ultimately lowering their living standards. Much less convincing evidence was offered to support the IT-related nature of the supposed shift in relative demand.

The belief that demand shifted against low-wage workers was at its root based on the observation that both the relative supply and price of skill increased over the same period. Given a neo-classical framework, this conjecture is perfectly reasonable. But it ignores a sea-change over the 1980s that sharply lowered the price of low-wage work, and thus encouraged its growth.

For one, the minimum wage fell 30% in real terms over the decade, as Congress failed to increase it for nine years. Second, persistent trade imbalances led to continuous erosion of our manufacturing base, a sector wherein non-college-educated workers could earn middle-class compensation. Related to this was the eight percentage-point decline in union coverage over the 1980s (from 24% to 16%, including non-members covered by collective bargaining agreements). Low-wage immigration also expanded over this period, increasing the supply of less-skilled workers. And this was an era of significant deregulation of product and labor markets, which further exposed low- and middle-wage workers to market forces. Finally, the high rate of unemployment over the 1980s extending into the early 1990s was under-appreciated at the time. This dimension of the problem becomes particularly clear when we compare the low-wage labor market of the 1980s to that of the latter 1990s, when unemployment hit a three-decade low point. (We say more about this below.)

All of these developments served to reduce the bargaining power of low-wage workers, and are directly behind the negative wage trends shown above. As these factors worked to drive down real wages and job quality in the low-wage sector, economists recognized that relative wages were rising sharply and concluded, as noted above, that demand must have shifted against those at the bottom of the wage (and skill) scale. The policy solution to this, of course, was to raise their skills.

Again I stress that none of the above should be taken as an argument against skill enhancement. Higher-skilled workers almost always earn more than less-skilled workers, and any individual worker contemplating her future needs to appreciate that. But in terms of national policy, we had better think beyond this. While demand was supposedly shifting against low-skilled workers, the economy was generating millions of (ever cheaper) low-wage jobs. Net job creation over the 1980s was in the service-producing sector, of course, and the two lowest-paying industrial sectors within the service-producing sector (retail and the services sub-sector) accounted for 79% of the net new jobs (Mishel et al., 2002). Clearly, there was a good deal of demand for low-wage work.

The neoclassical story, with its sole focus on rising skill premiums, fails to adequately appreciate these trends and thus fails to grasp that skill enhancement alone cannot solve the problem of low-wage work. Our view is that the most important forces behind the secular increase in low-wage work are the structural changes noted above, which decimated the bargaining power of low-wage workers and sharply lowered the quality of their jobs.

As long as low-wage work remains absolutely and relatively cheap, we will continue to add many, if not most, of our jobs in this sector, as shown in the BLS projections. Furthermore, our large low-wage labor market is an integral part of our macroeconomy. Low-wage work is no more or less than another "factor input" in our economic lives, and as it has grown cheaper, we've bought much more of it. In fact, more than any other country, we've come to depend on low-wage, low-productivity services to sustain our life styles. In this sense, an inequality-generating structure has evolved in our economy/labor market of which low-wage service employment is an integral component. These jobs serve to reduce unemployment and raise employment rates, hold down prices, and serve an increasingly bifurcated (by income/class) society.

The question is: what do we do about it? That is, what can we do to raise the quality of low-wage jobs and the living standards of working-poor and near-poor families (beyond raising their human capital)? Do we seek to reduce the number of low-wage jobs, perhaps by pursuing policies to raise their price, such as much higher minimum wages? Or should we avoid trying to alter prices and instead focus our policy efforts on redistribution through progressive taxes and transfers? In other words, where is the best intervention point: the primary distribution (market outcomes), the secondary distribution (post-tax and transfers), or some combination therein?

I explore both intervention points and, not surprisingly, settle on elements of both. Essentially, the recommended approach comes down to, first, making sure the primary distribution is delivering the highest wage possible given productivity constraints. Unions, higher minimum wages, and full employment are the key factors here. Second, refundable tax credits and work supports are used to close the remaining gap between earnings and needs. Though the safety net is vital, I say little about it here because the focus is on working families. There is, however, a greater need for a safety net for those unemployed or out of the labor force, especially when the economic fate of low-income families is ever more dependent on the market.

Raising Pretax Wages

Three "tools" should be applied to ensure that market outcomes are as favorable as they can be for low-wage workers—unions, minimum wages, and low unemployment. I will say the most about the latter because it is the most important and because much more has already been said about the other two.

Mishel et al. (2002, 187–194) present empirical evidence about both the various wage and benefits premiums received by those covered by unions relative to noncovered workers with similar characteristics. We also cite literature showing that unions tend to compress wages and thus that the decline in their share is implicated in the increase in wage inequality over the last few decades. In our policy context, they are a useful piece of the puzzle because they can raise wages above the market rate and thus counteract many of the negative forces that have lowered compensation in low-wage employment over the past few decades.

However, as shown in Table 1.1, unions remain a small force among low-wage workers. The numbers of low-wage workers covered by unions are probably growing; the Service Employees International Union, for example, is the fastest growing union. But unions continue to decline as a share of the workforce, especially in the private sector, where they are currently down to 9% (9.7% including nonmembers covered by collective bargaining).

A good bit of activity is afoot to change this, though it is beyond our scope to describe it. Two interesting models are worker centers and living wage campaigns. Worker centers are organizations representing workers who are for various reasons, traditionally out of reach of unions (e.g., day laborers, temp workers). Living wage campaigns typically have a fairly narrow occupational/industry target, but a secondary goal of some campaigns is to generate interest among low-wage workers in representation.

Minimum wages are another important addition to the policy set, especially for low-wage women (the female 10th percentile tends to move closely with the minimum). By providing a floor on wages below which they cannot fall, the minimum wage has the potential to compensate for the loss of bargaining power suffered by low-wage workers. On the other hand, the minimum wage itself can become part of the problem if the wage floor "caves in" due to congressional neglect.

Unlike increasing union density, raising the minimum is—politics aside—a fairly straightforward legislative initiative. Despite two increases in the 1990s, the real minimum wage remains 21% below its 1979 peak, before it was allowed to slide to a 34-year low over the 1980s. Unfortunately, the politics of minimum wage increases remain fractious as affected firms lobby hard against this increase in their labor costs. To some extent, research over the last ten years, which quite thoroughly debunks the textbook notion that a minimum wage increase of any magnitude will be disemploying, has helped advocates for this cause.

We discuss some of these issues in a paper on current legislation to raise the minimum from its current level of $5.15 to $6.65 by 2004 (Bernstein & Chapman, 2002). Our analysis suggests that given reasonable assumptions about future wage and labor force trends, a three-year phase-in to $6.65 would affect a significantly smaller share of the workforce than prior increases.[9] A shorter phase-in would reach more workers and, we argue, could be absorbed without disemployment.

Perhaps the least appreciated policy for lifting bargaining power and thus the wages of low-wage workers is also the most effective: full employment. The best evidence for this is the trajectory of low wages over the latter 1990s, as unemployment fell to a thirty-year low of 4% in 2000. The ensuing tight labor market forced employers to bid up wages for the first time in decades, and, as seen in the earlier figures, real low wages reversed course.

Bernstein and Baker (forthcoming) have written a book on the benefits of low unemployment over this period. We examine the increase in low wages and go through all the potential reasons for the turnaround. The most compelling explanation is a sharp increase in demand for low-wage work, caused largely by

---

[9] For example, while the last federal minimum wage increase reached about 10% of the workforce, this one is predicted to reach about 5%.

an acceleration in output and accompanied by an acceleration in productivity growth. The faster growth was accommodated by the Federal Reserve, which to its everlasting credit tested the terribly destructive theory that unemployment could not fall below 6% without triggering an inflationary spiral. The fact that support for that particular theory (the non-accelerating inflationary rate of unemployment, or NAIRU) has been weakened considerably (at least as far as it can be counted on to generate a reliable point estimate of the unemployment rate associated with full employment) may be one of the most important legacies of the period.

Bernstein and Baker (forthcoming) focus on full employment's positive impact on wages, incomes, inequality, employment, and even a few non-economic trends such as crime rates, which also seemed to fall as more remunerative legitimate opportunities appeared. Here we show the results of one simulation in which we estimate how low wages (nominal, in this case) might have trended in the absence of the post-1995 decline in unemployment.

Figure 1.7 is derived from a "wage curve" model wherein (logged) quarterly nominal wages are regressed on lags of the dependent variable, unemployment, and productivity growth. The data shown are for the male 10th percentile wage, but other gender/percentile simulations show similar results. The dynamic simulation of the actual series ("dynamic" in this context means that we predict the lagged dependent values) shows that the model tracks the data well.

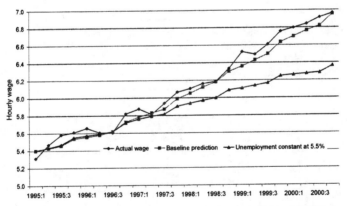

Figure 1.7. Male 10th percentile nominal wage, unemployment constant 1995 forward.

Note that when we simulate the trajectory of low male wages holding unemployment at its 1995 level of 5.5%, instead of letting it fall to 4% in 2000, wage growth flattens considerably. The actual increase in nominal wages for this decile, 1995–2000, was 25% (the predicted series also grows this much); the increase in the simulation is 15%. The RS deflator increased 12% over the period.

Thus, according to this simulation, in the absence of lower unemployment, real 10th male wages would have grown 3% over the period instead of 13%, underscoring the important role played by falling unemployment over the period.[10]

Figure 1.8 (a and b) provides another look at the impact of low unemployment on low wages, this time using variation between the states in two time periods. The two figures plot annualized state real wage changes for low-wage workers against change in state unemployment rates in the 1980s and latter 1990s. Thus, the highlighted state in Figure 8b represents a state in which unemployment fell about 3 points and real low wages grew close to 2% per year. An (unweighted) regression line is plotted through the dots.

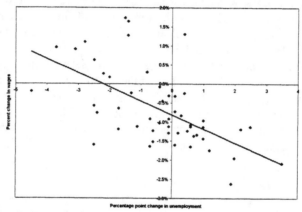

Figure 1.8a. The relationship between changes in 20th percentile wages and unemployment (1979-1989).

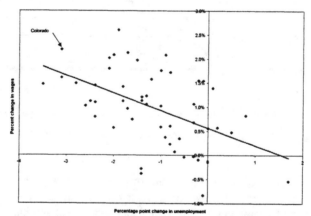

Figure 1.8b. The relationship between changes in 20th percentile wages and unemployment (1989-2000).

The most interesting feature of the graphs is the very different scatter of dots over the two periods. Our expectation would be that states that experienced falling unemployment also would be those that experienced faster real wage growth, as tight labor markets in those states bid up wages relative to states with weaker labor markets (e.g., areas of the country with an oversupply of low-wage workers relative to the available number of jobs, for example). In these graphs, this would mean that most of the dots would be in the upper left (rising wages and declining unemployment) or lower right hand (vice versa) quadrants.

The figures reveal, however, that this is much more the case in the 1990s than over the prior decade. In the 1980s, when demand for low-wage labor was generally slack, many of the states locate in the lower left-hand section, which corresponds to both falling unemployment and declining real wages, or the lower right hand section: falling real wages and rising unemployment. Over the 1990s, however, the majority of states shift to the upper left quadrant (rising wages/falling unemployment), a minority of states saw both falling unemployment and falling wages, and only one state (Hawaii) had rising unemployment and falling low wages.

Note also that the regression line is placed higher in the 1990s graph than in the 1980s figure. This intercept shift around a constant slope (the slopes are statistically indistinguishable) implies that the same change in unemployment in either decade led to higher wage growth in the 1990s. For example, a state in which unemployment fell by 2 points in the 1980s is predicted to have a -0.3% annual decline in real wages. For the 1990s, that same decline in unemployment translates into a 1% average increase in real 20th percentile wages.

Most readers will agree that full employment is a highly desirable state, but how do we get and stay there? The speed with which the economy grows, and thus the actual level of unemployment that corresponds to full employment, is largely a function of the rate of productivity and labor force growth. Macroeconomic strategies to influence these growth rates, particularly productivity, are both not well understood and far beyond our scope. Instead, we think monetary and fiscal policy should emphasize a full employment goal, with 4% unemployment as a demonstrable full employment level of unemployment.

Still, a few ideas regarding full employment policy are worth mentioning. At the top of the list, of course, are the actions of the Federal Reserve Board (the Fed), which can accommodate economic growth by maintaining low interest rates. As noted above, in the 1990s, the Fed showed a remarkable willingness to tolerate low unemployment. As we leave the current downturn behind, however, it is unclear whether Fed economists judge 4% unemployment as a benchmark against which to evaluate its monetary stance. Note that according to the Congressional Budget

---

[10] As Bernstein and Baker (forthcoming) note, a more realistic simulation might call for relaxing the ceteris paribus condition in the above, particularly regarding inflation. Thus, under the simulation, the fact that unemployment does not fall might have led to slower price growth, and thus real wages would have grown more quickly. However, the fact is that even as unemployment fell sharply over the simulation period, inflation actually decelerated so this limitation does not seem too serious.

Office, full employment translates into 5.2% unemployment. So, while they deserve rich praise for their accommodation in the latter 1990s, there is still an open question: does the Fed believe that our economy can sustain a 4.0% unemployment rate without accelerating inflation?

One potential mechanism for enshrining this message in public policy might be to renew the recently "sunsetted" Humphrey-Hawkins Act, which governed the conduct of the Fed and required it to target 4.0% unemployment as part of their mission. Given the importance of full employment to the nation, and particularly to the low-wage labor market, the renewal of the Act could require that when the unemployment rate is above 4%, the Federal Reserve Board Chairman must explain to Congress the actions he or she will take to bring the economy to full employment.

Four percent unemployment should be a goal of fiscal policy as well. An excellent example of what this might mean in practice can be taken from current economic conditions, when the unemployment rate is stalled at 6% and there are few visible sources of private-sector demand stimulus on the horizon. In fact, virtually all forecasters agree that unemployment is likely to remain stuck around its current level for at least the short term. A federal government committed to full employment would quickly engage in stimulative spending at this point, with little regard for short-term deficits.

Of course, how this is done is highly controversial, but putting aside partisan politics (which quickly get bogged down in tax cuts versus spending), and anti-deficit spending fetishes, there are well established ideas about how best to use federal spending to provide a short-term stimulus and lower unemployment.[11]

Filling the Gap Between Earnings and Needs

For numerous reasons, it makes no sense to depend fully on market outcomes to guarantee that the working poor and near poor can achieve economic self-sufficiency. First, we cannot count on the labor market to operate at or even near full employment. As of this writing, for example, the unemployment rate is stalled at 6%, African American unemployment is in double digits, and the largest declines in employment rates have been among African American women (Mishel et al., 2002, Table 3.7). Over most of the last 30 years, the economy has operated with considerable slack, particularly in the low-wage sector; the 1995–2000 period has been the exception. Second, though there is little available evidence to make this case, it is likely true that the low-productivity levels of many firms in our low wage sector constrain their ability to pay wage levels needed for working families to make ends meet. This is especially the case given that in many areas of the country, working families need incomes that are closer to twice the poverty line in order to meet their basic needs.[12]

---

[11] Two ideas worth pursuing in the current context are new fiscal grants-in-aids to states, most of which are constrained by balanced budget amendments, and an increase in temporary unemployment insurance benefits.

[12] Bernstein, Brocht, and Spade-Aguilar (2001).

We focus on two important gap closers: refundable tax credits tied to earnings and work supports.

The EITC has been mentioned throughout and stands as one of our most important programs for raising the incomes of low-wage workers in low-income families. We currently spend around $30 billion on this federal refundable tax credit. As discussed above, it has the potential to be far more important to low-income working families than any other source of cash or near-cash assistance.[13]

The policy already lifts millions out of working poverty, but numerous analysts have suggested extensions.[14] These generally involve some stretching of the inverted '\＿/' shape of the EITC schedule. By lengthening the upward slope and the plateau, and reducing the phase-down range, this politically popular program could further raise the incomes of working-poor and near-poor families, while further encouraging work (the flatter phase-out reduces the increase in marginal taxation as the credit fades). Of course, this would also make the program more expensive.

One particularly interesting approach is the "Simplified Family Credit" discussed in numerous pieces by Max Sawicky and Robert Cherry, which replaces the dependent exemption in the federal income tax, the EITC, and the new child tax credit.[15] Along with the type of changes mentioned above to the EITC schedule, they also add successively higher maximum benefits for each child (the current EITC provides benefits for no children, one child, and two or more). Most importantly, they try to smooth out some of the marginal rate problems caused by the interaction of these various components of the current federal tax code. They show, for example, that for low-income families in the $20,000 range, the phase-out in the EITC overlaps with the federal income tax to increase marginal tax rates, such that their after-tax income increases more slowly than would be the case with a more integrated and considerably simplified system.

Work supports are the other policy set that we stress as a way to help fill the earnings/needs gap faced by low-income working families. A work support is any policy that helps pay for an expense associated with work, such as childcare or transportation. However, it also is reasonable to include assistance for expenses faced by working families that are not directly tied to work, such as health insurance and housing (unlike, say, childcare; poor non-working families need these supports as well). We discuss these as direct and indirect work supports.

At this point, our system of work supports is much improved but still very ad hoc, with too much state variation and too little access for working families. Interestingly, the improvement stems in large part from welfare reform, as the fixed funding structure of the program, in tandem with sharply declining caseloads, meant that states had many more dollars to spend per case than they did

---

[13] On the shift in federal spending from cash assistance to the EITC, see Sholz and Levine (2002).

[14] This table—http://www.census.gov/hhes/poverty/histpov/rdp05.html—shows the extent to which the EITC lowers poverty rates. For examples of extensions, see Sawhill and Thomas (2001).

[15] See Sawicky and Cherry (2001).

pre-reform. In addition, the structure of the law gave states the opportunity (with waivers from the federal government) to provide assistance to low-income families who were not on the welfare rolls. Also, the introduction of CHIP—the Child Health Insurance Program—provided access to Medicaid for children (though not for their parents) in low-income families with incomes up to more than 200% of poverty in some states.

Of course, not every state jumped at the opportunity to develop or expand their system of work—as usual, there were good and not-so-good actors. Here again a large evaluation literature exists that we have not reviewed in detail. But some themes do emerge that are worth noting in our context.

We focus on childcare as this is potentially the largest expense for many low-income working families. Federally, childcare subsidies to low- and moderate-income families are provided through the Childcare and Development Block Grant (CCDBG), though TANF and the Social Services Block Grant also provide funding. (In fact, most of the growth in federal spending on childcare, 1997–2000, was due to state use of TANF funds for this purpose [Mezey, Greenberg, & Schumacher, 2002].) Under the CCDBG, states can provide childcare assistance to working families with incomes up to 85% of the state's median income, though the vast majority of states eligibility is below that level.

The most important fact to know about the current system is that the federal subsidies are currently assisting only about 15% of the eligible children.[16] This is clearly a very serious constraint to the living standards of low-income working families. Reliable and safe childcare is critical both to children's well-being and parents' ability to move into the workforce and build a consistent work history. The fact that states lack the resources to raise eligibility and cover more families is thus a major flaw in the current system of work supports.

These issues are surfacing in the current debate regarding the reauthorization of welfare reform. Conservatives, including the administration, have proposed raising the TANF work requirements—the share of the caseload expected to work and the hours per week they're required to spend in work or training—without committing any new funds for childcare, an approach that many other policy makers are firmly rejecting.

But as the data above on the income composition and levels of low-income single mothers reveal, regardless of the outcome of reauthorization, the cost of childcare will continue to seriously cut into the incomes of working families. In the example shown in Figure 1.6 about gross versus net (of work expenses) income, childcare expenses for low-income single-mother families reduced income by close to $1,500.[17] The average annual cost of center-based care for a young child is more than twice that in many parts of the country.

---

[16] This number is considerably lower than a government estimate of 30%, but that value is biased up by using state, not federal, eligibility guidelines (Mezey et al., 2002).

[17] These expenses were simulated using the method and values described by Short (2001). Since not every mother in this sample has children less than 12 (Short's cutoff for childcare), some families will not incur this expense. Also, the costs are a function of actual weeks worked per year, as report on the CPS.

What level of resources would it take to fully fund childcare for all eligible families? According to Mezey et al. (2000), $3.45 billion was spent on the CCDBG in 2000, reaching, as noted, 15% of eligible children. A simplistic back-of-the-envelope calculation suggests that going from 15% to 100% would involve a huge increase to $23 billion, practically another EITC program.[18] Given the complexities of the issue—tough questions about take-up rates, cost variation, the impact of such an expansion on costs and provision—this number should not be taken very seriously, but it is probably not too far from the ballpark (it's quite close to a much more detailed calculation by Helburn and Bergmann [2002], Table 9.1). In any event, an initiative to fully fund childcare through the CCDBG would be expensive relative to current expenditures, but current expenditures are totally inadequate. Given strong public and political support for work supports, the coverage gap could be somewhat, if not significantly reduced.

Ultimately, if we want to ensure that the earnings gap is reliably closed, we need to begin to contemplate a more universal approach to the provision of key work supports, such as child and medical care.[19] As some other industrialized economies have found, both of these services would benefit from being "taken out of the market place," as their provision is problematic in a market-based setting. Working-poor families are likely to underconsume childcare based on their children's needs and the demands of current policy. An even stronger market failure argument could be made for health care consumption. (Recall from Table 1.6 that one third of those in the lowest wage fifth were covered by employer-provided health insurance.)

There are many difficulties in pursuing such a path, of course. Figuring out the best methods for approaching universal provision of health or childcare is one major challenge (recall the confusion generated around the Clinton health care plan). Another challenge would be to build the political will to engage in such large-scale policy formulation. And of course, even the ideas we've briefly cited— expanding refundable tax credits tied to work, and requiring states to raise CCDBG eligibility to the federal level—call for considerable additional resources above current spending. On the other hand, the market-based policies we mentioned do not have direct budget costs, and full employment is of course a huge revenue-enhancer relative to running the economy below its potential.

For now, however, a coherent policy set to reduce the problem of working poverty (and near-poverty) is not necessarily out of reach. Incremental improvements to existing work supports, such as expanding CHIP to parents and boosting the funding and coverage of the CCDBG, are not only possible but are actively debated in Congress, as is an increase in the minimum wage. Expanding

---

[18] This is just 3.45/.15=23.
[19] See Helburn and Bergmann (2002) for a detailed presentation of a universal childcare program for the United States.

refundable tax credits is also frequently on the agenda—even the generally regressive Bush tax cut included a child tax credit that, through the efforts of low-income advocates, was made refundable. Add to this policy set the maintenance of full employment, and we have potentially powerful public/private program to ameliorate working poverty in the short to medium term.

Conclusion

The empirical portion of this chapter shows that low-wage work is by no means an uncommon experience in America. About one fourth of the workforce earned low wages in 2001 (about 30% for female workers), and about 30% of working families with children had incomes below twice the poverty line in 2000. Even at the peak of the last boom, one third of these workers had employer provided health insurance and just under one fifth had any sort of pension plan.

What's more, while the tight labor market of the latter 1990s helped to reduce the share of low-wage work, it's fair to say that over the long term, little progress has been made. Over this same period, welfare reform led to a sharp increase in low-wage employment among low-income mothers, whose income is now much more dependent on earnings (and earnings supplements) than was the case prior to TANF. Looking ahead, ten-year occupational projections by the BLS suggest that contrary to the notion of large-scale skill upgrading, low-wage work will continue to comprise a similar share of our workforce.

The rest of the chapter examines whether this is a problem and if so, what should be done about it. Economists and policy makers often frame the issue as one of skill deficits, that is, the problem of low-wage work could be ameliorated if low-wage workers received more training and education. This is no doubt true in the sense that higher levels of education are clearly associated with higher earnings, but as a sole or even central policy stance it is much too reductionist. The fact is that much has changed to sharply reduce the bargaining power of low-wage workers—the focus in this chapter is on unions, minimum wages, trade, and high unemployment—and these factors need to be considered as seriously as education. I stress the demonstrable importance of full employment, which led to dramatic gains in wages and incomes in the latter 1990s and had nothing to do with skill improvements.

These insights into the nature and causes of low-wage employment growth lead to a policy set that stresses intervening in both the primary distribution (market outcomes) and the secondary distribution (post-tax and transfers) to generate the growth needed to ensure that working families and their children are well above poverty. The goal is to make sure the primary distribution mechanism is the delivery of the highest wage possible given productivity constraints, and to use refundable tax credits and work supports to close the remaining gap between earnings and needs.

This agenda is ambitious and, if fully implemented, is a potentially costly one relative to current expenditures on tax credits and work supports. (On the other hand, it is very costly *not* to be at full employment.) We should not let the best be the enemy of the good, however. Despite current budget constraints, a coherent policy set that reduces the problem of working poverty (and near poverty) is not necessarily out of reach. Incremental improvements to existing work supports, such as expanding CHIP to parents and boosting the funding and coverage of the CCDBG, are not only possible but are actively debated in Congress, as are an increase in the minimum wage and the expansion of refundable tax credits. Add full employment to the mix and we have the ingredients of a potentially powerful program that can make some real inroads against working poverty.

References

Acs, G., & Danziger, S. (1993). Educational attainment, industrial structure, and male earnings through the 1980s. *Journal of Human Resources, 28*(3), 618–648.

Bernstein, J., & Baker, D. (in press). *The benefits of full employment and the costs of not being there*. Washington, DC: Economic Policy Institute.

Bernstein, J., & Chapman, J. (2002). *Time to repair the wage floor: Raising the minimum wage to $6.65 will prevent further erosion of its value* (Issue Brief No. 180). Washington, DC: Economic Policy Institute.

Bernstein, J., Brocht, C., & Spade-Aguilar, M. (2001). *How much is enough? Basic family budgets for working families*. Washington, DC: Economic Policy Institute.

Bernstein, J., & Hartmann, H. (1999). Defining and characterizing the low-wage labor market. In *The low-wage labor market: Challenges and opportunities for economic self-sufficiency*. Washington, DC: U.S. Department of Health and Human Services.

Boushey, H., Brocht, C., Gundersen, B., & Bernstein, J. (2001). In *Hardships in America: The real story of working families*. Washington, DC: Economic Policy Institute.

Harrison, B., & Sum, A. (1979). The theory of 'dual' or segmented labor markets. *Journal of Economic Issues, 13*(3), 687–706.

Helburn, S. W., & Bergman, B. R. (2002). *America's childcare problem: The way out*. New York: St. Martin's Press.

Mezey, J., Greenberg, M., & Schumacher, R. (2002). *The vast majority of federally-eligible children did not receive childcare assistance in FY 2000*. Washington, DC: Center for Law and Social Policy.

Mishel, L., Bernstein, J., & Boushey, H. (2002). In *The state of working America, 2002-03*. Ithaca, NY: Cornell University Press.

Piore, M. (1975). Fragments of a sociological theory of wages. In *Proceedings of the 25th Annual Meeting of the Industrial Relations Research Association*. Madison, WI: IRRA.

Sawhill, I., & Thomas, A. (2001). *A tax proposal for working families with children* (Welfare Reform and Beyond Brief No. 3). Washington, DC: Brookings Institution.

Sawicky, M. B., & Cherry, R. (2001). *Making work pay with tax reform* (Issue Brief No. 173). Washington, DC: Economic Policy Institute.

Scholz, J. K., & Levine, K. (2002). The evolution of income support policy in recent decades. In S. Danziger & R. Haveman (Eds.), *Understanding poverty*. Cambridge, MA: Harvard University Press.

Short, K. (2001). *Experimental poverty measures: 1999* (U.S. Census Bureau Current Population Reports P60-216). Washington, DC: US Government Printing Office.

2

LABOR MARKET AND FAMILY TRENDS AND PUBLIC POLICY RESPONSES

Paula England
Northwestern University

The last three decades have seen an increased proportion of families with children supported by low-wage workers. Many such families have inadequate incomes by most Americans' standards. Bernstein (this volume) argues that this situation arises because of changes in labor markets and in public policy. Although not discussed by Bernstein, the adverse trend in the adequacy of the incomes of many families with children is also exacerbated by the rise of single motherhood, given that the American system of child support, market, and public provision leaves many single mothers and their children poor. Bernstein discusses public policies that would help bring working families to a reasonable level of income. Below, I comment on Bernstein's analytic arguments and policy suggestions.

Understanding the Changing U.S. Labor Market

Bernstein shows that since 1973, there has been a decline in the proportion of American men who earn wages that, assuming full-time work, could support a family of four above the poverty line. In a similar vein, he shows how the real wage associated with the 20th percentile of men's wages has fallen. The biggest declines occurred in the early 1980s and the early 1990s. In contrast, the 20th percentile of men's wages increased from 1995–2000, but by the end of the century were still lower than in 1973. (All trends discussed here and in Bernstein apply to "real" increases or decreases, that is, they are after adjustments for changes in the cost of living.) These trends are part of a larger change in U.S. labor markets marked by a fall in the bottom half or more of the male wage distribution, and increases in pay at the very top of the distribution. Together, these changes substantially increased inequality within the distribution of men's earnings (Bernhard et al., 2001, chapter 1). Although he doesn't discuss it, inequality within the women's wage distribution also increased (Morris, Bernhardt, & Handcock, 1994).

Whether the situation looks better or worse for women than for men depends upon whether one focuses on wage levels or trends. Focusing on levels highlights the remaining gender inequality in the labor market; as Bernstein shows, in each year, a higher proportion of women have below-poverty wages than men (Figure 1.1), and the 20th percentile of women's wage distribution is always well below the 20th percentile of men's distribution (Figure 1.4). But if we focus instead on trends, women's wages by either measure trend upward over the period, rising especially during the 1980s, a period when men's wages were declining. Of course these wage figures pertain only to those who are employed, but here too women's situation trended upward while men's trended downward (Casper & Bianchi, 2001). Thus, gender inequality in market earnings decreased significantly but is still marked.

We have a better understanding of explanations for the decline in gender inequality than we do for the increased inequalities within each of the male and female distributions. Bernstein states that women's relative wages increased in part because of increases in the relative human capital of women, and due to a shift in the occupational distribution. Actually, sex differences in years of education have never been an important part of the sex gap in pay, particularly toward the bottom of the distribution. More men than women have dropped out of high school for a century, but where college is the issue, women were previously behind but are catching up quickly (Casper & Bianchi, 2001). More important to the sex gap in pay is the gender gap in experience, which results from women leaving the labor market to rear children. As women's employment has become more continuous, women's experience and seniority has increased relative to men's, lessening this source of the gender gap (Wellington, 1993, 1994). The second part of the declining sex gap in pay is occupational desegregation, owing to declines in hiring discrimination against women aspiring to enter predominantly male occupations, along with shifts in women's aspirations toward less sex-typed occupations (Blau, 1998). Bernstein refers to the shift in women's occupational distribution as "occupational upgrading". While the shifts in jobs were clearly upgrading with respect to pay, it is not clear that there has ever been a difference in the quantity of education or skill required by "male" versus "female" jobs. Occupational sex segregation is much more a matter of women's jobs paying less despite requiring a comparable amount albeit different types of skill than men's jobs. Policy initiatives for "comparable worth" (sometimes called pay equity) were animated by this finding of the low pay of female occupations relative to their skill demands and the human capital of their incumbents (England, 1992; Sorensen, 1994; Steinberg, 2001). But these initiatives never made it into law that affects the private sector. Thus, there has been no diminution in the extent to which female occupations pay less (England, Thompson, & Aman, 2001), just a decrease in women's concentration in traditionally female jobs.

Bernstein's analyses are driven by what is happening in the lower half of the distribution of jobs and earnings. I was interested to see so much progress on gender inequality even here since other work shows that both desegregation and experience increases have been greater among well educated women than in the rest of the distribution (Casper & Bianchi, 2001; Jacobs, 1989). Women have entered male professions and managerial jobs in much greater proportions than they have entered male skilled blue-collar trades, construction, and manufacturing jobs that are traditionally male (e.g., steel, automobiles). Whether this is because discrimination by employees is more severe in blue-collar jobs (it is unclear why this would be), men resist female coworkers more in these fields, or women are less interested in integrating these fields is not clear. Given this lack of progress in desegregation in the blue-collar world, the closing of the gender pay gap here is probably driven mostly by the steep fall in pay in blue-collar, predominantly male jobs in recent decades.

How do we explain the increased inequality within each of the male and female earnings distributions? Is there a theory of labor markets that offers a coherent explanation for these trends and suggests mechanisms for them? Bernstein says that his analysis is guided by the dual (or segmented) labor markets perspective. Although it is less popular in economics, many sociologists have adopted the segmentation perspective. The central idea is that some industries or firms offer higher wages, steeper wage trajectories with seniority, and better benefits because they are bigger, have higher profits, are more sheltered from vicissitudes of product markets by regulation or oligopoly, or have production processes that give labor more power (e.g., capital intensity gives workers a threat to sabotage equipment). Researchers have never come up with an agreed-upon operationalization of sectors. Yet, most ways of operationalizing the concept suggest wage differences between workers whose measured human capital is the same. In contrast, the differences in returns to seniority that the theory predicts have never really been adequately tested. The enduring contribution of the segmented labor market perspective is the insight that characteristics of positions affect wages quite apart from the skill levels of those holding the positions. While Bernstein claims to be guided by this perspective, his explanations of wage trends do not really stand or fall on the validity of the theory.

The deindustrialization thesis can be seen, loosely, as a dynamic version of segmented labor market theory. The idea is that jobs in the core were shifted abroad as capital became more mobile, increasing international competition. Either core jobs disappeared, or their wages went down as employers forced concessions on unions. Clearly, this is part of the story. But, as Bernstein points out, some of his own and others' decompositions attribute only about 15% of declining male wages or increasing inequality to industry composition shifts. If we include women in the analysis, another part of the restructuring story lies in the economy's shift toward the importance of care services, such as hospital, nursing home, and childcare workers. These sectors are expanding and pay extremely low wages to their largely women workers. The labor intensivity of the services makes it hard to use technology for productivity increases.

Bernstein's argument about what explains the erosion of wages hinges less on dual economy theory than on politics. He argues that workers lost power because Congress failed to increase the minimum wage and its real value fell drastically, unions declined in strength, the federal government became more anti-union, and 1980s monetary policy sustained high unemployment rates. Immigration and globalization also pulled wages down at the bottom. All these forces remained in place in the last half of the 1990s, but wages rebounded strongly. He attributes this in large part to the Federal Reserve Board's low interest rate policies, which encouraged full employment. While the rebound in wages at the bottom did not restore them to their 1973 level, the progress was impressive.

Changing Family Patterns

Bernstein talks little about family structure or women's employment, but there have been profound shifts in both that affect the trends in family income that he discusses in his chapter. Two compositional shifts in family patterns are important: (1) increasing women's employment leading more married couple families to have two earners, and (2) increasing single motherhood. Single motherhood was fueled in the 1960s and 1970s largely by increases in divorce. More recently it has been driven largely by later marriage combined with nonmarital childbearing (Casper & Bianchi, 2001). If we care about incomes out of concern for whether children are growing up in households with adequate incomes, then we should be concerned about family constellations as well as individuals' wages, as both affect the availability of income to children.

What has been the effect of the increases in women's employment and earnings? Ceteris paribus, this should help the adequacy of families' incomes. Indeed, from the point of view of adequate income for children, the decrease in men's wages, while of concern in its own right, would not necessarily increase the proportion of families with children facing inadequate incomes because husbands' decreases could have been offset by increases in wives' earnings. However, women's employment and earnings have grown most among well-educated women (Cancian & Reed, 1999), at least till until the mid-1990s when welfare reform, low unemployment, and the incentives of the Earned Income Tax Credit (EITC) combined to increase women's employment disproportionately (Meyer, 2002). Despite the high earnings of women whose husbands are also affluent, Cancian and Reed (1999) show that trends in women's employment did not contribute to increases in the distribution of household incomes (even before 1995). And women's employment has helped families at the bottom be above cutoffs for adequate income.

The rise of single motherhood, on the other hand, has contributed to inequality in household income and to inadequate incomes for children. More children are growing up largely disconnected from men's wages (given the inadequacy of child support), and supported by women's earnings. While women's earnings have increased relative to men's, they are still lower (Blau, 1998). Given our nation's paltry public support for single-mother families, this leaves many children below or near poverty.

Single motherhood comes about in two ways—divorce and nonmarital births. Divorce increased dramatically during the 1970s and has been level or slightly decreasing since 1980. Nonmarital births have been increasing steadily. About one third of births in the U.S. are now to unmarried parents. This is the main cause of the increase in single motherhood in the 1980s and 1990s (Casper & Bianchi, 2001; Ellwood and Jencks, 2001). In an accounting sense, a big part of the explanation is the retreat from marriage; one is not at risk to have a nonmarital birth if one is married. Part of what has changed is the lesser frequency of resolving a premarital pregnancy with a wedding. While many such pregnancies are resolved by abortion, many others lead to single women raising children alone. The bottom two thirds of the educational distribution has seen a steadily increasing rate of single motherhood, with women having children long before marriage (Ellwood & Jencks, 2001). Declining male wages, reducing the number of what Wilson and Neckerman (1986) referred to as "marriageable men" is part of the explanation for the decline in marriage. But Ellwood and Jencks (2001) argue that declines in male wages are too small to explain the very large portion of the increases in nonmarital child bearing. Moreover, explaining both the retreat from marriage and the accompanying nonmarital child bearing in terms of the fall in men's wages does not really make sense. After all, children are much more expensive than unemployed husbands because the former need childcare. An alternative explanation is the "women's independence effect," focusing on women's greater ability to support a child than in the past given increases in women's employment and wages, although this squares badly with the fact that nonmarital births have increased most among less-educated women. The fact is that we do not fully understand which side of the marriage "market" the retreat from marriage is coming from, how much is a cultural shift that raises the bar for marriage, and how much of the increase in single motherhood is explained by trends in the relative wages of men and women. What is clear is that the increase in single-mother families has contributed to the increase in household income inequality (Cancian & Reed, 1999) and to the inadequacy of the incomes in the households in which many children live (Christopher et al., 2001).

The Role of Public Policy

A major initiative of the Bush administration, linked closely with welfare reform, has been to promote marriage as a way to reduce single motherhood, child poverty, and other social problems. In one sense the policy makes sense. Clearly the increase in nonmarital births has encouraged child poverty, given the low wages of women and the low levels of and imperfect enforcement of child support. However, it must be noted that pronouncements coming from the Bush administration seem to assume that all the problems *correlated* with single motherhood are *caused by* single motherhood. This ignores the powerful forces of selectivity into single motherhood; generally, women with backgrounds that nearly guarantee their future socioeconomic disadvantage are most likely to become single mothers. At the same time, it is important not to go to the opposite extreme and think that the increase in single motherhood is all about the decrease in marriageable men (Ellwood & Jencks, 2001). The evidence suggests that a cultural shift has taken place and people see financial security as well as a certain quality of relationship as a prerequisite for marriage—more so than as a prerequisite for having children.

Children seem to be the less optional proposition, particularly for women without access to interesting or lucrative jobs. Moreover, unplanned pregnancies still happen frequently, and many cannot get or do not believe in abortion. About half of nonmarital births today are to cohabiting couples, and another 30–40% are to couples who are romantically involved (Carlson, McLanahan, & England, 2002). Some of these couples will get married eventually, but many will break up. While I share many liberals' and sociologists' opposition to removing money from direct transfers to the poor for marriage promotion, I do favor programs teaching relationship skills. We do not know if these will encourage stable, happy two-parent families, but the question is worth studying. Meanwhile, given that couples who have a child out of wedlock are more likely to stay together and marry if either partner's earnings are higher, policies that increase the incomes of low-wage workers, male or female, would be very pro-marriage (Carlson, McLanahan, & England, 2002). Policies that raise the incomes of low-wage workers would also help single-mother families, as well as two-parent families supported by low-wage workers.

In this vein, Bernstein recommends policies that encourage full employment (because they especially boost incomes at the bottom) as well as policies that supplement the income of working families from government transfers. Such supplementation could come through the EITC and public subsidies of childcare or healthcare. I agree with these recommendations.

Let us consider the underlying normative and scientific propositions from which these policy recommendations flow. On the scientific side, Bernstein is convinced that a high level of low-wage work is an enduring feature of our economy. The U.S. economy "produces" more low-wage work—but less unemployment and nonemployment—than Europe. The preponderance of low-wage work is the reason we need nonmarket sources of income for families supported by such workers.

What are the normative assumptions underlying this? They are presumably either that all people (or at least all children) deserve to live above some minimum adequate income (either absolutely or relative to other families). Thus, if this can be achieved only through nonmarket transfers, such a commitment implies that those of us with adequate incomes should be willing to tax ourselves to provide these transfers. An alternative formulation is founded more on opportunities for children than in terms of results. Inequality of results might be all right in a world of adults only but when they impact the opportunities of children they cut into the equality of opportunity that most Americans believe in. In this formulation, we need more equality of results not because this is a value in its own right, but to support more equality of opportunity.

What does the American public believe about this? If they agreed, why would welfare be so unpopular? I used to think that the median voter was operating out of simple narrow self-interest, not wanting to be taxed to redistribute income to others. But this is hard to square with the growth of the EITC, which redistributes much more income than AFDC ever did, with little negative political fallout, and with the increases in recent years in expenditures for child care and other "work supports" for working parents. Implicit in Bernstein's formulations, it seems to me, is a recognition that Americans' opposition to welfare is tied up with a work ethic in which paid work (not child rearing) is what counts. In this view, what is objectionable is to ask one family to transfer income to another if the receiving family doesn't have a paid worker. The typical voter *does* seem to have some willingness, however, to redistribute income conditioned on paid work. This is what the EITC does; one can get it only if there is earned income. It pains me to see the work of parenting not acknowledged as "counting" toward what would make one eligible for help from a safety net. But I think that those who favor redistribution for either of the reasons discussed above will have to tailor programs to be consistent with these "pro-paid-work" sensibilities or they will not be politically feasible. I am still hopeful that it may be politically feasible to change credit toward Social Security to reflect parenting (as opposed to marriage as they now do), and it may be feasible to make transfers larger to parents than to others, but some participation in paid work is probably a sine qua non of future transfers.

The progressive agenda needs to build on citizens' willingness to favor programs that transfer income to help encourage a decent standard of living and more equal opportunity only to families where at least one person is willing to work for pay. Of course, skirmishes remain about the terms of the redistribution— how much is offered, how many hours must be worked. For example, many in Congress currently want to require welfare mothers to work more hours for pay than do most middle-class mothers. And despite some willingness to make childcare funds available to families conditional on paid work effort, such programs are drastically short of making universal childcare available to all working parents— or even to low-income working parents. Still, it is interesting that the EITC has received little challenge. Thus, transfers (EITC, childcare, etc.) conditioned on paid work may be the main game in town to help poor families outside the market. This will not work for families headed by a single parent who cannot realistically work because of the mother's or a child's disability, but perhaps some revised version of SSI-Disability is more appropriate here.

Those who care about the well-being of families at the bottom can build on this "contingent social contract." Agreeing that we should do this, I nonetheless want to suggest two problems. First, consider the inverse U shape that defines the EITC benefits families get according to their earned income. The upward sloping part of the curve is where increased earned income yields more benefits. In this portion of the curve, those who are neediest get the least. Having some part of the range taking this shape is an inescapable consequence of having benefits work-conditioned in a way that is not just 0–1; more work yields more earnings and more benefit. In this range, the EITC creates a negative tax rate that encourages families to increase their hours of paid work. But holding hours of paid work constant between families, this upward sloping section also has the inegalitarian feature of giving more to higher-wage than lower-wage families. Given what we know about women's versus men's earnings, for example, it is likely to pay more to a family supported by a man toward the low end of the male distribution than a woman toward the low end of the female distribution. We could get around this by conditioning it on hours worked rather than earnings, but part of the simplicity of the EITC is that it can be administered by the IRS based on tax returns where earnings are documented with W-2s or other such documents. Documenting hours is not part of what the IRS does and is considerably more difficult. Thus, the EITC is limited in how much it can contribute to equality, and to boosting the incomes of those at the very bottom of the earned income distribution.

A second problem with the EITC is the "notch effect." Notches refer to places where an incremental increase in market income causes one to lose eligibility to an "all or nothing" in-kind program (such as health benefits), so that one loses more than was gained by the earnings increase. Such notches create work disincentives. At first glance, the EITC does not seem to have this problem because its means-testing uses a smooth sliding scale. However, the articulation of such income transfers with means-tested all-or-nothing in-kind transfers creates notches. For example, childcare and medical care in many states are means-tested and shut off entirely at a certain income level. Falling off a financial cliff or losing medical or childcare because a parent gets a raise or married can cause havoc for families, and creates disincentives for either paid work or marriage to an employed partner.

The negative income tax (of which the EITC is a special work-conditioned version) was proposed in part to get rid of this patchwork of programs. But without additional childcare and healthcare, they are likely to be inadequate, especially for families with several children or children with special needs. A European way to avoid notches is to make in-kind programs such as childcare and medical care universal. Bernstein advocates moving in this direction, and I agree. This, of course, increases the cost of health and childcare programs many times, but also increases the benefits and their political popularity once established. It bears repeating that we are the only industrialized nation without universal healthcare, and many nations have near universal preschool. There is a good investment-in-human-capabilities argument for such expenditures, which are one way that one generation loans money to the next, to be repaid when the younger generation becomes wage earners (England & Folbre, 1999). The best public policy response to low wages is a combination of transfers and universal benefits that ensure adequate support for children in all kinds of families.

References

Bernhard, A. D., Morris, M., Handcock, M. S., & Scott, M. A. (2001). *Divergent paths: Economic mobility in the new American labor market.* New York: Russell Sage Foundation.

Blau, F. D. (1998). Trends in the well-being of American women, 1970–1995. *Journal of Economic Literature, 36,* 112–165.

Cancian, M., & Reed, D. (1999). The impact of wives' earnings on income inequality: Issues and estimates. *Demography, 36,* 173–184.

Carlson, M., McLanahan, S., & England, P. (2002). Union formation and dissolution in fragile families. Unpublished manuscript, Columbia School of Social Work.

Casper, L. M., & Bianchi, S. M. (2001). *Trends in the American family.* New York: Russell Sage Foundation.

Christopher, K., England, P., McLanahan, S., Ross, K., & Smeeding, T. (2001). Gender inequality in poverty in affluent nations: The role of single motherhood and the state. In K. Vleminckx & T. Smeeding (Eds.), *Child well-being, child poverty and child policy in modern nations* (pp.199–220). London: Policy Press.

Ellwood, D. T., & Jencks, C. (2001). The growing differences in family structure: What do we know? Where do we look for answers? Unpublished manuscript, John F. Kennedy School of Government, Harvard University.

England, P. (1992). *Comparable worth: Theories and evidence.* New York: Aldine de Gruyter.

England, P., & Folbre, N. (1999). Who should pay for the kids? *Annals of the American Academy of Political and Social Sciences, 563,* 194–209.

England, P., Thompson, J., & Aman, C. (2001). The sex gap in pay and comparable worth: An update. In I. Berg & A. Kalleberg (Eds.), *Sourcebook on labor markets: Evolving structures and processes.* New York: Plenum.

Jacobs, J. A. (1989). *Revolving doors: Sex segregation and women's careers.* Stanford, CA: Stanford University Press.

Meyer, B. D. (2002). Labor supply at the extensive and intensive margins: The EITC, welfare, and hours worked. *American Economic Review, 92,* 373–379.

Morris, M., Bernhardt, A. D., & Handcock, M. S. (1994). Economic inequality: New methods for new trends. *American Sociological Review, 59,* 205–219.

Sorensen, E. (1994). *Comparable worth: Is it a worthy policy?* Princeton: Princeton University Press.

Steinberg, R. J. (2001). Comparable worth in gender studies. In N. J. Smelser & P. B. Baltes (Eds.), *International Encyclopedia of the Social & Behavioral Sciences* (Vol. 4, pp. 2393–2397). London: Elsevier.

Wellington, A. J. (1993). Changes in the male-female wage gap, 1976–1985. *Journal of Human Resources, 28,* 383–411.

Wellington, A. J. (1994). Accounting for the male/female wage gap among whites: 1976 and 1985. *American Sociological Review, 59,* 839–884.

Wilson, W. J., & Neckerman, K. M. (1986). Poverty and family structure: The widening gap between evidence and public policy issues. In S. H. Danziger & D. H. Weinberg (Eds.), *Fighting poverty: What works and what doesn't.* Cambridge, MA: Harvard University Press.

3

BEYOND LOW WAGES: UNDEREMPLOYMENT IN AMERICA

Leif Jensen
Tim Slack
The Pennsylvania State University

Jared Bernstein (this volume) has pulled together a rich array of statistical information, much of it from his own work at the Economic Policy Institute, to address some basic issues regarding the past, present, and future of low-wage work in the United States. His analysis provides signs of both hope and despair. On the hopeful side, the economic boom and tight labor markets of the later 1990s were good for the wages of those with so-called "bad jobs." Working poverty among women declined steadily over recent decades, narrowing the gender gap in this regard. The black disadvantage in the prevalence of working poverty relative to whites also diminished during the Clinton expansion. Even more promising perhaps is the suggestion that the very low unemployment rates of this period were non-inflationary, giving rise to the hope that federal policy might recognize and institutionalize a lower full-employment unemployment rate.

On the downside, Bernstein calls attention to the increasingly integral role that low-wage service work plays in our daily economic lives. He seems to suggest that the centrality of low-wage work is both little appreciated and little understood, at least among those lucky enough to have good jobs. Obviously it goes much further than our own shores. Every time we go into a Wal-Mart we are surrounded by plastics and gadgetry manufactured by workers whose wages are dwarfed by the $8.70/hour that Bernstein uses as a threshold to define low-wage work. And Bernstein tells us that much of future employment growth is expected to be in the low-wage sector, raising the prospect that trends toward increasing income inequality will only increase. While some might wonder what's wrong with a little income inequality so long as all the boats are rising, research by Diane McLaughlin and Shannon Stokes suggests that net of other characteristics, the income inequality of places is associated with higher levels of mortality (McLaughlin & Stokes, 2002). There are other troubling signs in Bernstein's analysis as well. One is the apparently deteriorating circumstances of Latinos, at least relative to whites and blacks. On the policy side, federal subsidies for childcare are reaching a paltry percentage of all eligible children at a time when more and more single parents are being asked to show personal responsibility through work. And also on the policy side, if history is any guide, it is hard to be optimistic that minimum wages will be raised appreciably, or that EITC schedules will be made more generous, particularly if the country decides it wants to purchase a war in Iraq instead.

Along the way there are important lessons in Bernstein's analysis. For example, while it may seem obvious to a roomful of social scientists, it is not always clear to others that there is a difference between absolute and relative change. To be sure, some of the fastest growing jobs in relative terms will be high-skilled IT positions, but the base of such jobs is quite small. In absolute terms the greatest number of additional jobs over the next ten years are projected to be lower skilled and poor paying.

Bernstein's chapter leaves very little to criticize. As social scientists we often wrestle with the methodological trade-off between faceless numbers and numberless faces. Some might be unsettled by the barrage of graphs and charts based on statistics that are, after all, aggregates of real-life day-to-day struggles. I suspect other presentations at this conference will provide the faces and the stories of those striving to eke out a living with marginal employment.

Bernstein could only do so much in one chapter, but in one sense his story is constrained. By focusing on low-wage labor, he necessarily confines himself to only one dimension of the much broader concept of employment hardship. One line of research has empirically approached employment hardship via the concept of underemployment. With its roots in the Labor Utilization Framework of Philip Hauser (1974), and as refined by the work of Terry Sullivan, Cliff Clogg, and associates (Clogg, 1979; Clogg & Sullivan, 1983; Sullivan, 1978) researchers developed a measure of employment hardship that was more inclusive and comprehensive than mere unemployment. The operational definitions of states of underemployment used here are as follows:

> *Sub-unemployed* is a proxy for "discouraged workers" and includes individuals who are not currently working and who did not look for work during the previous four weeks because they felt no jobs were available;
> *Unemployed* follows the official definition and includes those not working but who (1) have looked for work during the previous four weeks, or (2) are currently on lay off;
> *Underemployed by low hours* (or involuntary part-time employment) parallels the official definition of those who are working "part-time for economic reasons" and includes those who are working less than 35 hours per week because they cannot find full-time employment;
> *Underemployed by low income* (or working poor) includes those whose labor market earnings during the previous year, adjusted for weeks and hours worked, were less than 125% of the official poverty threshold for an individual living alone.

All other workers are defined as *adequately employed*, while those who are not working and do not want to be working are defined as *not in the labor force*.

What we would like to do here then is to complement Bernstein's work with some additional analysis of underemployment in the U.S. for roughly the same two-decade period he was concerned with—more faceless numbers. Our analysis constitutes an extension of a line of research on trends and causes of underemployment conducted by Jensen in collaboration with Jill Findeis and our students (Jensen et al., 1999). Some of our past results echo Bernstein's findings. For example, with respect to trends in the prevalence of underemployment, we have documented increasing Latino-White inequality—a result that is partly accounted for by increases in Latino immigration—and like Bernstein we also document decreasing black-white inequality (Slack & Jensen, 2002). With respect to industry, we corroborate higher underemployment in services than manufacturing, but there are even greater disadvantages for those employed in retail trade and extraction. Finally, our past work has revealed distinct spatial disparities, with nonmetropolitan residents being more prone to underemployment than those living in metropolitan areas (Jensen et al., 1999). The spatial dimension of low-wage work is something Bernstein's paper touches on briefly through a state-level analysis, but it would be interesting to explore spatial differentiation in low-wage work in much greater detail. In *this* analysis, however, we focus on gender differences in underemployment.

While not emphasized perhaps as much as it could be, the gender dimension of Bernstein's findings is intriguing. On the one hand, he documents improvement in the circumstances of working women over recent decades; on the other, female workers remain more vulnerable than their male counterparts. Clearly also, the changing behavior of women is at the center of the striking shift in income packaging during the 1990s away from public assistance and toward earnings. To a significant degree this shift was induced by the welfare reform of 1996, a piece of legislation focused squarely on low-income single women and their children.

We analyze data from the March Current Population Surveys (CPS) for every third year spanning the period 1977–2001. Collected by the U.S. Bureau of the Census on behalf of the Bureau of Labor Statistics, the CPS is a monthly survey of approximately 50,000 U.S. households and all individuals residing within them. As the official source of the nation's unemployment statistics, the CPS contains key employment variables needed to operationalize the concept of underemployment as defined above.

Figure 3.1 shows the distribution of all workers across states of underemployment for the period 1977–2001. Those who are truly out of the labor force, that is, are not working and do not want to be, are excluded from the analysis for now. This figure shows that the large majority of all workers—ranging from 76% to 87%—are adequately employed. Among those who are underemployed, working poverty and unemployment are the most common forms of underemployment, followed by involuntary part-time workers and, lastly, discouraged workers. Also, mirroring a number of Bernstein's findings, the prevalence of underemployment is clearly countercyclical—rising during periods of recession such as the early 1980s and early 1990s. Finally, note that the prevalence of underemployment is roughly the same today—a couple of percentage points lower—than it was at the end of the 1970s. So as Bernstein also concludes in his analysis, we simply have not made that much progress over the long term.

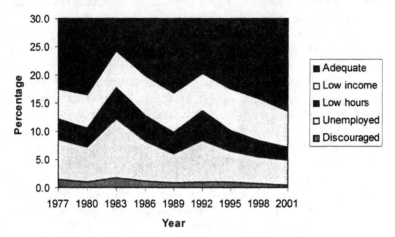

Figure 3.1. Underemployment by type, 1977-2001.

Figure 3.2 shows the same distribution for three years—1977, 1989, and 2001—but broken down by gender. In each of these years women are more likely to be underemployed, owing largely to the fact that they are more likely to be working poor. Overall, the gender difference in underemployment prevalence appears to be on the decline, a possibility that is confirmed in Figure 3.3. This figure shows underemployment rates for women and men, along with the excess

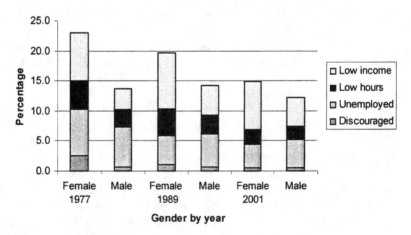

Figure 3.2. Underemployment by type by gender, 1977-2001.

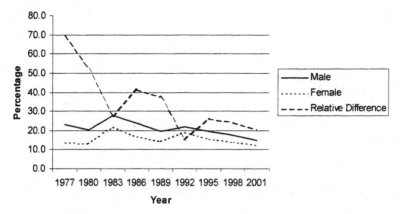

Figure 3.3. Underemployment by gender, 1977-2001.

of female-to-male underemployment expressed in relative terms. The pattern suggests a somewhat bumpy but nonetheless clear decline in gender inequality in underemployment. In 1977, the prevalence of underemployment among women exceeded that of men by some 69%. By 2001, this difference was only 21% (and only about 2.5 percentage points). Interestingly, this decline in gender inequality, coupled with the rise in women's labor force participation, has meant that over these years the share of all underemployed people who are women has remained fairly constant, hovering at just over one half.

Figure 3.4 shows trends in underemployment prevalence among women in one of four family status categories: unmarried with children present (where unmarried means never married, divorced, or separated), unmarried without children, married with children, and married without children. (An "other" category consisting of a small number of widows is not included here.) Not surprisingly, the figure reveals much higher underemployment among unmarried women with children, whose percentage underemployed is usually in excess of 30%. While the countercyclical trend in underemployment is clearly in evidence, note that among those unmarried with children, the dip between 1998 and 2001 seems to be in excess of what one would expect even taking into consideration the strong economy. Women who are married without children are the least likely to be underemployed over the years. Those in the remaining two categories fall between these extremes, hovering around the same rates as one another, at least until the 1990s when it appears those unmarried without children became worse off relative to those married with children.

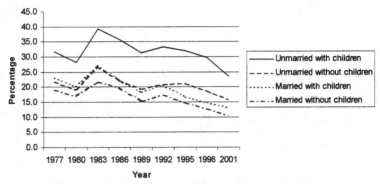

Figure 3.4. Underemployment among women by family status, 1977-2001.

As calculated here, the base of these underemployment rates excludes women who are not in the labor force and do not want to be. In Figure 3.5 we focus on single mothers but include those not in the labor force, and examine their distribution across three possible labor force states: not in the labor force, underemployed, and adequately employed. In most years about 30% of single mothers were not in the labor force. Adequate employment is always the modal category, with the smaller remaining portion consisting of the underemployed. Consistent with Bernstein's finding of a dramatic rise in reliance on earnings (versus public assistance) in the later 1990s, note the decline in the proportion of single mothers who are not in the labor force, but also the decline in the proportion underemployed. By the late 1990s and into the new millennium, the majority of all single mothers became adequately employed (58% in 2001).

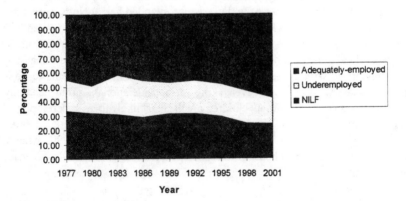

Figure 3.5. Employment status among unmarried women with children, 1977-2001.

Bernstein describes in his chapter the analytic question of whether one should examine low-wage work among the poor, or all low-wage work. For the most part he is concerned with the poor. To conclude our analysis we follow an analogous course by examining underemployment among women who are in families whose annual incomes were below 150% of the poverty threshold—the near poor. Figure 3.6 shows underemployment rates by family type among women in near-poor families. Not surprisingly, underemployment rates are uniformly higher for near-poor women than for all women (see Figure 3.4). By and large their underemployment rates exceed 50%, sometimes substantially so. However, even among near-poor women the pattern is one of decline in underemployment rates since the later 1980s, and especially during the later 1990s. Also interesting is that by restricting the analysis to those near-poor and below, there is much more homogeneity across family types in the prevalence of underemployment. Indeed, it is *not* single mothers with children who have the greatest likelihood of underemployment. Rather, in general it is poor women without children, whether single or married, who have the highest prevalence of underemployment. It is plausible that this reflects a kind of selectivity, such that poor women with children are more likely to endure the costs of entering the labor force only if their job prospects are somewhat better.

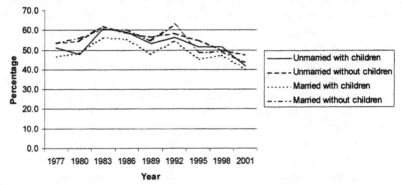

Figure 3.6. Underemployment among near-poor women by family status, 1977-2001.

Finally, Figure 3.7 shows the distribution of all poor and unmarried women with children across the three labor force states: not in the labor force, underemployed, and adequately employed. Compared to the same results for all such women regardless of poverty status (see Figure 3.5), poor unmarried women with children are less likely to be in the labor force, and more likely to be underemployed if they are. However, even among these near-poor women the pattern is similar to that seen previously. That is, the percentage not in the labor force drops appreciably during the later 1990s, reflecting the well-known influx of poor single mothers into the workforce, and the percentage adequately employed increases correspondingly.

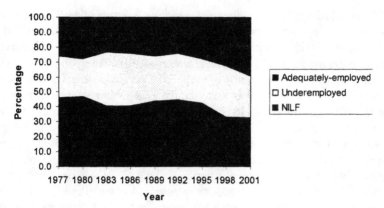

Figure 3.7. Employment status among near-poor unmarried women
with children, 1977-2001.

That so many and near-poor single mothers could be defined as adequately
employed exemplifies an inherent shortcoming in the algorithm we use for defining
underemployment with the CPS. Underemployment status is first determined by
current labor force status. Only if someone is currently employed full-time, or
part-time voluntarily, do we then assess whether they are working poor, and that
status is based on the previous year's earnings adjusted for weeks and hours worked.
Someone otherwise adequately employed at present could have worked just a few
weeks in the previous year, but if their wages during that stint were above the low-
wage cutoff, they would *not* be defined here as working poor even if their family
income was the below poverty level. The point is, that those we define as adequately
employed here may include many who are currently working in low-wage jobs, as
defined by Bernstein.

So, like Bernstein's analysis, our modest descriptive treatment of
underemployment has both positive and negative implications. On the bright side
gender disparities in underemployment have declined, and the strong economy of
the 1990s clearly helped to reduce underemployment, especially among women.
At the same time, however, women remained disadvantaged relative to men, and
single women with children remain especially vulnerable to underemployment.

In a sense it is unfortunate that our analysis does not include post-2001 data,
because certainly one worries how the current recession will affect prospects for
underemployment. Indeed, upward ticks in both poverty and unemployment rates
have been much in the news lately. Will the healthy gains of the 1990s simply
evaporate? If so, such that folks at the bottom find it harder and harder to make
ends meet, and if welfare reform is re-authorized (perhaps with an even tougher
love than before), what will working families do? Bernstein offers an excellent
package of policy options that needs to be embraced. Expanding health insurance
coverage and child care support, increasing the minimum wage and earned income

credits, and stimulating the economy to achieve a fuller full employment all make sense. That this package seeks to ameliorate poverty through work and "playing by the rules" may be sufficiently alluring to political moderates that it has half a chance. But, again, it's hard to be terribly optimistic.

If such an array of policy options is not enacted, again we are left with the question of what folks will do. One intriguing possibility is that they will increasingly turn to the informal economy to make ends meet, something that Tim Slack is exploring in his dissertation research. But even here there is evidence from a study in Vermont by Nelson and Smith (1999) which suggests that working families with at least one good job are in a better position to profit from participation in the informal economy than are those families whose jobs are in Bernstein's low-wage sector. Apparently, therefore, another double jeopardy faced by those with low-wage jobs is constraints against meaningful participation in the informal economy as well.

To conclude, the problems of working families today go beyond low wages to include a range of types of inadequate employment. Working poverty and other forms of underemployment are to an ever-increasing degree at the heart of the poverty debate. It is critical for Jared Bernstein's message and others like it to be central in that debate. What happens over the next few years will determine whether we should look to the longer-term future with hope or despair.

References

Clogg, C. C. (1979). *Measuring underemployment: Demographic indicators for the United States*. New York: Academic Press.

Clogg, C. C., & Sullivan, T. A. (1983). Demographic composition of underemployment trends, 1969–1980. *Social Indicators Research, 12*, 117–152.

Hauser, P. M. (1974). The measurement of labor utilization. *The Malayan Economic Review, 19*, 1–17.

Jensen, L., & Slack, T. (in press). Underemployment in America: Measurement and evidence. *American Journal of Community Psychology.*

Jensen, L., Findeis, J. L., Hsu, W., & Schachter, J. P. (1999). Slipping into and out of underemployment: Another disadvantage for nonmetropolitan workers? *Rural Sociology, 64,* 417–438.

McLaughlin, D. K., & Stokes, C. S. (2002). Income inequality and mortality in U.S. counties: Does minority racial concentration matter? *American Journal of Public Health, 92,* 99–104.

Nelson, M. K., & Smith, J. (1999). *Working hard and making do: Surviving in small town America*. Berkeley, CA: University of California Press.

Slack, T., & Jensen, L. (2002). Race, ethnicity and underemployment in nonmetropolitan America: A thirty-year profile. *Rural Sociology, 67,* 208–233.

Sullivan, T. A. (1978). *Marginal workers, marginal jobs: Underutilization of the U.S. work force*. Austin: University of Texas Press.

4

CHANGING FAMILIES, SHIFTING ECONOMIC FORTUNES, AND MEETING BASIC NEEDS

Lynne M. Casper
Rosalind B. King
National Institute of Child Health and Human Development

Dr. Jared Bernstein has written a very interesting and thought-provoking paper (Bernstein, this volume) and has done a superb job of bringing together data from different sources to describe the landscape of the low-wage labor market. Much research concerned with labor force participation, low-income families, and economic inequalities across families focuses on the supply side of the labor market, describing who occupies what types of jobs, how much they work, what they earn, and the attendant economic outcomes. Bernstein offers a refreshing look at low-wage jobs from the demand side, focusing on trends in low-wage jobs over time, the abundance and quality of these jobs, the important role they play in sustaining our economy, and their future outlook in 2010.[1] He also provides a thoughtful discussion of the effects of welfare reform and potential policy interventions that could be implemented to eliminate the gap between resources and need among low-wage workers.

Defining low-wage employment is complicated and somewhat arbitrary as Bernstein suggests in his chapter. The meanings and implications of a low-wage job are likely to differ depending on an individual's characteristics and circumstances. A high school student may be thrilled with a part-time job paying $6.00 per hour, whereas an unemployed aerospace engineer who is only able to locate a job teaching engineering at a technical school that pays $15.00 per hour would likely consider her new job to be low wage. Family structure, the changing composition of families over time, the age of the individual, and his or her attachment to the labor force affect the economic well-being of workers and their families. Earnings from a low-wage job are more or less adequate depending on the number and characteristics of the people they support. We argue that these characteristics should be taken into account in any examination of low-wage labor and how it affects economic well-being.

Family structure is very important in examining the implications of low-wage jobs across families. Two components related to family structure help to determine a family's economic status: (1) the total income of the family and (2) the ratio of dependents to earners in the family. The number of members in the family, and

---

[1] See Appendix A for a discussion of how the categorization of occupations affects the projections of types of jobs that will experience the most growth from 2000 to 2010.

each member's age, gender, marital status, and labor force status influence both of these components (Casper & Bianchi, 2002; Casper, McLanahan, & Garfinkel, 1994; McLanahan, Casper, & Sørensen, 1995). Each of these characteristics is related to family structure. For example, the more adult earners in the family, the more income the family is likely to have, all else being equal. Also, the more dependent children or other nonearners a family has, the more people there are to support. In general, men earn more than women. On average then, households with fathers do better financially than those with only mothers. Thus, a low-wage job means something very different in a single-mother family in which a mother is supporting herself and two children than it does in a dual-earner family in which the husband has a high-wage job and his spouse supplements his income with a part-time, low-wage job.

In addition, household and family structure have witnessed dramatic changes in the past three decades. Household and family sizes have declined, the number of single-mother and dual-earner families has grown, and more people are living by themselves. Shifts in family composition can affect economic inequality across households over time even if the proportion of low-wage jobs remains constant.

The age of the worker also matters because workers at either end of the age distribution depend more heavily on other sources of income. Earnings from a low-wage job do not have to stretch as far for a teenager whose parents provide food and shelter as they do for a middle-aged worker who is the only earner in the family and must support two children on her earnings. Similarly, older people generally have some economic support through the government, and/or pension or retirement funds and are not as dependent on their own earnings.

People generally have different degrees of attachment to the labor force. Research in this area has typically focused only on persons with a strong attachment to the labor force¾those who usually work full-time, year-round. While this approach supposedly controls for variability in the labor supply and provides a more precise measure of the wage rate, workers in households at the low end of the income distribution are not as likely to be represented in these traditional measures because they are more likely to experience unemployment, job market discouragement, and intermittent employment (Ryscavage, 1996). (See chapter 3 by Jensen and Slack for a thorough description of the extent and implications of underemployment.)

Given that the implications of low-wage jobs differ for people, we first discuss the importance of family and household structure in assessing economic disparity across families. We examine the change in household and family composition over time and illustrate how these changes parallel increasing economic inequality across families with different characteristics, and the relationship between age and occupation to demonstrate the importance of considering age in looking at low-wage jobs.

We conclude this chapter with an examination of the ability of low-wage workers and minorities to meet basic needs. Earnings, health insurance, and pensions are important indicators of economic well-being among low-wage workers, as Bernstein has shown, but they are not the only important indicators. In this chapter, we provide further evidence of the gap between earnings and needs among low-wage workers, looking at the ability of people across income quintiles and race to pay for necessities (e.g., rent, heat, electricity, etc.). We also examine their food sufficiency.

In this chapter, we provide a complimentary perspective to Bernstein's. We believe both approaches provide valuable insight and are indispensable for understanding low-wage work and its consequences for economic disparity across families.

The Changing Landscape of Families and Households

The question, 'What's Happening to the Family?' is one that demographers have been asking for a long time and their perspective has been both historical and dynamic (Bumpass, 1990). Five key demographic trends are relevant to understanding family change (Casper & Bianchi, 2002; DaVanzo & Rahman, 1993; McLanahan & Casper, 1995).

1. The delay in forming marriages, increasing the time adults spend outside marriage, often living in their parents' home, with friends, or unmarried partners;
2. The increase in heterosexual cohabitation, either as a precursor or substitute to marriage or as an alternative to living alone;
3. The growth in single-parenting due to widespread divorce but, more recently, a growing tendency for births to occur outside marriage as marriages are postponed;
4. The steady increase in women's labor force participation, especially among married women, in the second half of this century and the accompanying decline in the one-wage-earner, two-parent family; and, finally,
5. Delayed and declining fertility and declining mortality resulting in fewer children, smaller families, and also a lengthening of life, adding to the time adults spend "post-children."

This has fueled growth in the number of married couples without children and elderly who increasingly live independently, apart from their children or extended kin. These behaviors, when aggregated to the population-level, create changes in household and family structure that in turn affect income inequality.

The changes in household structure that result from these five trends are evident in Figure 4.1, Panel A. Traditionally, families have accounted for the large majority of households, but the "family" share of households has been declining.

Panel A: Households 1960-1998

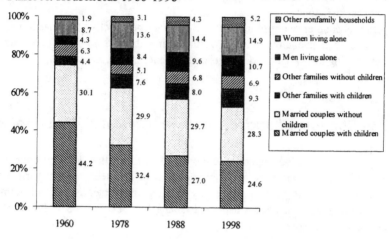

Panel B: Families 1978-1998*

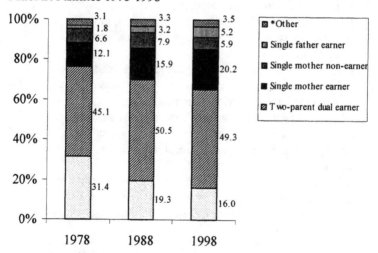

Source: Current Population Survey, March Supplements 1960-1998.
Note: Families are family groups
*Includes two-parent, mother-only earner families; two-parent neither-earner families; and single-father non-earner families
The proportions of these families are small and have not changed substantially over the past 20 years.

Figure 4.1.   Households and families by type.

A large component of the decline in family households was the decrease in the proportion of married-couple households with children. These households dropped dramatically from 44% of the total in 1960 to 25% in 1998. The proportion of households made up of married couples without children remained relatively stable over this 40-year period, as did the proportion of other families without children (e.g., two adult sisters living together, a mother living with her adult daughter or an uncle living with his adult nephew).

Another factor contributing to the decreased share of households that included children was the growth in nonfamily households, especially persons living alone. Those who live only with nonrelatives compose the other type of nonfamily household. These households have also grown substantially since the 1960s, although they account for a much smaller component of the growth in nonfamily households. Cohabiting households are included in this category and have experienced tremendous growth since 1960.

Changes in fertility, marriage, divorce, and mortality and growth in persons living alone have resulted in smaller households on average. The most profound differences occurred at the two extremes—the largest and smallest households. Between 1960 and 1998, the share of households with 5 or more people decreased from 23% to 10% (Casper & Bianchi, 2002, Figure 1.2). During the same period, the share of households with only one or two people increased from 41% to 58%. Between 1960 and 1998, the average number of people per household declined from 3.3 to 2.6, as did the average number of children under 18 years of age per family household.

What is Happening to the Two-Parent Family?

Much of the concern about the "disappearing" two-parent family centers on the well-being of children: the worry that children are less adequately supported when they do not live with both parents. Figure 4.1, Panel B shows the change during the past two decades in the distribution of family groups (hereafter referred to as families) with children by the parents' labor force status.[2] An important change in families is the increased likelihood that all parents in the home are employed. There has been a substantial decline in what some consider the "traditional" family—two parents with only the father employed. Meanwhile, two-parent families in which both parents worked outside the home increased slightly as a percentage of all families with children (from 45% to 49%). Between 1978 and 1998, the proportion of families with single mothers increased from 19% to 26%, and most of these mothers were employed. While this is an appreciable increase in single-mother families over the 20-year period, the proportion reached 26% in 1993 and

---

[2] Family households can contain more than one family group. The Census Bureau definition of a family group includes all family households plus related subfamilies (i.e., families within families, either married couples or parent-child units living in a family household) and unrelated subfamilies living in someone else's household. In the remainder of this chapter we refer to family groups with children under the age of 18 as families.

has remained there since. Moreover, about two thirds of single mothers were employed over the entire 20-year period. And, beginning around 1994, this proportion began to increase so that by 1998, more than three fourths of single mothers were employed.

Not only has the likelihood increased that all parents in the household are employed, but parents and other household members are working longer hours as well. In fact, hours of employment have grown for all types of households and families. Figure 4.2 presents the average annual number of hours worked for all individuals in the household by selected household and family types. The mean number of hours worked by all working members in the household in family households with children increased 11% between 1978 and 1998 (from 2,893 hours to 3,219 hours). For households the increase was 8%, from 2,329 to 2,504 hours per year. (The average hours worked per household is less than that per family because households are more likely to contain one person.) Both of these increases are particularly impressive when we consider that they occurred over a time period in which the average number of adults in families and households declined.

In 1998, dual-earner families with children in the home averaged the most work hours (4,147 per year). Single-father, earner families worked an average of 3,059 hours per year. Some may be surprised that single-father, earner families work so many hours. However, about 60% of single fathers are either cohabiting, living with their parents, or living with other adults (Casper & Bianchi, 2002, Table 5.1); the number of hours these individuals work is included in the calculations presented in Figure 4.2. It is interesting to note that by 1998, the average annual hours of work was similar for two-parent, father-only, earner families (2,570) and single-mother earner families (2,549). People who live alone worked the fewest average annual hours: 1,462 for men and 845 for women. They tend to work fewer hours both because by definition they are in homes with only one potential earner, and because a large proportion of them are retired.

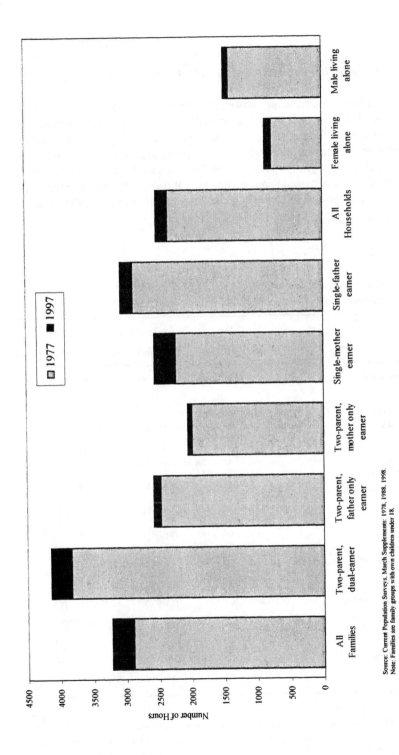

Source: Current Population Surveys, March Supplements: 1978, 1988, 1998.
Note: Families are family groups with own children under 18.

Figure 4.2. Increases in mean annual hours worked for selected household and family types, 1977-1997.

61

Racial Differences in Household and Family Structure

Variations in household structure constitute one of the most significant differences among black, Hispanic, and white families in the United States (Casper & Bianchi, 2002; McLanahan & Casper, 1995; Ruggles, 1994; Spain & Bianchi, 1996). Despite differences in levels of single-parenting, the patterns of family change have been similar for all of these groups over the past four decades. Since the 1960s, white, black, and Hispanic household composition has followed the same general pattern of declining married-couple and rising one-parent households with the majority of the change occurring in the 1960s and 1970s (Table 4.1).

Table 4.1

Types of Households and Family Groups with Children under Age 18, by Race: 1978, 1988, and 1998

	White			Black			Hispanic		
	1978	1988	1998	1978	1988	1998	1978	1988	1998
Total Households (%)	100	100	100	100	100	100	100	100	100
Married Couples	64.9	59.7	55.7	40.8	36.2	31.3	63.7	56.3	55.9
-With Children	32.6	27.0	24.2	23.8	19.8	16.4	45.6	37.3	36.3
-No Children	32.3	32.7	31.5	17.0	16.4	14.9	18.1	19.0	19.6
Female Householder	23.3	25.5	26.9	42.7	45.6	49.1	24.3	27.6	27.6
-With Children	4.6	4.6	5.0	20.0	19.7	20.5	12.7	13.3	13.1
-Living Alone	14.1	15.2	15.9	13.2	14.2	16.0	6.7	7.5	7.2
-Other	4.6	5.7	6.0	9.5	11.7	12.6	4.9	6.8	7.3
Male Householder	11.8	14.9	17.4	16.4	18.2	19.5	12.1	16.2	16.6
-With Children	0.6	1.0	1.7	1.2	1.6	1.7	1.0	2.0	2.7
-Living Alone	8.1	9.6	10.8	10.9	11.7	12.9	7.0	7.3	7.3
-Other	3.1	4.3	4.9	4.3	4.9	4.9	4.1	6.9	6.6
Total Family Groups with Children <18 (%)	100	100	100	100	100	100	100	100	100
Two-Parent, Dual Earner	47.8	56.6	55.9	31.0	29.6	28.6	37.3	36.5	36.9
Two-Parent, Only Father Earner	34.2	20.8	16.2	13.1	7.9	6.0	33.3	25.5	23.7
Single-Mother, Earner	9.9	12.9	15.8	27.4	32.2	44.3	10.5	15.1	19.4
Single-Mother, Non-Earner	3.8	3.9	3.6	21.5	23.4	13.1	13.3	14.3	10.4
Single-Father, Earner	1.6	3.2	5.4	2.6	3.0	4.2	1.9	3.6	5.2
Other*	2.8	2.7	3.1	4.4	4.0	3.8	3.6	5.1	4.5

Source: Casper & Bianchi 2002.

Note: Race/ethnicity categories are White, non-Hispanic; Black, non-Hispanic; and Hispanic.

*Includes two-parent, mother only earner; two-parent, neither earner; and single father non-earner. The proportions of these families are small and have not changed substantially over the past 20 years.

Restricting attention to all families rather than all households, the most dramatic racial difference in families is the contrast in the proportion that includes a married couple versus those with a single mother. This difference has sparked controversy dating back almost a half century to the infamous Moynihan Report (1965) that argued that the high rate of unemployment among black males was propelling "family disintegration" within the black community. Although many took issue with Moynihan's characterization of the black family, the likely causal relationship between lack of labor force opportunity and family formation decisions continues to be a theme in theory and research on poor and minority families to this day (Wilson, 1987, 1996).

Historically, men and women's work patterns have varied by race with higher labor force participation among black than white women and lower labor force participation among black than white men (Spain & Bianchi, 1996). For all races, a declining proportion of children live with two parents but the likelihood of having both parents employed has increased (Table 4.1, bottom panel). Similarly, the type of single-parent family that is increasing is one in which the single mother, or in a smaller proportion of cases the single father, is employed. Single-mother, non-earner families experienced minimal growth between 1978 and 1988 and then declined as a percentage of families with children between 1988 and 1998. The decrease was relatively small among white families, but quite substantial for black and Hispanic families.

Figure 4.3 graphs the ratio of black and Hispanic percentages in each family type to the white percentages. A dramatic difference among the three race groups is in the prevalence of the two-parent, father-earner family. Black families were about 40% less likely than whites to be in this group in all three periods. By contrast, Hispanic families were relatively similar to whites in 1978, but as time went on, were increasingly more likely than whites to be in this group.

Compared with whites, the most dramatic difference in family structure for both blacks and Hispanics is in the proportion of single-mother, non-earner families. Black and Hispanic families were also more likely to be single-mother, earner families. Single-father, earner families were more common among black and Hispanic families than among white families in 1978. But by 1998, this pattern was reversed with single-father, earner families as or more common among white families.

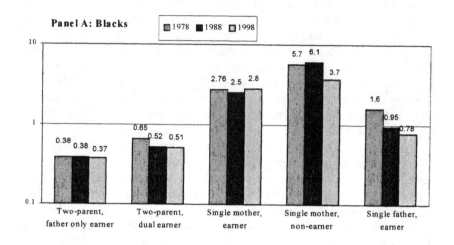

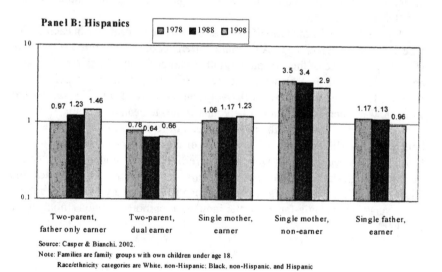

Source: Casper & Bianchi, 2002.

Note: Families are family groups with own children under age 18.

    Race/ethnicity categories are White, non-Hispanic; Black, non-Hispanic, and Hispanic

Figure 4.3. Changes in the ratios of family structure proportions of Black and Hispanic families to White families: 1978, 1988, and 1998.

Changing Families, Growing Economic Inequality Income

To illustrate the implications of low-wage work for different types of families, we describe how the economic fortunes of families with children vary by family structure and how they have changed as family structure and labor force participation have changed.[3] Table 4.2 shows data on income growth in families with employed and nonemployed parents.[4] In both absolute and relative terms, married-couple families with both parents employed fared best over the entire period. These families had the highest average household and per-capita income at each point in time,[5] changes in income were positive in both decades, and percent increases in income tended to outpace those in other types of families. In 1997, individuals in two-parent, dual-earner families had the highest per-capita income, followed by those in single-father, earner families, those in two-parent, father-only earner families, and those in single-mother, earner families. Those in single-mother, non-earner families fared the worst.

Figure 4.4 compares the per-capita income level a child, mother, or father would enjoy, on average, if he or she lived in different types of families. In 1997, a child in a two-parent family with only the father employed had a per-capita income level about two thirds that of a child in a dual-earner, two-parent family. Interestingly, two decades earlier, in 1977, such a child would have had an average per-capita income about 82% that of a child in a dual-earner, two-parent family. Thus, married-couple families with only the father employed lost ground vis-à-vis families with two earners.

Similarly, individuals who lived in single-parent families in 1997 had lower per-capita income levels than those in two-parent, dual-earner families. Most disadvantaged of all were individuals who lived in single-mother, non-earner families. All of these families lost ground to two-parent, dual-earner families; the income gap separating those in the least economically advantaged from those in the most economically advantaged families grew over the period.

---

[3] Of course, living arrangements are endogenous and often jointly determined with labor force decisions. Our point is simply that household and family structure matters, that individuals live in collectives, and that these living arrangements are linked to economic well-being. It is an empirical fact that people living in some arrangements, on average, fare better than those in other arrangements.

[4] The economic well-being of households also has changed. Due to space limitations, we do not discuss these changes here. For a discussion of income inequality across households, see Casper and Bianchi (2002), chapter 9.

[5] In 1977, the per-capita income of families with single fathers who were employed was actually $64 more than the per-capita income of two-parent, dual-earner families.

Table 4.2

*Changes in Median Household Income and Per Capita Income for Families
with Children by Employment Status of Parents: 1977 to 1997*

	1977	1987	1997	Percent change 77-87	Percent change 87-97
Two-Parent, Dual-Earner					
Household income	50,999	55,723	59,900	9.3	7.5
Per capita income	12,402	14,058	15,004	13.4	6.7
Two-Parent, Father Only Earner					
Household income	43,680	42,959	42,040	-1.7	-2.1
Per capita income	10,190	10,158	9,930	-0.3	-2.2
Single Mother, Earner					
Household income	24,024	25,968	25,306	8.1	-2.5
Per capita income	7,619	8,229	8,005	8.0	-2.7
Single Mother, Non-Earner					
Household income	11,535	8,731	9,332	-24.3	6.9
Per capita income	3,223	2,422	2,621	-24.9	8.2
Single Father, Earner					
Household income	40,933	36,310	35,976	-11.3	-0.9
Per capita income	12,464	11,903	11,600	-4.5	-2.5

Source: Casper & Bianchi, 2002.

Note: In 1997 dollars. Families are family groups with own children under 18. Employment status refers to employment last year. Data are shown for all family types that accounted for at least 5 percent of families in 1998. Not shown
are married-couple families with only the mother or neither parent employed and single-father families where the father
was not employed. Combined, these groups accounted for only about 3.5 percent of families in 1998 -- 1.8 percent of
families were two-parent with only a mother employed, 1.2 percent were two-parent neither employed, and 0.5 percent
were single-father families without an employed father.

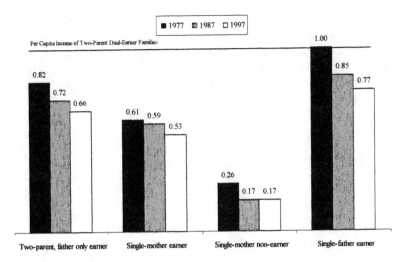

Figure 4.4. Ratios of per capita income of selected family types relative to two-parent, dual-earner families: 1977, 1987, and 1997.

Poverty

Household and per-capita income assess how families are doing, *on average*, but no assessment of family economic well-being is complete without a look at those families who are at the bottom of the income distribution and experience substantial material hardship. A comparison of poverty levels across families shows that chances of falling into poverty vary greatly by family type and employment status of the parents.

Table 4.3 shows that two-parent families who are buffered against poverty by earnings from both the mother and father have poverty rates that are extremely low (2.4% in two-parent, dual-earner families in 1997). By contrast, when the father is the only earner in a two-parent family, poverty rates rise considerably¾to almost 15%. Similarly, almost 14% of single, employed father families are in poverty. Single-mother families with an employed parent are even more disadvantaged with a poverty rate of 30%. Families with no parents in the labor force run an extremely high risk of living in poverty.

The table also shows the change in poverty rates over time for different types of families. Overall, for all families with children the poverty rate rose from 13.4% in 1978 to 19.1% in 1988, but fell again to 16.1% in 1998. Regardless of family type, all families experienced increasing in poverty from 1978–1988. However, between 1988 and 1998, all families, except two-parent, father earner families, experienced declines in poverty levels. Looking at the ratios of poverty for each family group relative to the two-parent, dual-earner family, we see that the ratios increase in each decade for each family type. These numbers indicate that overall, other families are increasingly falling behind the most well-off type of family— two-parent families with both parents employed. Put another way, income inequality across families is increasing.

Table 4.3

Changing Poverty Levels for Selected Family Types: 1977-1997

	Percent in Poverty			Ratio to Dual-Earner, Two-Parent Family		
	1977	1987	1997	1977	1987	1997
All families	13.4	19.1	16.1	NA	NA	NA
Two-parent, dual-earner	3.4	3.6	2.4	1.0	1.0	1.0
Two-parent, father only employed	7.3	12.7	14.7	2.1	3.5	6.1
Single mother, employed	26.1	33.7	30.0	7.7	9.4	12.5
Single mother, not employed	76.4	92.1	74.4	13.6	25.6	31.0
Single father, employed	12.3	16.3	13.7	3.6	4.5	5.7

Source: Current Population Survey, March Supplements: 1978, 1988, 1998.

Note: Families are family groups with own children under 18. Employment status refers to employment last year. Data are shown for all family types that accounted for at least 5% of families in 1998. Not shown are married-couple families with only the mother or neither parent employed and single-father families where the father was not employed. Combined, these groups accounted for only about 3.5% of families in 1998 -- 1.8% of families were two-parent with only a mother employed, 1.2% were two-parent neither employed, and 0.5% were single-father families without an employed father.

The level of income in minority families is significantly lower and the likelihood of poverty much higher than in non-Hispanic white families. Table 4.4 shows per-capita income and the percent in poverty for selected types of families with children in 1997. Within each race, minority two-parent, dual-earner families are advantaged relative to other types of minority families. However, minority families are disadvantaged relative to comparable white families.

Table 4.4

Changing Poverty Levels for Selected Family Types: 1977–1997

	Per Capita Income			Poverty Rate		
Selected Family Types	Median	Ratio to White Family of Same Type	Ratio to White Dual-Earner, Two-Parent Family	Percent in Poverty	Ratio to White Family of Same Type	Ratio to White Dual-Earner, Two-Parent Family
Two-Parent, Dual Earner						
White	16,061	1.00	1 00	1.6	1 00	1 00
Black	12,750	0.79	0 79	2.3	1.44	1.44
Hispanic	9,691	0.60	0.60	8.4	5.25	5.25
Two-Parent, Father Only Earner						
White	12,025	1.00	0.75	8.0	1.00	5.00
Black	6,615	0.55	0.41	22 7	2.84	14.19
Hispanic	5,280	0 44	0.33	34.8	4.35	21.75
Single-Mother, Earner						
White	9,698	1.00	0.60	24.8	1.00	15.50
Black	6,193	0.64	0.39	35 8	1 44	22.38
Hispanic	6,387	0.66	0.40	35 6	1 44	22.25
Single-Mother, Non-Earner						
White	3,900	1.00	0.24	65 8	1.00	41.13
Black	1,832	0.47	0.11	80.8	1.23	50.50
Hispanic	2,069	0.53	0.13	82.6	1.26	51.63
Single-Father, Earner						
White	12,333	1.00	0.77	11.5	1.00	7.19
Black	9,585	0.78	0.60	15.2	1.32.	9.50
Hispanic	7,333	0.59	0 46	26.1	2.27	16.31

Source: Casper & Bianchi, 2002.

Note: Families are family groups with children under 18. Race/ethnicity categories are White, non-Hispanic; Black, non-Hispanic; and Hispanic.

Components of Rising Household Income Inequality

Given this picture of increased income inequality, one of the important questions is, why has this happened? The answer, it turns out, is complex and involves a mix of factors, some having to do with marriage and living arrangements and others having to do with how well certain types of workers are doing in the labor force. For example, the number of one-person households has grown, as has the proportion of families that have only one parent present. Mother-only families, as we have seen, have low incomes relative to two-parent families. But single-person households, in which income rose substantially in the 1980s, also have lower incomes than married-couple families with two earners. Hence, the changing composition of families and the labor force participation rates of members within those families require increased scrutiny.

But this is not the whole story. At the same time that household structure has changed, earnings inequality has also grown. For example, it is now well established that inequality in the earnings distribution has increased with less well-educated workers, male and female, falling behind college-educated workers. Families relying on earnings from high school (or less) educated householders are increasingly disadvantaged.

Several studies document the role that changing household structure has played in trends in income inequality. The movement away from married-couple families and the increase in dual earning within married-couple families are compositional shifts that have contributed to rising income inequality across households (Karoly & Burtless, 1995; McLanahan & Casper, 1995; Ryscavage, 1995). Levy (1998) estimates that these compositional changes explain as much as two fifths of the growth in inequality. Change in income and earnings account for the other three fifths, according to Levy. The largest wage factor is men's earnings.

One caveat is in order. Most of these studies took place before welfare reform, and hence, before women with low human capital began to enter the labor force. It is unclear how the increasing labor force participation among low-income women, most of whom are single-mothers, has affected income inequality across families.

Age and Low-Wage Jobs

The implications of low-wage work differ across the life course. As teens age they pass from dependence on their parents to financial independence, supporting themselves and most likely a family. As they age still further, they enter retirement and come to depend less on their own earnings and more on income from social security, pensions, and retirement savings. The need for personal earnings is greater in mid-life when obligations to support a family are also greater and other sources of income are not as easily obtained. As Bernstein argues, low-wage jobs are necessary to sustain our economy, but they are also useful for some younger workers to help support themselves before they become established and for older workers who may want or need to supplement their income.

Bernstein shows (Bernstein, this volume, Table 1.2) that low-wage workers are most often found in "other" service, sales, and clerical occupations. In Table 4.5, we use 2000 Current Population Survey data to examine the age distribution of workers within occupations and to investigate the extent to which younger and older workers are found in typically low-wage occupations. As one might expect, teenagers comprise a greater proportion of these low-wage occupations than other occupations. They are also more likely to be laborers, or providing household services, occupations that also pay relatively poorly (Table 4.5, bottom panel). Older workers are also most often found in poor paying jobs: farm, private household services, sales and transportation. Workers aged 25–54 are more likely to be found in higher paying professions—managerial, professional, and technical. By contrast, younger and older workers are not well represented in these occupations. Hence, low-wage jobs do contain a higher proportion of younger and older workers who may have more income from other sources and fewer financial obligations.

Table 4.5
Age Distribution and Total Average Annual Earnings
by Major Occupational Group

Age Distribution		Age Group				
		15-19	20-24	25-54	55-64	65+
Occupational Division	N					
Managerial	8,889	0.7	4.1	79.1	12.3	3.8
Professional	9,479	1.5	6.0	77.3	11.4	3.7
Technical	2,195	2.4	10.8	78.0	7.7	1.1
Clerical	9,673	5.1	12.2	68.1	10.3	4.2
Sales	7,879	13.1	13.1	59.8	9.4	4.5
Protective Services	1,218	4.9	10.4	71.2	9.6	3.9
Other Services	8,280	16.6	14.7	56.2	8.9	3.6
Craft	6,725	2.7	8.7	76.7	9.7	2.2
Operatives	3,860	3.6	11.3	73.8	9.2	2.2
Transportation	2,772	3.4	8.2	70.7	12.4	5.3
Laborers	3,022	17.7	19.6	54.3	6.6	1.8
Private Household Services	543	19.1	10.2	48.6	13.9	8.2
Farm	1,579	12.8	10.6	55.9	11.1	9.6

Table 4.5 cont'd.

Average Annual Earnings		Age Group				
		15-19	20-24	25-54	55-64	65+
Occupational Division	N					
Managerial	8,889	$13,424	$21,327	$52,627	$57,545	$35,887
Professional	9,479	$4,866	$16,946	$46,267	$52,441	$37,654
Technical	2,195	$8,752	$15,695	$36,621	$39,593	$23,751
Clerical	9,673	$5,766	$13,216	$24,037	$24,607	$14,342
Sales	7,879	$4,727	$11,362	$37,830	$35,884	$22,484
Protective Services	1,218	$3,600	$15,219	$39,377	$31,455	$9,980
Other Services	8,280	$4,220	$9,781	$16,206	$15,542	$11,003
Craft	6,725	$10,311	$18,642	$35,013	$36,590	$22,921
Operatives	3,860	$8,360	$16,815	$25,587	$25,493	$14,491
Transportation	2,772	$10,884	$15,613	$29,641	$30,799	$11,783
Laborers	3,022	$5,247	$11,915	$20,361	$22,395	$14,140
Private Household Services	543	$962	$7,074	$11,072	$8,637	$4,175
Farm	1,579	$3,927	$10,624	$19,757	$19,384	$10,080

Source: Current Population Survey, March Supplement: 2000.
Note: ----- Ns are unweighted, percents are weighted. Major occupational group refers to
the longest job held last year.

   The bottom panel in the table also shows that average annual earnings vary
over the life course within occupations. The 25–54 age group includes the prime
years in which workers would be supporting a growing family. When we compare
earnings in these years to earnings in the teen years, we find that the ratio of
earnings of teen workers to those ages 25–54 ranges from 0.09 in private household
and protective services to over 0.33 among operatives and transportation workers.

When we compare earnings of retirement-aged workers to those ages 25–54, the earnings ratios range from lows of less than 0.40 among private household and protective services to a high of 0.81 among professionals. Even in low-wage jobs, workers earn more when they are most likely to be supporting a family. Thus, age differences are important to keep in mind when thinking about the implications of low-wage jobs.

Meeting Basic Needs

Bernstein described the inequality in wages, health insurance, and pension coverage between workers in low- and high-wage jobs. Changing families and their shifting economic fortunes also lead to inequalities across families in their abilities to meet basic needs. Some families have difficulties paying for the basic necessities of food, shelter, and clothing, while others don't go to the doctor or dentist when the need arises. The Survey of Income and Program Participation (SIPP) collects information about the difficulties people have in meeting basic needs. People who did not meet essential expenses, did not pay utility bills, did not pay rent or mortgage, needed to see the dentist but did not go, needed to see the doctor but did not go, had phone service cut off, had utilities shut off, were evicted, or did not get enough to eat are defined as having difficulty in meeting at least one basic need (Bauman, 1999). Overall, one in five people reported having difficulty meeting at least one basic need in 1995 (Table 4.6).

People living in low-wage households with household incomes in the lowest quintile were almost 6 times more likely to experience difficulties in meeting at least one basic need compared with those in high-wage households with incomes in the highest quintile (37.8% versus 6.5%). People in the lowest quintile were also more likely than those in any other quintile to have difficulty meeting each specific need presented in the table. For example, almost 20% of people in the lowest quintile lived in households that could not pay their full electric bill compared with 12% of those in households in the second quintile. They were also more likely to report that they sometimes didn't get enough food to eat. Eleven percent of those in the lowest quintile didn't get enough to eat compared with 7% in the second quintile, 3% in the third quintile, 2% in the fourth quintile, and under 1% in the highest quintile.

Inequalities in basic needs also exist across race. Blacks and Hispanics were far more likely to experience difficulties; approximately one in three had difficulties meeting at least one basic need compared with only 17% of whites. Minorities were also more likely to experience difficulties satisfying each of the separate needs listed in the table.

Table 4.6

People Living in Households with Difficulties Meeting Basic Needs, by Income Quintile and Race: 1955 (in percent except where noted)

Type of Difficulty with Basic Needs	Total	Income Quintiles					Race		
		Lowest Quintile	Second Quintile	Third Quintile	Fourth Quintile	Fifth Quintile	White	Black	Hispanic
Didn't meet essential expenses	12.8	25.0	15.8	10.9	6.5	4.2	10.9	21.3	18.2
Didn't pay full gas, electric, oil bill	9.9	19.9	12.2	8.5	4.4	2.8	7.8	18.2	16.2
Didn't pay full rent or mortgage	6.8	14.0	8.2	6.0	3.0	1.5	5.5	11.0	11.6
Needed to see dentist but didn't go	7.0	12.1	9.2	6.7	3.8	2.1	6.5	7.0	10.6
Needed to see doctor but didn't go	5.7	10.7	7.9	4.8	2.8	1.7	5.3	6.6	8.2
Had telephone disconnected	3.7	8.8	5.2	2.1	1.3	0.6	2.5	9.5	6.8
Had gas, electric, oil disconnected	1.9	4.0	2.1	1.5	1.0	0.4	1.3	4.2	3.4
Evicted from house or apartment	0.4	1.1	0.4	0.5	0.1	0.0	0.3	1.0	0.4
Not enough or not the kind of food wanted	18.8	35.1	24.8	15.1	9.8	6.4	14.6	30.4	35
Not enough food									
Percent	4.8	11.2	6.6	3.2	1.5	0.8	3.2	9.3	11.7
Avg. number of days without food in last 30 days	9	9	9	9	6	6	10	7	7
Avg. budget shortfall in last 30 days (dollars)	95	86	110	98	115	42	107	59	104
Experienced at least one difficulty	20.2	37.8	24.5	18.4	11.3	6.5	17.0	32.3	32.1

Source: Bauman, 1999.

Note: Income quintiles are calculated on household income. Race/Ethnicity categories are White, non-Hispanic; Black, non-Hispanic; and Hispanic.

Conclusion

Bernstein provides an important and useful description of the low-wage labor market and some innovative suggestions for dealing with the gap between income and needs of low-wage workers. Examining the low-wage labor market from the demand side is very important, but it is equally as important to point out that it only tells part of the story. When considering low-wage work and how it affects the well-being of workers, their families, and their children, we have argued that it is important to take into account differences in the structures of households and families, including the age, gender, marital status, and employment status of each occupant. Why? Because the implications of low-wage employment for workers can be quite different for people in different types of families and households. Also, compositional shifts can affect income inequality among households, families, and individuals. We presented evidence to support the claim that household compositional change did play a role in increasing family income inequality over time.

Bernstein also assesses the quality of low-wage work and discusses the relative lack of health insurance and pension benefits in low-wage occupations. We added to this discussion by examining how many people have problems meeting basic needs. Making ends meet is difficult for many families, especially for minority families and those in the lowest income quintile.

Income inequality has been rising just as the government has removed or reduced many of the supports that low-wage workers depend on to make ends meet. That these families are having difficulties paying for food, shelter, and utilities has been well documented. In the last part of his chapter, Bernstein suggests some policy interventions that could help ameliorate these problems. Only time will tell if these interventions are adopted and, if so, whether they have the intended result.

Appendix A

While we acknowledge and appreciate Bernstein's point about the difference between the fastest-growing occupations and those adding the most jobs and the relative quality of those jobs, we think that this point requires a caveat. The numbers cited by Bernstein refer to specific occupations. These numbers should be viewed within the context of the occupational classification scheme used by the Bureau of Labor Statistics (BLS).

The BLS projections reflect the 2000 Standard Occupational Classification system. This system begins with ten major occupational groups (e.g., professional and related occupations). These groups are eventually broken out into nearly 700 detailed occupations (e.g., computer support specialists) (Hecker, 2001). This process of disaggregation occurs across up to four levels and thus often splinters a substantial occupational group into a large number of small detailed occupations.

The left panel of Table 4.A shows the top ten detailed occupations projected to add the most jobs from 2000–2010 as presented in Bernstein. He asserts that most of the jobs to be added to the economy between 2000 and 2010 are low-wage jobs. As we show in the third column of the table, these particular detailed occupations vary in their levels of disaggregation from one to four levels. We thus investigated whether this ordering in terms of greatest number of jobs added remains the same when comparisons are made within the same level of disaggregation. Since "retail salespersons" is only one level of disaggregation within its major occupational group, we went back to the first disaggregation within major occupational group for the other nine detailed occupations as well. The BLS report does not provide a term to refer to the first disaggregation, so for our purposes we refer to the first disaggregation as an occupational division. Bernstein's ten detailed occupations fit within eight occupational divisions. Of those eight, the right panel of Table 4.A shows that, in contrast to Bernstein's findings, computer and mathematical occupations are projected to add the most jobs between 2000 and 2010, followed by healthcare practitioners and technical occupations.

This exercise also highlights the variation in levels of disaggregation among the detailed occupations. As we have noted, "retail salespersons" is both a detailed occupation and an occupational division. "Cashiers, except gaming, " a second-level disaggregation, forms the vast bulk of new jobs to be added among "cashiers" whereas "computer support specialists," a third-level disaggregation, forms approximately one quarter of new jobs to be added among "computer and mathematical occupations."

Besides being the occupational division with the greatest projected numerical job growth, "computer and mathematical occupations" includes seven of the top ten fastest growing detailed occupations. This occupational division has two subdivisions: computer specialists and mathematical science occupations. Computer specialists includes computer programmers, software engineers, database administrators, and systems analysts, among others. Mathematical science occupations include actuaries, mathematicians, and operations research analysts. Data processors are located under a different major occupational group, "office and administrative support occupations".

We agree with Bernstein that substantial increases in low-paying service jobs will likely occur over the next ten years. But as this exercise demonstrates, claims about the relative numbers added in different categories are highly subject to the classification scheme used.

Table 4.A
BLS Occupational Projections: Differing Categorizations of Those Adding Most Jobs

Specific Occupations Adding Most Jobs	New Job Openings	Level of Disaggregation	Occupational Divisions Containing Those Occupations	New Job Openings
Combined food preparation and serving workers, including fast food	673	3	Computer and mathematical occupations	1,996
Customer service representatives	631	3	Healthcare practitioners and technical occupations	1,599
Registered nurses	561	3	Food preparation and serving related occupations	1,577
Retail salespersons	510	1	Financial information and record clerks	1,172
Computer support specialists	490	3	Protective service occupations	809
Cashiers, except gaming	474	2	Secretaries, administrative assistants, and other office support occupations	592
Office clerks, general	430	2	Retail salespersons	510
Security guards	391	4	Cashiers	488
Computer software engineers, applications	380	4		
Waiters and waitresses	364	3		
Total	4,904		Total	8,743

Source: BLS Projections web page
(http://www.bls.gov/emp/home.htm#tables)

Source: Hecker, D. (2001). Occupational employment projections to 2010.
Monthly Labor Review (November), 57-84.

Acknowledgments

We are grateful to Suzanne Bianchi for providing comments on an earlier draft of this chapter. We thank Philip Cohen for providing the numbers presented in Table 4.5 and Matthew Hayden for his help with the tables and figures in this chapter. The findings and opinions expressed are attributable to the authors and do not necessarily reflect those of the NICHD.

References

Bauman, K. J. (1999). Extended measures of well-being: Meeting basic needs. *Current Population Reports, P70-67.* Washington, DC: U.S. Bureau of the Census.

Bianchi, S. M., & Casper, L. M. (2000). American families. *Population Bulletin, 55*(4). Washington, DC: Population Reference Bureau.

Bumpass, L. (1990). What's happening to the family? Interactions between demographic and institutional change. *Demography, 27,* 483–493.

Casper, L. M., & Bianchi, S. M. (2002). *Continuity and change in the American family.* Thousand Oaks, CA: Sage.

Casper, L. M., McLanahan, S. S., & Garfinkel, I. (1994). The gender-poverty gap: What we can learn from other countries. *American Sociological Review, 59,* 594–560.

DaVanzo, J., & Rahman, M. O. (1993). American families: Trends and correlates. *Population Index, 59,* 350–386.

Hecker, D. E. (2001). Occupational employment projections to 2010. *Monthly Labor Review, 124,* 57–84.

Karoly, L. A., & Burtless, G. (1995). Demographic change, rising earnings inequality, and the distribution of personal well-being. *Demography, 32,* 379–406.

Levy, F. (1998). *The new dollars and dreams.* New York: Russell Sage Foundation.

McLanahan, S. S., & Casper, L. M. (1995). Growing diversity and inequality in the American family. In R. Farley (Ed.), *State of the Union: America in the 1990s, Volume 2* (pp. 1–45). New York: Russell Sage Foundation.

McLanahan, S. S., Casper, L. M., & Sørensen, A. (1995). Women's roles and women's poverty in eight industrialized countries. In K. Mason & A. M. Jensen (Eds.), *Gender and family change in industrialized countries* (pp. 258–278). Oxford, England: IUSSP and Oxford University.

Moynihan, D. P. (1965). *The Negro family: The case for national action.* Washington, DC: U.S. Department of Labor, Office of Policy Planning and Research.

Ruggles, S. (1994). The transformation of American family structure. *American Historical Review, 99,* 103–127.

Ryscavage, P. (1996). A perspective on low-wage workers. *Current Population Reports, P70-57.* Washington, DC: U.S. Bureau of the Census.

Ryscavage, P. (1995). A surge in growing income inequality? *Monthly Labor Review, 118,* 51–61.

Spain, D., & Bianchi, S. M. (1996). *Balancing act: Motherhood, marriage, and employment among American women.* New York: Russell Sage Foundation.

Wilson, W. J. (1996). *When work disappears.* New York: Alfred A. Knopf.

Wilson, W. J. (1987). *The truly disadvantaged: The inner city, the underclass, and public policy.* Chicago: University of Chicago Press.

II

What Features of Work Timing Matter for Families?

5

EMPLOYMENT IN A 24/7 ECONOMY: CHALLENGES FOR THE FAMILY

Harriet B. Presser
University of Maryland

Introduction

Over recent decades, the U.S. labor force has been experiencing greater diversity in the nature of employment. The total number of weekly hours people are employed has been spreading to both ends of the continuum so that more people are working very few as well as very many hours (Smith, 1986; U.S. Department of Labor, 2002). *Which* hours people are working has also been changing with flex-time on the rise (Golden, 2001; U.S. Department of Labor, 1998) and more people working the "fringe times" of the traditional 9–5 work day (Hamermesh, 1999). Interestingly, the increasing diversity in work hours has been occurring while the cumulative number of weekly hours people are employed has remained virtually unchanged between 1970 and 2001 (Rones, Ilg, & Gardner, 1997; U.S. Department of Labor, 2002).[1]

An important but often neglected aspect of temporal diversity is employment that occurs mostly in the evening or night, or on a rotating basis around the clock. Although we do not have comparable data over time to rigorously assess the trend in non-day work shifts, there are strong indications that such employment is on the rise as we move toward a 24-hour, 7-days-a-week economy. As of 1997, only 29.1% of all Americans worked mostly during the daytime, 35–40 hours per week, Monday through Friday—the "standard" work week. Removing the limitation of 35–40 hours, and including those working part-time and over-time, the percentage increases to 54.4%—a bare majority (Presser, 1999).

As consumers, we witness the movement toward a 24/7 economy by observing that stores are increasingly open evenings and nights, it is easier to make travel reservations or order goods with a live voice on the phone at any time of the day or week, and we increasingly expect medical care and other services to be available to us at all times. A new phrase, "24/7" has quickly become common parlance to denote around-the-clock availability. From a consumer perspective, there seem to be few complaints about "colonizing the world after dark," to borrow Melbin's (1987) phrase.

---

[1] As Jacobs and Gerson (1998) note, the changes in cumulative work time have been essentially in the number of weeks worked per year, and the extent of this increase is under considerable debate.

But what does this expansion of economic activity around the clock mean for workers who provide their labor in the evenings, nights, and weekends? And what does it mean for families? While there is a considerable body of research on the individual consequences of shift work, particularly its health consequences (for reviews, see U.S. Congress, 1991; Wedderburn, 2000), there is a paucity of research on the family consequences of late hour shifts and weekend employment—what I mean by nonstandard schedules.

In this chapter, I document the prevalence of nonstandard work schedules among employed Americans and consider what this implies for the functioning and stability of family life. I do this drawing primarily upon findings from my forthcoming book and my earlier publications, along with reviewing the work of others. The challenges that families with preschool and school-aged children face when parents work nonstandard schedules is discussed in the context of these findings, particularly as they relate to low-income families. I also list some important research needs to fill major gaps in our knowledge.

It is important to acknowledge at the outset that the temporal nature of work life for families is being driven primarily by factors external to the family. As I have described elsewhere (Presser, 1999), there are at least three interrelated factors that increase the demand for Americans to work late or rotating shifts and weekends: a changing economy, changing demography, and changing technology. The growth of the service sector of the economy (which has higher proportions working nonstandard schedules than the goods-producing sector) is a critically important factor underlying all of these changes. This growth has been remarkable: In the 1960s, employees in manufacturing greatly exceeded those in service industries, whereas by 1999, the percentage was over twice as high in services as in manufacturing (Hatch & Clinton, 2000; Meisenheimer II, 1998). A related change has been the dramatic increase in women's labor force participation during this period, especially among married women with children, 70% of whom are now employed (U.S. Bureau of the Census, 2001, Table 578). Not only have women moved disproportionately into the service sector, responding to the growing demand for such workers, but their increased employment in all sectors contributed to this growing demand, as people needed more services at late hours and weekends. For example, the decline in full-time homemaking with greater *daytime* employment of women has generated an increase in the extent to which family members eat out and purchase other homemaking services. (For elaboration of other relevant factors, see Presser, forthcoming.)

We have then a process whereby macro changes external to the family affect the temporal nature of employment, offering more job opportunities at late and rotating hours as well as on weekends. Out of necessity or preference (and the data suggest mostly the former; Presser, 1995), employees increasingly take such jobs, which in turn affect the temporal nature of family life, particularly the "at home" structure of American families in the evenings, nights, and weekends. This is the context in which we should view the challenges of American families generated by the 24/7 economy.

Prevalence of Nonstandard Work Schedules: May 1997 Current Population Survey

National studies describing the prevalence of shift workers—those who work most of their hours in the evening or night—go back to the early 1970s and are based primarily on special supplements added to the U.S. Census Bureau's Current Population Surveys (CPS; see, for example, Hedges & Sekscenski, 1979). These surveys are based on very large samples (over 50,000 households), making them ideal for assessing prevalence. However, over the years, the way the work schedule questions have been asked and the response options allowed have often changed, precluding a rigorous determination of trends over time in the prevalence of work schedules.[2] Also, weekend employment was not asked until 1991. I report here what we know about the prevalence of nonstandard work schedules—both with regard to shifts and weekend employment—for the most recent year data are publicly available, 1997.

Definitions of Work Schedules

First, an important note about defining work schedules. As used in this chapter, work shifts refer to when people work *most* of their hours. Accordingly, people who work mostly in the day, but also in the evening or night, are considered here to be daytime workers. Estimates of the extent to which people work evenings and nights, whether or not they primarily work days, would be substantially larger than the estimates for evening and night shifts shown here. I prefer to use work shifts denoting *most* hours, as this provides a sharper distinction between various patterns of employment around the clock, differences that are expected to substantially alter the temporal nature of family life.

In determining what constitutes a specific shift, I have modified the definition used by the Bureau of Labor Statistics (Hedges & Sekscenski 1979; U.S. Department of Labor, 1981) to include the recently "hours vary" response option used in 1997.[3]

---

[2] For example, between 1973 and 1980, people were asked the hours they began and ended worked most days in the prior week but there was no question as to whether are rotators who happen to be on the day shift in the prior week. Since about one-third of those who work other than fixed daytime schedules are rotators, this seriously underestimates the prevalence of nonday shifts. Changes in the CPS were made in 1980 asking specifically about shift rotation, but the response options on hours work began and ended varied in other ways in the special CPS supplements on work schedules that followed (1985, 1991, and 1997), presenting comparability problems. Ignoring this issue, the data have been presented to show there has been little change in shift work between 1985 and 1997 (Beers, 2000). I do not believe one can draw this conclusion from these data.

[3] The BLS used these shift definitions when analyzing only full-time wage and salary workers. I use this designation for all workers, both full- and part-time and both self-employed and wage and salary workers.

Fixed day: At least half the hours worked most days in the prior week fall between 8 a.m. and 4 p.m.

Fixed evening: At least half the hours worked most days in the prior week fall between 4 p.m. and midnight.

Fixed night: At least half the hours worked most days in the prior week fall between midnight and 8 a.m.

Rotating: Schedules change periodically from days to evenings or nights.

Hours vary: An irregular schedule that cannot be classified in any of the above categories.

I define persons as working *nonstandard hours* when they work other than fixed-day schedules the previous week on their principal job.[4] (The percent employed who are multiple job holders is 7.6%; inclusion of the hours of employment on secondary jobs would make little difference in designating shifts, since the definition refers to most hours.)

The specific days of the week worked were asked for the principal job, although no reference to last week or usual week is included in the question.[5] However, this information was asked after other questions relating to the usual week. The specific work days are categorized by specific weekday or weekend combinations. Those who work *nonstandard days (weekends)* are defined as working on Saturday and/or Sunday.

It should be noted that we are not addressing here the issue of flex-time, in which employees are given the option to vary their beginning and ending hours within a confined range according to their personal preferences. Rather, we are considering the work shift that is typically mandated by employers.

Estimates of Prevalence

Table 5.1, based on these definitions, shows the prevalence of non-day employment for all employed Americans aged 18 and over in 1997. One fifth of the employed do not work a fixed daytime schedule on their principal job. Two fifths of the employed do not work five days a week, Monday through Friday. Part-time workers (fewer than 35 hours a week on all jobs) are more likely than full-time workers to work nonstandard hours and days. Most of the diversity in work schedules, however, is contributed by full-timers because part-timers make up less than one fourth of all employed.

---

[4] The shift definition used for my analysis of data from the National Survey of Family Growth, to be discussed later in this paper, excludes "hours vary," as detailed information on work schedules for every day of the week were provided without this response option, permitting the allocation of individuals into the other categories as appropriate.

[5] The question reads: AWhich days of the week (do you/does name) work [ON THIS JOB/FOR THIS BUSINESS] [ONLY]? (Check all that apply.)

Table 5.1
The Work Schedules of Employed Americans Age 18 and Over by Gender an Number of Hours Employed: May 1997, CPS.

Work Schedules	Total			Males			Females		
	Total	>= 35 hours.	< 35 hours.	Total	>= 35 hours.	< 35 hours.	Total	>= 35 hours.	< 35 hours.
Hours									
Fixed day	80.1%	83.0%	70.4%	78.9%	81.1%	67.5%	81.4%	85.9%	72.0%
Fixed evening	8.1	6.3	14.4	8.1	6.9	15.2	8.1	5.5	14.0
Fixed night	4.1	4.3	3.7	4.5	4.5	4.5	3.7	3.9	3.3
Hours vary	4.2	3.2	7.7	4.4	3.7	8.5	3.9	2.5	7.2
Rotating*	3.6	3.2	3.8	4.1	4.0	4.4	2.8	2.2	3.5
Number	49,570	38,272	11,201	25,916	22,067	3,800	23,654	16,205	7,401
Days									
Weekday only, 5 days	60.3	65.7	42.4	59.7	62.3	45.6	61.1	70.6	40.6
Weekday only, <5 days	8.0	3.6	22.9	5.3	3.4	16.1	11.0	3.9	26.6
7 days	7.9	7.7	8.0	8.7	8.4	9.5	6.9	6.7	7.2
Weekday and weekend, < 7days	23.1	22.9	24.3	25.7	25.8	26.2	20.1	18.7	23.3
Weekend only, 1 or 2 days	0.7	0.1	2.4	0.5	0.1	2.6	0.9	0.1	2.2
Number	50,275	37,827	10,771	26,167	21,802	3,635	24,108	16,025	7,136
Combination									
Fixed day, weekdays only, 5 days	54.4	59.6	36.5	52.9	55.5	38.6	56.2	65.4	35.3
Rotators or hours vary and weekend*	5.3	4.6	7.2	5.9	5.4	8.6	4.5	3.5	6.5
All others	40.3	35.8	56.3	41.1	39.2	52.8	39.3	31.1	58.2
Number	48,672	37,813	10,765	25,469	21,790	3,631	23,203	16,023	7,134

* This includes 74 individuals designated as 24-hour workers

The total number of cases is more than the sum of those working 35 or more hours last week and less than 35 hours because of missing data on the number of hours worked last week on all jobs. Also, differences in number of cases by type of work schedules are due to missing data for these variables. All percentages are weighted for national representativeness; the number of cases reports unweighted samples for each category. Work schedules refers to the principle job; total hours refers to all jobs.
Percentages may not add exactly to 100.0 because of rounding.
Source: Presser, 1999.

Although the labor force is highly segregated occupationally by gender (Reskin & Roos, 1990), gender differences in work schedule behavior among all those employed are not great. With regard to *hours*, men are somewhat more likely than women to work other than fixed daytime schedules (21.1% and 19.6%, respectively). The gender difference is seen specifically in the higher percentages of men than women working fixed nights and variable and rotating hours. There is no gender difference in the prevalence of evening work (both 8.1%). Among part-time workers of both sexes, substantial proportions work evenings (15.2% of men and 14.0% of women). Part-time workers are the subgroup showing the highest percentages with variable hours.

As for work *days*, men are only slightly more likely than women to work during nonstandard times—that is, other than a five-day work week, Monday through Friday (39.7% and 38.9%, respectively). The distribution of nonstandard work days, however, varies considerably by gender. In particular, men are more likely than women to work weekends (34.9% and 27.9 %, respectively); women are more likely than men to work weekdays but fewer than five days a week (11.0% vs. 5.3%, respectively). Very few employed Americans, men or women, work weekends only. As might be expected, workdays are most likely to be nonstandard when people work part-time.

When work hours and days are combined, Table 5.1 shows the figure cited earlier—that only 54.4% of employed Americans work Monday through Friday, 5 days a week, on a fixed-day schedule. The counterpart is that 45.6% do not— 47.1% of men and 43.8% of women. Moreover, the large majority of part-timers work other than this 5-day weekday pattern.

If individuals have this high prevalence of nonstandard schedules, it follows that couples as a unit—with both spouses "at risk" of working such schedules— will have a higher prevalence. We see in Table 5.2 that almost one fourth (23.8%) of all couples with at least one earner have at least one spouse who works a non-day shift. The percentages are higher for those with children, and particularly those with preschool age children (30.6%).

When focusing on dual-earner couples only, the prevalence of non-day shifts is higher than for all couples, since either spouse is "at risk" of working non-days. Over one fourth (27.8%) of dual-earner couples have a spouse who works a non-day shift. Again, those with children are most likely to have such a schedule, and particularly those with preschool aged children (34.7%). Rarely do both spouses work non-day shifts. Although there are usually some overlapping hours of employment among couples with one spouse working non-days, there is considerable nonoverlap, and thus it is appropriate to characterize such couples as essentially working "split-shifts." (An alternative term used is "tag-team.")

Table 5.2

Percentage of Married Couples with at Least One Spouse Who Works Non-day Shifts by Family Type and Age of Youngest Child: May 1997 CPS.

Family Type and Age of Youngest Child	% Non-day
At least one earner*	23.8
At least one earner and:	
Child <age 14	25.8
Child <5	30.6
Two earners only**	27.8
Two earners and	
Child <age 14	31.1
Child <5	34.7

Note: Non-day shifts include work schedules in which the hours most days of the reference week

*Couples with at least one employed spouse on the job during the reference week in nonagricultural occupation, including all rotators, and both spouses aged 18 and over.

**Couples with both spouses on the job during the reference week, including all rotators, both in nonagricultural occupations, and both aged 18 and over.

Single mothers (non-married and separated) are more likely to work nonstandard schedules than married mothers—as well as longer hours. For single mothers with children under age 14, 20.8% work nonstandard hours and 33.2% work weekends; for married mothers with children under age 14, it is 16.4% and 23.9%, respectively (Presser, forthcoming). For both marital statuses, having younger children increases the percentages as well as having low individual earnings.

With such widespread prevalence of nonstandard work schedules among American families, what do we know about the consequences? I address this issue first with regard to the existing literature, and then report on some findings from my previous research and forthcoming book.

Social Consequences of Nonstandard Schedules: Literature Review

Although there is an abundant literature on the effect of women's employment per se on family life, particularly relating to issues of marital quality, childcare, and child well-being, there is a paucity of research on the effects of employment at nonstandard work schedules (by either employed mothers or fathers) on the family. The following reviews many of these findings for the U.S., although it is not meant to be an exhaustive review.[6]

Quantitative Studies

The most thorough national study, and one that considered weekend employment as well as non-day shifts, is based on data now 25 years old, the 1977 U.S. Quality of Employment Survey (Staines & Pleck, 1983). The authors found that for all married couples as well as dual-earner couples specifically, shift work was associated with difficulties in scheduling family activities; moreover, working weekends and variable days was linked with less time in family roles and higher levels of work-family conflict and family adjustment. Some of the negative family outcomes were reduced when a worker=s control over his or her work schedule was taken into account.[7] This study was an ambitious effort to explore the impact of work schedules on families, although the way non-day shifts were defined and grouped together is problematic as well as the different sampling procedure for main respondents and spouses.[8]

Other less intensive national studies that consider the relationship between nonstandard work schedules and family life include the longitudinal study on the effects of shift work on marital quality and stability by White and Keith (1990), based on a 1980 survey with a follow-up component in 1983 (White & Keith, 1990). This study also has definitional problems.[9] The study found that marital happiness, sexual problems, and child-related problems were negatively affected by shift work, although the effects were of relatively low magnitude. The longitudinal analysis revealed that among marriages that remained in tact over the three-year period, entry into shift work significantly increased marital disagreements and entry out of shift work significantly increased marital interaction and decreased child-related problem. Looking specifically at marital breakup, the investigators found that being a shift-work couple in 1980 significantly increased the likelihood of divorce by 1983—from 7% to 11%.

Neither of these two studies were designed to study shift work in depth; rather, they were secondary analyses of surveys undertaken for more general purposes.

---

[6] For a more extensive review of the literature on shift work, separately by topic, see Presser (forthcoming).

[7] Using the same data source, Kingston and Nock (1985) found among dual-earner couples that there was no strong relationship between the combined *number* of hours couples worked or the amount of time one or both spouses worked and marital or family satisfaction. (This study excludes those who work "irregular hours," and thus presumably excludes rotators.)

[8] Those working afternoon schedules were combined with evening and night workers, and together were categorized as non-day shift workers. (Those working in the morning were among the day workers.) The effects of different non-day shifts were not separately considered (nor the gender of the shift worker). Also, the main respondents in the sample were eligible only if they worked at least 20 hours a week, but the number of hours of employment was not restricted for spouses.

[9] The researchers asked respondents if they were shift workers but did not define the range of hours that constitute a shift nor the type of shift.

Another secondary analysis by Blair (1993), based on the National Survey of Families and Households (the same data source to be reported in the next section), considered the effects of employment (and family) characteristics on various dimensions of marital quality for both husbands and wives, and included shift status as one aspect of employment. The operational definition of shift status (a dichotomous variable) is not provided, but having a "shift" was found to significantly reduce marital quality only in terms of "daily contact," not other measures considered. A smaller longitudinal study of 92 working-class dual-earner couples recruited from prenatal classes at hospitals in Western New England (about one half with spouses working the same shift and one half different shifts; Perry-Jenkins & Haley, 2000) showed that during the first year of parenthood, working different shifts helped couples manage child care but often had negative consequences for the mental health of the parents and their marital relationship.

Empirical studies designed specifically to study the impact of shift work on employees, while not national in scope, suggest some negative family effects. The most extensive U.S. study of this type dates back to the early 1960s (Mott et al., 1965), and was designed to investigate the social, psychological, and physical consequences of shift work for white, blue-collar men in selected continuous processing industries. Analyzing three dimensions of marital quality, the investigators concluded that shift work led to "some reduction in marital happiness and an even greater reduction in the ability to coordinate family activities and to minimize strain and friction among family members" (Mott et al., 1965, p. 146).

More recently, some empirical studies have addressed issues of parent-child interaction and child care use as related to nonstandard work schedules in studies about family life for certain populations. With regard to parent-child interaction, the 1999 National Survey of America's Families (Phillips, 2002), which focuses on low-income households, found that married couples with children aged 6–11 who worked late hours were more likely to be involved in their children's school, but the children of such parents were less likely to be engaged in extracurricular activities. This study does not distinguish type of shift, defining "night hours" as employment mostly from 6 p.m. to 6 a.m. Another study, more broadly inclusive of all married couples (not just low-income), is based on the 1981 Study of Time Use; this study found little relationship between work schedules—the amount of minutes husband and wife are employed within certain ranges of hours around the clock—and the amount of parental time with children, but children here include all those under age 20 (Nock & Kingston, 1988).

The type of childcare arrangements that people working nonstandard hours make for their children has been studied at the national level, showing a heavy reliance on relative care. Among dual-earner couples, much of this relative care is by resident fathers (Brayfield, 1995; Casper, 1997; O'Connell, 1993; Presser, 1986). This is essentially "split-shift" parenting, whereby mothers and fathers work very different hours: one mostly days and the other mostly non-days. While mothers are more likely than fathers to report "better childcare arrangements" as their main reason for working nonstandard hours, only a minority of either spouse do so; most parents report reasons related to their jobs, not their families (Presser, 1995).

We know very little about child outcomes related to shift work, either from quantitative or qualitative studies. A cross-tabular analysis of data from the National Longitudinal Survey of Youth (Heymann, 2000), without controls, showed that school-aged children who had poor educational outcomes in 1996 were more likely to have parents who worked evening shifts some or all of their working years between 1990 and 1996 than were other children. (Evening shifts are self-defined by respondents without specification of which hours this encompasses.)

A three-city study (Boston, Chicago, and San Antonio) of low- and moderate-income families in 1999 found more problem behaviors and fewer positive behaviors among children aged 2–4 when parents worked nonstandard hours or weekends (grouped together) compared to fixed daytime schedules (Bogen & Joshi, 2001). Multivariate analyses suggested that nonstandard schedules may affect children directly as well as have a small indirect effect on children by increasing parenting challenges (decreasing satisfaction and increasing stress).

Qualitative Studies

Qualitative studies on how families cope when one or both parents work nonstandard schedules are rare. Rubin (1994), in her study of 162 working-class and lower-middle class families in the U.S., discusses the pressures on time for both husbands and wives when they work different shifts (about one fifth of her couples). She notes the lack of childcare options that result in each parent caring for their children while the other is employed.

Other qualitative studies offer a mixed message about positive and negative aspects of parents working nonstandard schedules. For example, Deutch's study of 30 dual-earner couples working different shifts finds parents speaking positively about such work schedules allowing both spouses to rear their children and have a joint income. Yet the author concludes, "… the loss of time together was a bitter pill to swallow. The physical separation symbolized a spiritual separation as well" (Deutch, 1999, p. 177).

Garey's (1999) interviews with seven nurses working the night shift full-time indicated that these mothers liked the fact that this late work schedule allowed them to maximize family time and do traditional maternal tasks at home, as though they were full-time "at-home moms." Such tasks included helping with homework and being able to participate or facilitate children's school and extracurricular activities. Moreover, they preferred the night to evening shifts because they were able to supervise dinner and bedtime and, for those married, have more time with their spouses. The cost to these mothers, which they were all willing to assume, was considerable sleep deprivation (most getting about 4–5 hours a night).

Problems of sleep deprivation among shift workers and the desire to be a "good mother" by working late hours are also relayed in interviews with women in the Midwest (sample size not provided; Hattery 2001). Another qualitative study of 90 male security guards on rotating shifts found that many fathers also deprived themselves of sleep in order to participate in family life, eating meals with their family "out of sync with their biological rhythm" (Hertz & Charlton 1989, p. 502).

Social Consequences of Nonstandard Work Schedules: The National Survey of Families and Households, 1986–1987 and 1992–1994

Building on this body of research, I have analyzed data from the National Survey of Families and Households (NSFH) on the relationship between nonstandard work schedules and family life. I present here some highlights of these findings (for more details, see the references cited).

First, a note on the NSFH. This representative survey of all American families was conducted in two waves; the first interview during the years 1987–1988 (N=13,007), and the second between 1992–1994 (N=10,007). Spouses and partners were asked to complete a separate questionnaire, so one can obtain couple data on selected variables.[10] The findings reported here are based on Wave 1, with an analysis of Wave 2 when considering marital instability, and relies on data from both spouses among those married. The shift definition is the same as that reported earlier for the CPS, except that the "hours vary" is not a response option and thus all nonstandard work shifts are "non-day" (see endnote 4). For some analyses, non-day shifts had to be combined as a single group because of the small numbers in each type of shift. In analyses that permit a separate examination of different non-day shifts, the results typically present a complex picture.

Marital Quality

Four dimensions of marital quality at Wave 1 were examined as separate dichotomous dependent variables in regressions: general marital unhappiness, low quality time, marriage in trouble, and assessment of an even or higher chance of divorce. The shift patterns of the couples (non-days grouped) and the family type were key independent variables. Control variables included the number of hours each spouse worked, the education of both spouses, the number of times each spouse has been married, whether either spouse cohabitated, difference in age between spouses, duration of marriage, whether children less than age 19 in household, and for some models gender ideology of each spouse and age of wife.

The results can be summarized as follows, separately for married single-earner couples (one fifth of these single earners are wives), and dual-earner couples.

Among single-earner couples, non-day shifts and weekend employment seem to pose a risk to the quality of the marriage relative to daytime employment—but only when it is the wife who is the single earner, not the husband. The negative relationships for wives are stronger when children are present.

Among dual-earner couples, couples with a spouse working nonstandard hours generally have higher levels of marital dissatisfaction relative to those in which both spouses work fixed days, but these relationships are specific to certain couple work schedules and certain indicators of marital quality. In most instances the relationships are stronger when children are present. Interestingly, adding the control for gender ideology of the spouses did not significantly alter these relationships for couples with or without children. Weekend employment was not significantly associated with marital dissatisfaction.

Marital Instability

Among couples married at Wave 1, their marital status at Wave 2—about five years later—was assessed in regression analyses that considered the work shifts and weekend employment of both spouses (with similar controls as above). It was found that only for couples with children did nonstandard work schedules increase the likelihood of marital instability—and only when the husband or wife worked the night shift. (There are some additional conditions relating to duration of marriage; see Presser, 2000.) One could speculate that this result occurs because spouses who choose to work late night hours are especially likely to be in troubled marriages before making this decision, but a separate analysis of the quality of marriages among those who enter into non-day shifts between Waves 1 and 2 does not support this view (Presser, 2000).

Gender Division of Household Labor

The NSFH data suggest that the functioning and stability of family life are affected by nonstandard work schedules. An important family function is household labor. Focusing specifically on dual-earner households, regression analyses show that when husbands work a non-daytime or rotating shift and their wives work a day shift, the men are significantly more likely to do traditionally female household tasks than couples in which both spouses work day shifts. These tasks include: preparing meals, washing dishes and cleaning up after meals, cleaning house, and washing, ironing, and mending clothes (Presser, 1994). The control variables included the husband's education, occupation, and earnings, both absolute and relative to his wife, the gender ideologies of both spouses, and their stage in the life course, including the number of preschool and school-aged children.

Parent-Child Interaction

Other aspects of family functioning include the frequency of parent-child interaction. In the NSFH, data are available on the extent to which parents eat meals with their children and do various one-on-one activities together.

As for meals, having dinner together is an especially important day-to-day ritual in most families. Both mothers and fathers who work evenings and rotating shifts are significantly less likely to have dinner with their children than parents who work days. Working nights, however, does not show less frequent family involvement in dinner relative to days (Presser, 2001). In contrast, nonstandard work schedules are associated with *greater* frequency in which parents eat breakfast with their children, but which nonstandard schedule has this relationship differs by gender of parent and whether a single or married mother (Presser, forthcoming).

As for one-on-one parent-child interaction, the NSFH asked questions about the frequency of the following parental activities with children ages 5–18: leisure activities outside the home, work on projects, private talks, and help with homework. Overall, there is a mixed picture, with differences evident by gender of parent and marital status of mothers. The findings (Presser, forthcoming) suggest the following: With regard to the frequency of leisure activities outside the home, working nights may minimize this for mothers, both single and married; rotating shifts seem to do this for married fathers and single mothers. With regard to parents working on projects with children, its frequency is higher when dual-earner mothers work rotating shifts and single mothers work evenings, as compared to days; shift status is not associated with this activity for fathers, with the exception of one near-significant relationship. As for the frequency of private talks, single, but not married, mothers show a relationship to shift status (more frequent when they work evenings and nights rather than days, less frequent when they rotate); married fathers show a reverse pattern from single mothers (less frequent with evening work and more frequent with rotating shifts). As for help with homework, the significant relationships for mothers of both marital statuses are negative when they are on rotating shifts, and positive for fathers when they work night shifts. The few significant or near-significant relationships with regard to weekend employment also show a mixed picture, with only some activities seemingly related and differences in direction by gender of parent. This is very much a complex set of results suggesting that nonday shifts matter for parent-child interaction both positively and negatively, but the different effects of different shifts, as well as the gender differences, are hard to interpret and need further study.

Childcare Arrangements.

Parents who work nonstandard hours and weekends rely more heavily on relatives for childcare for their preschool-aged children when mothers are employed. When mothers are married and working nonstandard schedules, the most frequent "relative" providing care is the child's father, clearly increasing that form of parent-child interaction. When mothers are not married and are working nonstandard schedules, the most frequent relative providing care is the grandparent. While this greater reliance on relatives when working nonstandard hours has been shown with other national data sources, as previously noted, analysis of the NSFH data takes into account weekend employment as well as work shifts and also considers patterns of multiple childcare use. Those working nonstandard schedules, weekends as well as non-day, are more likely to make multiple arrangements (Presser, forthcoming). This fact, along with the heavier reliance on informal providers, makes for more complex childcare arrangements for such parents, both married and single.

Among school-aged children ages 5–11, the presence of parents at home when children leave for and return from school is generally enhanced when mothers work evenings and nights, a clear advantage of such schedules. This relationship obtains for single mothers, but the overall presence of a parent at home during such times is less than for married mothers—which is to be expected given that the child's father is usually not living in these non-married households. For both family types, we do not know if the parents working late hours are awake or asleep before and after school. Typically, other childcare arrangements are made when parents are not present. However, about 15% of parents report their children aged 5–11 in self-care before school, and about 10% after school. Self-care is reported less by parents who work late rather than work daytime hours, but if parents working nights are more likely to be asleep when the child leaves and returns from school, parental supervision of children may be lacking and self care of such children may be greatly underestimated.

Implications for Low-Income Families

Both the existing research and my new NSFH findings summarized here suggest that employment at nonstandard times presents some major challenges to U.S. families. While there may be advantages, the data suggest that in many ways employment at nonstandard hours and weekends adds extra stress to families with children, and with regard to night work, may substantially increase the risk of separation or divorce among the married. There has been no research to date that rigorously assesses how low-income families cope with nonstandard schedules relative to those with higher incomes. Indeed, there is little research that rigorously assesses how those working nonstandard schedules cope relative to those working at standard times, regardless of income. Some of the qualitative studies are insightful but they report on too few cases to draw conclusions.

We know that although employment at nonstandard times occurs at all levels of income, it is disproportionately found among those with low incomes. For example, the top five occupations of non-day workers are cashiers, truck drivers, waiters and waitresses, cooks, and janitors/cleaners. It is not just that these jobs are low-paying in general—they are even more low-paying if you have these occupations and work at nonstandard times (Presser, forthcoming). Thus, people who work nonstandard hours have to deal with the joint stresses of managing with such low pay and with being "out of sync" temporally with other family members, including their children. As noted earlier, it does not appear that parents who work nonstandard schedules generally find this the preferred mode of child-rearing, despite the advantage of reduced childcare costs and greater involvement of fathers. Single mothers of low income who generally do not benefit from sharing childcare with fathers would seem to find working nonstandard schedules especially problematic.

It thus seems appropriate to conclude that while some parents may prefer such schedules, employment at nonstandard times is driven by demand and generally recruits those with limited job possibilities. This includes mothers moving from welfare to work who often experience a misfit between their required hours and days of employment and the availability of formal childcare, and have to put together a patchwork of informal arrangements to hold on to their jobs. My analysis of mothers in the labor force in 1997 with characteristics similar to those moving from welfare to work (high school education or less, aged 18–34, at least one child under age 14) revealed that about two fifths of these employed mothers did not work a fixed-day schedule on weekdays only (Presser, forthcoming). Moreover, many of those working fixed days had hours that extended into the "fringe"—that is, they started very early in the morning or ended in the evening, times when formal daytime childcare is typically not available.

The minimal attention to such issues reflects the general lack of attention in the social policy arena to the temporal frictions between work and family life that occur as a consequence of the widespread engagement of employed parents in nonstandard schedules. Two-parent families often look much like one-parent families in terms of parent-child interaction, and single-parent families much like no-parent families. Presumably "intact" families often are composed of spouses who hardly see one another. We need to be concerned about the special needs such situations generate for low-income families and how they might be addressed. One way to find this out is to do research that focuses specifically on this issue.

Research Needs

It is clear from the research to date that investigating the social consequences of nonstandard work schedules for individuals and their families is not an easy task. There are different work shifts, there is weekend employment, and the cumulative number of hours people work needs to be taken into account. Moreover, the consequences may be different for families with children versus no children, and between those with preschoolers versus older children. On top of such considerations are the special problems of low-income parents, particularly single mothers. And there is the question of short-term versus long-term costs and benefits (e.g., enhancing father-child interaction when spouses work split shifts but increasing the odds of divorce if one of the spouses works nights).

Such considerations reflect complex situations that need further study, and there are many ways to approach this. I offer my assessment of some important considerations for future research as specified in my forthcoming book, recognizing that we need many studies with multiple approaches.

1. *The need to do focused studies on the costs and benefits of working nonstandard schedules.* As we have seen, most of the research to date on the consequences of working nonstandard schedules has been based on large-scale surveys or on qualitative studies that were not designed with this focus. Thus we know very little about why people work these schedules, their perceived trade-offs, and the perceived impact on their lives and those of family members. It would be highly relevant to consider gender differences here as well as distinctions between single and married mothers, particularly with regard to the trade-offs being made.

2. *The need to distinguish different work shifts in studies of the consequences of nonstandard work schedules.* As the findings presented in this paper suggest, different nonstandard work shifts may have different effects on family life and on children. To more adequately assess this, we need large-scale studies that oversample those working nonstandard shifts so that there are sufficiently large numbers to make comparisons between those working evenings, nights, and rotating shifts, as well as days.

3. *The need to have precise measures of work shifts.* It has been noted that many of the shift work studies use ambiguous definitions of work shifts, often self defined by the respondent without clear instruction from the interviewer. It would seem

best to ask people the specific hours their work begins and ends (daily or for most days during a reference week), plus whether they rotate, and leave the derivation of the day, evening, and night shifts to the investigator (which is then reported with the findings). This approach would also allow investigators to compare different studies by deriving similar definitions of work shifts.

4. *The need to study the movement of employees in and out of different work schedules.* Studies of shift work have generally been cross-sectional rather than longitudinal, yet there is undoubtedly considerable flow in and out of different work schedules. It is important to know the duration of shift work for employees, and particularly employed parents, and how movement in and out of nonstandard work shifts relates to family concerns, employer demands, and the lack of alternative daytime job opportunities.

5. *The need to explore the effects of nonstandard work schedules on the physical and emotional health of individuals and how these effects on individual well-being interact with the functioning of family life.* Given the paucity of knowledge on this interaction, it would seem appropriate to start with intensive qualitative studies of families working late and rotating shifts. It would be especially interesting to explore the extent to which those working such schedules suffer from sleep deprivation, and the process by which this may interact with family functioning, affecting the quality and stability of marriages as well as the care of children. In the latter regard, it is important to know how well preschool-aged children are being cared for during the day by parents who work nights or rotating shifts.

6. *The need for research on married fathers who care for their children during most of the hours that mothers are employed.* It would be revealing to know how distinctive these fathers are from other fathers and the consequences (positive and negative) that they perceive for themselves of having taken on this responsibility as well as the actual consequences. In the latter context, it would be especially interesting to have longitudinal data to assess change over time.

7. *The need for intensive research on the reasons for working nonstandard work schedules, particularly those of parents with children.* To date, we rely on one question in the CPS for our knowledge of reasons people work nonstandard hours. Qualitative studies refer to some couples who report either positive or negative consequences of shift work, but we have no research that probes in depth as to why substantial numbers of parents have chosen these schedules. In addition to some preferring to arrange childcare this way, there may be other care-giving reasons that merit exploration (e.g., better arrangements for the care of disabled persons and the elderly). Also, it would be good to know what people really mean when they say their main reason is that it is a job requirement, and if there are gender differences in this meaning.

8. *The need for more research on the effects of nonstandard work schedules on children, including their development and school achievement.* While we have moved forward over the past decade in better understanding the effect of childcare on child development, we have generally ignored the issue of how the nonstandard work schedules of parents, and the more complex childcare arrangements this generates, affects child outcomes. This issue calls for studies of the children in addition to the parents, and both the frequency and quality of parent-child interactions as well as childcare quality. Such research would require substantial sample sizes in order to consider children of different ages and the different work schedules of parents. Good measures of child outcomes are also important.[10]

---

[10] For further methodological details, see Sweet, Bumpass, and Call (1988), and http://ssc.wisc.edu/nsfh/home.htm.

Future Expectations

Filling these issues needs is important not only to better understand today's families, but to better anticipate the future, as the number of American households with parents working nonstandard hours increases. I predict this increase will be experienced disproportionately by employed women, and to a lesser extent by employed blacks and Hispanics. This prediction is supported by job growth projections between 2000 and 2010, although I recognize that such projections essentially are educated guesses subject to error.

Table 5.3 shows the top ten occupations in 2000 that, according to the Bureau of Labor Statistics, are projected to have the largest job growth between 2000 and 2010 (Hecker, 2001, Table 4). Using the May 1997 CPS data, I have calculated the percentage in these top growth occupations that work nonstandard schedules. (As noted in the table's footnote, given the difference in occupational codes used for the projections and for the CPS, the matching of some occupations is not precise, and for one not possible.)

We see that most of these occupations—namely, food preparation and serving workers, registered nurses, retail salespersons, cashiers, security guards, and waiters and waitresse—are disproportionately high on the percentage working other than a fixed day (far exceeding the overall average for all occupations of 19.9%). The same occupations that are disproportionately high on nonstandard hours are disproportionately high on weekend employment.

We also see in Table 5.3 (far right) the percent female, the percent black, and the percent Hispanic in these top growth occupations. These percentages can be compared with the percentages in all occupations for the respective groups shown in the column headings. When the percentages for specific occupations exceed that for all occupations, the subgroups are disproportionately in those occupations.

This comparison reveals that the top growth occupations high on nonstandard work schedules are also high on percent female, with the one exception being security guards. The picture is more mixed for blacks and Hispanics, who are overrepresented in the top growth occupations of food preparation and servers, cashiers, and security guards, and for Hispanics, of waiters and waitresses. Hispanics are underrepresented as registered nurses; blacks, as waiters and waitresses.

Table 5.3

Largest Projected Job Growth Occupations (2000-2010) and Their Work Schedule, Gender and Race Characteristics.

Job Growth Rank	Occupation[b]	Employment (in 1,000's)		% in Occupation Working Non-Standard Schedules, May 1997 CPS			% of Group in Occupation May 1997 CPS		
		2000	2010[a] (Projected)	% Other Than Fixed Day (a)	% Weekend (b)	% (a) or (b) (c)	% Female (All occ. = 46.0)	% Non-Hispanic Black (All occ. = 10.5)	% Hispanic (All occ. = 9.8)
1	Food Preparaton and Serving Workers, Incl. Fast Food[c]	2,206	2,879	45.8	55.0	68.0	51.5	11.8	24.2
2	Customer Service Representatives[d]	1,946	2,577	NA	NA	NA	NA	NA	NA
3	Rgistered Nurses	2,194	2,755	34.6	42.9	55.1	94.5	7.5	3.2
4	Retail Salespersons	4,109	4,619	32.2	62.9	70.6	55.3	7.7	8.7
5	Computer Support Specialist[e]	506	996	20.0	15.9	26.5	56.1	19.9	3.1
6	Cashiers, Except Gaming	3,325	3,799	50.4	71.0	80.1	77.2	15.6	12.3
7	Office Clerks, General	2,705	3,135	16.2	15.7	23.5	76.3	13.6	8.9
8	Security Guards[f]	1,106	1,497	57.0	55.8	73.9	22.8	19.4	13.0
9	Computer Software Engineers, Applications[g]	380	760	5.2	13.5	16.9	31.5	6.6	2.4
10	Waiters and Waitresses	1,983	2,347	65.1	79.0	89.5	78.8	3.1	12.6

[a] Projections are derived by the Bureau of Labor Statistics (Hecker, 2001, Table 4).

[b] The BLS occupational classifications for job projections is based on the National Industry-Occupation Employment Matrix (NIOEM) and do not always correspond exactly with the CPS occupational classifications, as noted in the footnotes below.

[c] This category includes Kitchen workers, food preparation and 'Misc food preparation occupations' in the CPS.

[d] There is no separate classification in the CPS for this category.

[e] This category corresponds to Computer Equipment Operators in the CPS.

[f] This category includes Guards and Police, Except Public Service and Protective Service Occupations, n.e.c. in the CPS.

[g] This category includes Computer System Analysis and Scientists and Operations and Systems Researchrs and Aanlysts in the CPS.

Source: Presser, forthcoming.

In conclusion, employment in a 24/7 economy presents many challenges for U.S. families. The research to date hints at many of these, but we have much more to learn. We should not be turned away by the complexity of the issue. Indeed, I contend that when work and family research does not take into account the nonstandard work schedules of employed family members, it is likely to be missing some important explanatory variables for the outcomes of interest. Moreover, work and family policies cannot continue to ignore the temporal diversity of working families, especially those of low income. Failure to explicitly acknowledge such diversity compromises the effectiveness of such policies, as exemplified by the misfit between childcare availability and the work hours of many mothers moving from welfare to work.

The movement toward a 24/7 economy, in my view, will not be reversed in the decades ahead. It may be slow in pace or even stalled by a weakening economy, but I believe the long-term trend is toward more employment around the clock, particularly in the service sector. I hold this view because the 24/7 economy is driven by factors external to the family that are not likely to change in the foreseeable future. For better or worse, families will increasingly need to respond to these challenges. And so will we as scholars.

Acknowledgments

I am grateful to Kei Nomaguchi and Lijuan Wu for their very able research assistance in generating the data both for this paper and for my other publications upon which this paper draws. The analysis of the NSFH data summarized here was supported in large part by the W. T. Grant Foundation and a visiting scholarship at the Russell Sage Foundation.

References

Beers, T. (2000). Flexible schedules and shift work: Replacing the '9-to-5' workday? *Monthly Labor Review, 123*, 33–39.

Blair, S. L. (1993). Employment, family, and perceptions of marital quality among husbands and wives. *Journal of Family Issues, 14*, 189–212.

Bogen, K., & Joshi, P. (2001, November). *Bad work or good move: The relationship of part-time and nonstandard work schedules to parenting and child behavior in working poor families.* Paper presented at the Conference on Working Poor Families: Coping as Parents and Workers, Bethesda, MD.

Brayfield, A. A. (1995). Juggling jobs and kids: The impact of employment schedules on fathers' caring for children. *Journal of Marriage and the Family 57,* 321–332.

Brayfield, A. A., Deich, S. G., & Hofferth, S. L. (1993). *Caring for children in low-income families: A substudy of the National Child Care Survey, 1990* (Urban Institute Report 93-2). Washington, DC: Urban Institute Press.

Casper, L. M. (1997). *My daddy takes care of me! Fathers as care providers* (Current Population Reports P70-59). Washington, DC: U.S. Department of Commerce, Census Bureau.

Deutsch, F. M. (1999). *Halving it all: How equally shared parenting works.* Cambridge, MA: Harvard University Press.

Garey, A. I. (1999). *Weaving work and motherhood.* Philadelphia: Temple University Press.

Golden, L. (2001). Flexible work schedules. *American Behavioral Scientist, 44,* 1157–1178.

Hamermesh, D. S. (1999). The timing of work over time. *The Economic Journal, 109,* 37–66.

Hatch, J., & Clinton, A. (2000). Job growth in the 1990s: A retrospect. *Monthly Labor Review, 123),* 3–18.

Hattery, A. J. (2001). Tag-team parenting: Costs and benefits of utilizing nonoverlapping shift work in families with young children. *Families in Society: The Journal of Contemporary Human Services, 82,* 419–427.

Hecker, D. E. (2001). Occupational employment projections to 2010. *Monthly Labor Review, 124),* 57–84.

Hedges, J. N., & Sekscenski, E. S. (1979). Workers on late shifts in a changing economy. *Monthly Labor Review, 102,* 14–22.

Hertz, R., & Charlton, J. (1989). Making family under a shiftwork schedule: Air Force security guards and their wives. *Social Problems, 36,* 491–507.

Heymann, J. (2000). *The widening gap: Why America's working families are in jeopardy and what can be done about it.* New York: Basic Books.

Jacobs, J. A., & Gerson, K. (1998). Who are the overworked Americans? *Review of Social Economy, 56,* 442–459.

Kingston, P. W., & Nock, S. L. (1985). Consequences of the family work day. *Journal of Marriage and the Family, 47,* 619–629.

Meisenheimer, J. R., II. (1998). The service industry in the 'good' versus 'bad' debate. *Monthly Labor Review, 121,* 10–21.

Melbin, M. (1987). *Night as frontier: Colonizing the world after dark.* New York: Free Press.

Mott, P. E., Mann, F. C., McLoughlin, G., & Warwick, D. P. (1965). *Shift work: The social, psychological, and physical consequences.* Ann Arbor, MI: University of Michigan Press.

Nock, S. L., & Kingston, P.W. (1988). Time with children: The impact of couples' work time commitments. *Social Forces, 67,* 59–85.

O'Connell, M. (1993). *Where's papa? Father's role in child care* (Population Trends and Public Policy Report No. 20). Washington, DC: Population Reference Bureau.

Perry-Jenkins, M., & Haley, H. (2000, November). *Employment schedules and the transition to parenthood: Implications for mental health and marriage.* Paper presented at the annual meeting of the National Council on Family Relations, Minneapolis, MN.

Phillips, K. R. (2002). *Parent work and child well-being in low-income families* (Occasional Paper No. 56). Washington, DC: The Urban Institute.

Presser, H. B. (1986). Shift work among American women and child care. *Journal of Marriage and the Family, 48,* 551–563.

Presser, H. B. (1994). Employment schedules among dual-earner spouses and the division of household labor by gender. *American Sociological Review, 59,* 348–364.

Presser, H. B. (1995). Job, family, and gender: Determinants of nonstandard work schedules among employed Americans in 1991. *Demography, 32,* 577–598.

Presser, H. B. (1999, June 11). Toward a 24-hour economy. *Science, 284,* 1778–1779.

Presser, H. B. (2000). Nonstandard work schedules and marital instability. *Journal of Marriage and the Family, 62,* 93–110.

Presser, H. B. (2001). Toward a 24-hour economy: Implications for the temporal structure and functioning of family life. In *The Social Contract in the Face of Demographic Change: Proceedings. 2nd Renontres Sauvy International Seminar. Montreal, Quebec, Oct. 4–6.* (pp. 115–129). Paris: Institut National D'Éstudes Démographiques.

Presser, H. B. (in press). *Work schedules in a 24/7 economy: Challenges for American families.* New York: Russell Sage Foundation.

Reskin, B., & Roos, P. A. (1990). *Job queues, gender queues.* Philadelphia: Temple University Press.

Rones, P. L., Ilg, R. E., & Gardner, J. M. (1997). Trends in hours of work since the mid-1970s. *Monthly Labor Review, 120,* 3–14.

Rubin, L. B. (1994) *Families on the fault line.* New York: Harper Perennial.

Smith, S. J. (1986). The growing diversity of work schedules. *Monthly Labor Review, 109,* 7–13.

Staines, G. L., & Pleck, J. H. (1983). *The impact of work schedules on the family.* Ann Arbor: Institute for Social Research, University of Michigan.

Sweet, J., Bumpass, L., & Call, V. (1988). *The design and content of the National Survey of Families and Households.* Madison: University of Wisconsin, Center for Demography and Ecology.

U.S. Bureau of the Census. (2001). *Statistical abstract of the United States: 2001* (121st ed.). Washington, DC: Author.

U.S. Congress. (1991). *Biological rhythms: Implications for the worker* (Office of Technology Assessment, OTA-BA-463). Washington, DC: U.S. Government Printing Office.

U.S. Department of Labor. U.S. Bureau of Labor Statistics. (1998). Workers on flexible and shift schedules. In *Labor Force Statistics from the CPS* (USDL98-119). Washington, DC: Government Printing Office.

U.S. Department of Labor. U.S. Bureau of Labor Statistics. (2002). *Labor Force Statistics from the Current Population Survey: Household Data Annual Averages, Table 19.* Retrieved from http://www.bls.gov/cps/cpsaat19.pdf

Wedderburn, A. (Ed.). (2000). Shift work and health [Special issue]. *Bulletin of European Studies on Time* (BEST, Vol. 1). Luxembourg: Office for Official Publications of the European Communities; also available on web site: www.eurofound.ie

White, L., & Keith, B. (1990). The effect of shift work on the quality and stability of marital relations. *Journal of Marriage and the Family, 52,* 453–462.

6

THE TIME AND TIMING OF WORK: UNIQUE CHALLENGES FACING LOW-INCOME FAMILIES

Maureen Perry-Jenkins
University of Massachusetts, Amherst

Introduction

Past research (Staines & Pleck, 1983) and more recent findings by Presser (this volume) suggest that work hours and the scheduling of work is a major challenge for most U.S. families, but a particularly stressful one for two subgroups: low-income families and those with young children. A growing trend among parents of young children is to work alternating shifts, where spouses' paid work schedules are opposite and non-overlapping (Presser, 1989, 1994). Working alternating shifts is a strategy that enables some parents to avoid the high cost of childcare and/or to maintain values regarding the importance of exclusive parental care, especially with infants (Deutsch, 1999). Research suggests, however, that the potential benefits of shift work, especially for parents of young children, may be negated by its deleterious effects on the marital relationship (Presser, 2000) and individuals' physical and emotional health (Finn, 1981; Simon, 1990). Recent data made available from the May 2001 Current Population Survey (CPS) indicates that approximately 14.5 million, or 14.5 %, of all full-time wage and salary employees work non-day and/or non-fixed shifts, which includes evening shifts between 2 p.m. and midnight, night shifts, rotating shifts, and irregular shifts (U.S. Bureau of Labor Statistics, 2002). Among dual-earner couples in the United States, one in four includes at least one spouse who is a shift worker; this number rises to one in three if they have children (Presser, 2000). In addition, shift work is most common among blue-collar workers in the protective and food service industries and among those employed as operators, fabricators, and laborers (Beers, 2000). Given these demographic trends, important questions arise about how working nonstandard schedules affects the mental and physical health of employees and their family relationships, especially those employed in blue-collar and low-income occupations.

While shift work may provide a convenient childcare alternative for parents, it is not usually an occupational choice. According to the Current Population Survey (U.S. Bureau of Labor Statistics, 2002), more than one half (53%) of full-time employees who worked an alternating-shift reported doing so because it was "the nature of the job", 13.3% reported that it was a personal preference, 8.9% reported that it provided better arrangements for family or child care, 6.9% said the pay was better, and 3.3% worked shift so they could attend school. Thus, a relatively small percentage of all shift workers, about 9%, chose nonstandard work schedules for better childcare arrangements. However, for low-educated women, a full 30% report working nonstandard schedules for childcare reasons and another 10% did so to care for other family members (Presser & Cox, 1997). It appears that the reasons for working nonstandard hours vary by employee characteristics and need. As our society continues to move towards a 24-hour, seven days/week economy, the need for nonstandard work schedules will necessarily increase, making the question of how these schedules affect employees, their family relationships, and their children's development even more important.

The Time and Timing of Work: Measurement Issues and Methods

Assessing the hours and scheduling of hours that employees work is decidedly more complicated than appears at the outset. In a paper that specifically addresses challenges in accurately measuring work hours, Goldenberg (1994) recommends asking respondents about the context surrounding their responses, such as are the hours typical, when do they vary etc. It is also useful to know if employees use records or pay stubs to provide accurate information regarding work hours. In general, it is usually more straightforward to measure work hours than the schedule of those hours, in that the majority of workers can tell you what hours they worked last week. For the majority, that number represents their typical number of hours. Yet, the number of contingent workers, those who hold jobs without long-term contracts, and seasonal workers has grown sharply over the past decade (Polivka, 1996; Rogers, 2000). For these employees, the hours of work are far less straightforward, often dependent upon weather, number of available workers, and demand for service. Currently, these workers, unless the focus of a particular study, are categorized based on their work status of the previous week—an approach that misrepresents the instability and fluidity of their work experiences—or are excluded from analyses completely.

A second concern that has arisen in our own research in assessing work hours has to do with "under the table" jobs. Respondents may be reluctant to report the work they do that is not reported in their income taxes. In our project, in phase 1 the majority of spouses reported working one job, with 12% reporting a second job and 4% a third job. By the time of our fifth interview, however, 27% of the men in our sample reported having two jobs and 10% reported having three jobs. We discovered in all but three cases that these were not new jobs, but jobs they had not reported to us at the phase 1 interview for fear we might report them. Thus, our assessments of work hours may underestimate the work hours devoted to the "underground economy."

Turning to employment schedules, Presser points out that the concept of shift work is a complicated one. It is one of those concepts that we all know perfectly well until we have to describe it. At its most basic level, shift work refers to working "non-standard hours", meaning not 9–5 Monday through Friday. Non-standard hours could be the 3–11 shift, the graveyard shift 11–7, rotating shifts that combines all hours, and then of course weekends. An important contribution of Presser's work is her careful operationalization of nonstandard work schedules that assesses when employees start their workday and when they complete the majority of their hours on the job, be they days, evenings, nights, or weekends. This level of detail has proven important since certain types of shifts, particularly the night shifts, are related to more negative family outcomes than other shifts (Presser, this volume).

Another level of complexity arises when linking individual work schedules to the schedules of other family members. At the dyadic level, are there different implications for well-being or marital relations depending upon which partner works the non-standard schedule or whether we characterize a couple as split shift? Due to the nature of many of our nationally representative data sets, where the individual is the unit of analysis, a person is categorized based on their work schedule (e.g., evening, night, rotating). Then, either individual or family outcomes are examined in relationship to work schedules. One could argue that being part of an alternating shift couple, even if one partner does work a day schedule, may hold implications for both partners' well-being.

In an ongoing longitudinal study of 150 working-class, dual-earner families experiencing the transition to parenthood, we explored this methodological issue. Specifically, we examined how shift work, operationalized at both the individual level as well as at the couple level (e.g., where a family is characterized as a shift-work family when spouses work alternating shifts), was related to mental health and marital outcomes for a sample of new parents (Perry-Jenkins et al., 2002). Our findings revealed that individual shift work schedules were related to more negative mental health outcomes for wives working nonstandard schedules. For example, wives working nonstandard shifts report significantly higher depression prenatally and over the first year of the child's life. In contrast, at the couple level it was the overlap in the couples' work schedules that held stronger implications for the marriage. Specifically, at Time 1, the prenatal interview, there were no significant differences in spouses' reports of marital love; by Time 2, wives working nonstandard schedules reported significantly lower marital love; and by Time 3, both spouses in shift-work families reported significantly lower marital love. These findings suggest that the level of analysis we use in operationalizing shift work may hold different consequences for individual well-being and family relationships and they point to the importance of studying change over time. As Presser suggests, we need new, longitudinal, and representative data sets that allow us to explore shift work at multiple levels of analysis, including the individual and couple levels.

A final measurement issue that Presser raises and one that deserves special attention is the stability of one's work schedule. We often assess shift work at one point in time with little attention to variation in work schedules and hours despite the fact that we know work conditions vary constantly. Especially given the fact that shift workers are more likely to be employed in low-income, less secure jobs, it is likely that their jobs and job schedules change quite often. It may be that job instability is as critical a factor related to family outcomes as shift work itself.

The Context of Shift Work

From an ecological perspective, Bronfenbrenner and Morris (1997) propose that we must carefully attend not only to aspects of social context, such as race, class, gender, and family structure, but to the idea that family processes may differ within contexts, and ultimately hold different consequences for human development. As Presser's findings indicate, shift work appears to hold different implications for families of different structures (i.e., single-parent versus two-parent, single- vs. dual-earner) and families at different stages of the life span (e.g., having young children or not). Specifically, findings to date suggest that those most at risk for marital instability are shift work couples with young children. These data point to the importance of context as it interacts with work conditions to shape family life. What other contexts must we consider? Does shift work hold different consequences for low-income families versus high-income families? According to Presser (this volume), "Although employment at nonstandard times occurs at all levels of income, it is disproportionately found among those with low incomes" (p. 84). In particular, less-educated mothers are pulled into shift work due to the lack of other options (Presser & Cox, 1997).

Are there different costs and benefits of shift work for families of different economic means? For example, imagine a couple using nonstandard work schedules as a strategy to cope with the high costs of childcare by using parental care. A couple in our study used just such a strategy and their day ran something like this: Mom left for work at the local candle factory at 6:00 a.m., Dad was home with baby during the day until 2:30 p.m., at which time he packed up their son and had a rendezvous with Mom at 3:00 p.m. at a rest stop on the side of interstate 91. At this time they would check in, consult about the baby's day, and Mom would then head home with the baby while Dad headed off to his 3–11 p.m. job at a sub shop. This pattern worked five days a week; Dad worked Saturday as well while Mom covered childcare. Both parents reported that their primary reason for working their schedule out this way was to avoid the high cost of childcare. An added benefit was that their child was being raised by both parents. When asked what might make it easier to manage the demands of work and family, the couple mentioned three things: (1) more money, (2) health insurance, and (3) more flexible schedules. Money would allow them to buy minimal childcare services to give them a break. In terms of health care, the family's health care was covered by the mother since the father was uninsured, so she had to return to full-time employment sooner than she wanted to keep the family covered. Finally, both spouses worked in very inflexible settings where arriving late or leaving early resulted in the docking of pay and letters of reprimand. How might a higher-income family cope with the same scenario? A family with more financial resources might be able to buy more services such as childcare to ease the burden of parents' double shifts, or one parent might not have to work full-time.

Presser points out that we need to explore the costs and benefits of working nonstandard schedules. A high percentage of families in our study use relative care for childcare, a trend reflected in the national data. While there are clearly benefits to using relative care, these arrangements often have hidden costs in terms of social capital. Specifically, new parents often feel highly indebted to family and friends for the childcare service they receive and feel obligated to "pay back" in terms of services or care. Moreover, some parents find it "costly" to have grandparents and in-laws who have strong opinions regarding how children should be raised and feel entitled to express their views since they are providing care. As Presser suggests, we need research that examines the costs and benefits of nonstandard work schedules and we may need to be especially attentive to the social and psychological costs and benefits in our analyses.

How do aspects of race and ethnicity relate to the use of shift work and perhaps moderate the relationships between shift work and family life? The most recent CPS data from 2001 indicates that almost 20% of black employees work nonstandard schedules, meaning an evening, night, irregular, or rotating schedule, while significantly fewer white (13.6%) and Hispanic (14.8%) employees work alternate shifts. It will be important to see how these statistics break down by family structure and income as well. While attending to these multiple social contexts, attention to family life course issues might point to ways in which the relationship between shift work and family life differs for families with young children versus families with adolescents.

As Bronfenbrenner and Morris (1997) point out, much research in the social sciences begins at the "social address" level where we compare one social group to another. For example, research has explored differences in marital and child outcomes in dual-earner vs. single-earner families or in two- vs. single-parent families. In the case of work schedules, our social address has often been shift work, and we examine variation in families as a function of being in a shift work family or not. To date, the research indicates potential risks for parents and children of living in shift work households. Thus, the next question becomes: What are the processes within these families that predict more positive or negative outcomes?

As researchers in this area, our job has been to ask the important questions about how employment schedules shape the lives of families. A reporter, in a recent conversation about shift work, became quite frustrated with my complicated answer to how shift work may be related to marriage and parenting. He finally interrupted me and said, "Just tell me with a simple 'yes' or 'no' is shift work bad for families?" Of course, the logical extension to whatever answer I might have given him was a prescription for whether one should or should not work shifts. The implicit assumption in a question like this one is that workers have a choice about their schedules, which the data suggest is not really the case. Thus, we need to continue to explore the complexity of the relationships between employment schedules and family life because the solutions and supports lie in understanding the complexity.

Processes Within Families Working Nonstandard Schedules

As Presser (this volume) points out, the movement to a 24/7 economy is not likely to be reversed, suggesting that work schedules will continue to be varied and diverse. Since the data to date suggest that working nonstandard hours may be a risk factor not only for individual well-being but for family relationships, we are left to ask: What do we do to reduce the risk? It is unreasonable to expect or suggest to those who work nonstandard schedules, especially those with young children, that they should leave their jobs since they may be placing their family relationships at risk. Rather, it is incumbent upon researchers to start explicating the processes that link shift work to individual well-being and family relationships.

The critical question becomes, what variables predict why some couples cope well with varied work schedules and others seem to suffer? One could argue that perhaps couples who are already experiencing marital difficulty chose split shifts as a way to avoid marital interaction. This is an interesting hypothesis, but one that Presser tested using data from the National Survey of Family and Households and found not to be supported. Another hypothesis suggests that couples with split shifts simply have less time together and this lack of interaction leads to more troubled marital relationships. Or perhaps shift work takes a toll on the individual worker that leads to exhaustion and depression that, in turn, negatively affects family relationships. From a developmental perspective, important questions arise regarding whether couples in longer, more stable relationships are better equipped to cope with the demands of nonstandard schedules than newly married couples. Finally, while in our data we see a decline overall in parental well-being and marital quality, we do not know how these variables mediate the linkages between work schedules and children's development.

In a similar vein, does shift work reduce parents' ability to interact with their children and supervise their activities? Presser's work suggests that the answer to this question is complex and a function of the shift the parent works, the gender of the parent, the type of parent-child activity one is assessing, and the developmental stage of the child. If one has a preschooler, then parents working evening or night shifts could have more time with their child than those working day shifts. In contrast, working an evening shift would provide parents with school-age children little to no overlapping hours at home with their children during their workweek. By identifying parent-child interaction as an important mediator variable, our next step is to explore how parent-child interactions may mediate the link between nonstandard work schedules and children's developmental outcomes in multiple arenas, such as the social, emotional, and cognitive dimensions of development.

In our attempt to explore the processes that underlie the connections between shift work and family functioning, we would be wise to identify and explore multiple outcomes in our studies. Specifically, shift work may work in very different ways in affecting employees' mental health as opposed to their marital and parent-child relations. Thinking back to the cost-benefit analysis Presser proposes, it may be that parents are willing to sacrifice marital companionship for the financial and personal benefits of providing exclusive parental care for their children.

The time and timing of employment are the focus of this group of chapters, and the data we currently have available to us suggest that these aspects of one's job hold consequences for the individual worker, for his or her family relationships, and for children. Research also has shown us that there are multiple aspects of work beyond its time and timing that have implications for well-being and family relationships. For example, Parcel and Menaghan's (1994) findings support the notion that holding a job low in complexity, or entering such a job, may drain parental energy, discourage mothers' intellectual growth, and discourage child-rearing values and practices that teach children to internalize norms. Since nonstandard work schedules are more likely to occur in low-income service occupations and we know that such jobs are also more likely to lack autonomy and complexity, then the potential risk factors for employees and their families may become additive. In contrast, more positive job conditions, such as greater autonomy and control at work, more complexity, and supportive supervisors and co-workers may mitigate the effects of working nonstandard schedules.

Another important finding from Parcel and Menaghan's research is evidence for lagged effects whereby work and family conditions have greater effects over time than concurrently. Thus, we need longitudinal databases that include detailed information on both work schedules and work conditions, as well as information on employees' well-being and family relationships. Ideally, when possible we would benefit from experimental research designs. As workplaces start to experiment with initiating new procedures and practices, researchers need to be there to capitalize on these natural social experiments. In doing so we will be better able to pinpoint those factors that make a difference in workers' lives and make it possible to examine selection effects that play a large role in the types of individuals who choose particular types of jobs.

Workplace Responses and Policies:
A Time for Creative Thinking

Thus far my comments have focused primarily on better understanding the processes linking nonstandard work schedules and work hours to employee well-being and family outcomes. The findings to date, however, are quite compelling in their consistency. They suggest that nonstandard work schedules may be a serious risk factor for negative family outcomes, especially for low-income families with young children. This conclusion is especially worrisome when one considers that employers' decisions regarding who works nonstandard schedules are most often based on a seniority system in which young workers, with the lowest seniority and who are the most likely to have young children, most often work evening or night shifts. How we deal with equity issues on the job while also developing work systems that do not undermine employee and family well-being is a significant challenge. When we asked couples working alternating shifts in our study to tell us what would make it easier to manage work demands and family life, they had some important suggestions. First, the majority said higher pay, especially higher differential pay for working night shifts. Second, the majority felt that longer shifts over fewer days would be helpful, so four 10-hour nights would be preferred over five 8-hour nights. Third, more schedule flexibility in start and end times would be beneficial. Some parents mentioned that being able to be home to help get children off to school in the morning would be helpful, but since most shifts run until 7 a.m., by the time the commute is added in most employees cannot be home to help during this busy time of day. Finally, a number of mothers reported that receiving health insurance for part-time work would have made it possible for them to cut back on work hours to manage childcare; however, in many families where only one spouse has health benefits, full-time work is a necessity.

In closing, I agree with Harriet Presser's conclusion that, "For better or worse, families will increasingly need to respond to these challenges and so will we as scholars" (Presser, this volume, p. 102). In our efforts to respond, we must continue to talk across disciplines to use multiple methodologies, and we must listen to multiple voices, especially the voices of those who have not been heard before.

References

Beers, T. M. (2000). Flexible schedules and shift work: Replacing the "9-to5" workday. *Monthly Labor Review, 123*, 33–40.

Bronfenbrenner, U., & Morris, P. A. (1997). The ecology of developmental processes. In W. Damon (Ed.), *Handbook of child psychology* (5th ed.) (pp. 993–1028). New York: Wiley.

Deutsch, F. M. (1999). *Halving it all: How equally shared parenting works*. Cambridge, MA: Harvard University Press.

Finn, P. (1981). The effects of shift work on the lives of employees. *Monthly Labor Review, 104*, 31–35.

Goldenberg, K. L. (1994). Answering questions: Questioning answers: Evaluating data quality in and establishment survey. Proceedings of the section on Survey Research Methods. Washington, DC: American Statistical Association.

Parcel, T. L., & Menaghan, E. G. (1994). *Parents' jobs and children's lives*. New York: Aldine de Gruyter.

Perry-Jenkins, M., Goldberg, A., Pierce, C., & Haley, H. L. (2000). *Employment schedules and the transition to parenthood: Implications for mental health and marriage*. Paper presented at the National Council on Family Relations, Minneapolis, MN (November).

Polivka, A. E. (1996). Contingent and alternative work arrangements, defined. *Monthly Labor Review, 119*, 3–9.

Presser, H. B. (1989). Can we make time for children? The economy, work schedules, and child care. *Demography, 26*, 523–543.

Presser, H. B. (1994). Employment schedules among dual-earner spouses and the division of household labor by gender. *American Sociological Review, 59*, 348–364.

Presser, H. B. (2000) Work schedules and marital instability. *Journal of Marriage and the Family, 62*, 93–110.

Presser, H. B., & Cox, A. G. (1997). The work schedules of low-educated American women and welfare reform. *Monthly Labor Review, 120*, 25–34.

Rogers, J. (2000). *Temps*. Ithaca, NY: Cornell University Press.

Rubin, L. B. (1994). *Families on the fault line*. New York: Harper Perennial.

Simon, B. L. (1990). Impact of shift work on individuals and families. *Families in Society: The Journal of Contemporary Human Services*, 342–348.

Staines, G. L., & Pleck, J. H. (1983). *The impact of work schedules on the family*. Ann Arbor, MI: University of Michigan, Institute for Social Research.

U.S. Bureau of Labor Statistics, U.S. Department of Labor. (1997). Current Population Survey. Washington, DC: U.S. Government Printing Office.

U.S. Bureau of Labor Statistics, U.S. Department of Labor. (2002). Current Population Survey. Washington, DC: U.S. Government Printing Office.

7

EXPLORING PROCESS AND CONTROL IN FAMILIES WORKING NONSTANDARD SCHEDULES

Kerry Daly
University of Guelph

Introduction

Presser (this volume) sets out to examine the implications of nonstandard work schedules for "the functioning and stability of family life" (p. 84). She identifies factors contributing to the increased prevalence of nonstandard work schedules and outlines the negative repercussions for marital quality, family scheduling, educational outcomes for children, and eating together. In short, it seems clear that nonstandard schedules have *de-stabilizing* effects on family life. These findings themselves are critically important for thinking about workplace policies and practices and the provisions of supports and services to families. Embedded in the goal of this chapter, however, is an invitation for us all to explore more fully what these nonstandard schedules imply for the functioning and stability of family life. As Presser comments, there is a paucity of research on the effects of nonstandard work schedules on families.

As a qualitative researcher who is particularly interested in the meaning of family processes and experiences, I would like to respond to that invitation by opening the curtain a little wider on the dynamics that are played out in these families. To that end, it is my intention to explore paths of inquiry that might begin to provide a better understanding of the meanings, practices, and strategies that are used as a way of creating and sustaining family life in the face of nonstandard schedules. In other words, if we are to understand why nonstandard schedules have such a detrimental impact on marriages and families, then we need to understand at a more concrete level the way that stresses, conflicts, and divergent realities develop over time. If we have a clearer window on the patterns of interaction and decision-making in these families, then we are in a more confident position for making recommendations in practice and policy. To this end, I shall focus my comments on two issues: the *processes* involved in living through nonstandard schedules; and the *dynamics of control* that are characteristic of these families.

Focusing on Process

One of the unique and central dynamics of working nonstandard shifts in two-parent families is the manner in which partners make transitions between shifts. Unlike 9–5 families who ritually disperse together in the mornings and ritually reconvene in the late afternoon hours, these are families for whom more elaborate strategies and temporal structures are called for. Metaphorically, parents working nonstandard shifts have been referred to as "tag team" parents or "split-shift parents". However, we know little about how this kind of parenting works and the kinds of negotiations and strategies that are used in managing these more complex schedules.

One way of examining these timing and scheduling efforts is to use Hochschild's concept of the *"third shift"*. This refers to the growing importance of families devoting time and energy to the organizational activities associated with making everyday schedules run smoothly. The underlying premise of the third shift is that partners create structured opportunities for schedule planning and the accompanying orchestration of tasks. Empirical research that has examined the gendered nature of these planning activities indicate that women carry more responsibility and exert more control over the way that the family schedule is worked out (Arendell, 2001; Daly, 2002; Mederer, 1993). For couples working nonstandard schedules, we know little about the organization of the third shift. One area of inquiry would be to examine the degree to which couples are deliberate about finding time for third-shift activities. A variety of questions arise with respect to the form and shape of these organizational activities, including whether they occur at all, but if they do, when they are scheduled, how they are conducted, and whether they are prospective or reactive.

Given the challenges of nonstandard schedules for finding overlapping time, however, one might expect fewer opportunities for third-shift organizational work in these families. As a result, the focus then shifts to the manner in which these couples find ways to communicate with each other about the organization of everyday routine. Of particular interest here would be to examine the way that parents in tag team relationships actually pass on the "tag". Specifically, how many tags or transitions are there in the course of day? One could imagine that in some families there is one focused tag where key information is passed between partners. Also possible is a model involving multiple tags throughout the course of the day. What forms do these transitions take? In its most standard form, third-shift discussions are most likely to include face-to-face meetings or interactions in which instructions, appointments, or special requests are sorted out and responsibility delegated and taken. When face time is at a premium, however, one could expect other kinds of strategies to be used. For example, to what extent does technology play a role in carrying out the tag in a more remote fashion? With the prevalence of cell phones, e-mail, and pagers, one might expect that these have become more important instruments in the passing of the "informational baton" at any time between shifts. Furthermore, it would also be valuable to look at the way that women and men deal with scheduling gaps, hot points (where timing is very tight), and transitions.

Although it is tempting only to focus on the ways that parents "tag" with one another with respect to the communication of responsibilities, it may well be that the game of tag being played in these families is far more complex, with all members of the family passing tags, interpreting tags, and in some cases strategically diverting tags. Perhaps the term "tag team parenting" is in itself misleading. Instead, we should be looking at the more complex dynamics of "tag team *families*". Given the complexity of these schedules and the kind of temporal disorientation that may accompany them, there is the potential in these families for very complex patterns of communication. Take, for example, how children mediate telephone messages from one parent to another, how children are given responsibilities in between parents being home, and how children then "give" instructions to the other parent upon their arrival.

While the third shift refers specifically to the ways that families find to cope with scheduling and time demands in families, there is a much broader question that opens up about how families in nonstandard schedules communicate with one another in a variety of other functional domains. Organization of tasks and responsibilities is one domain, but how do these families communicate about parenting strategies and expectations? Given the finding reported by Presser (this volume) that nonstandard shifts have a negative impact on marital quality but only when there are children present, it would seem that the management of parenting responsibilities is particularly challenging. Therefore, it is essential to look at the dynamics of parenting in families living with complex schedules. In contrast with families where both parents are at home at similar times and may have an agreed upon division of labor, in these families both parents have periods where they are not only required to work at home autonomously but also in a more generalized role where they are responsible for dealing with all situations that arise. Although this might serve the values of interchangeability and a balanced gender contribution to parenting, it might also result in greater levels of conflict resulting from the development of separate parenting styles.

One of the fundamental challenges for understanding process in families who work nonstandard schedules is the way that they create and sustain a sense of cohesion as a family. When family face time is limited, a question arises about how they share the mundane ups and downs of everyday living that are so important to the construction of a shared family identity. In my own work on the meaning of "family time" (Daly, 1996, 2001), even couples working standard schedules are feeling challenged to find sufficient opportunity to be together to create the kinds of sustaining and defining activity that we think of as "family time". For families working nonstandard shifts, it would be interesting to examine the kinds of expectations they have for family time and the kinds of strategies that they use in trying to align their expectations for, and realities of, family time.

Many of our notions of "family time" have some of the same nostalgic biases as the term "the family" itself. Hence when we think of "nonstandard schedules" we think of "nonstandard families" and think of them as some kind of deviation from our inherited traditions and ideologies about who the family is or who we expect it to be. If we embrace post-modern ways of thinking about diversity, globalization, and the constant changing of forms, then "family time" is a term that we must open up to broader scrutiny. When we do this, we must examine both expectations and ideologies for what this should be, and diverse family practices that tell us what families actually do when they are together and what it means to them. For families working nonstandard schedules, there must be different constructs of family time-different definitions of togetherness, different ways of constructing routines, different ways of evaluating their strengths and weaknesses as a family. Do these families create different kinds of rituals as a way of contending with nonstandard schedules?

An exploration of process as it relates to families in nonstandard schedules has a number of conceptual guideposts to draw on. Several decades ago, Kantor and Lehr (1976) talked about "clocking" in families as the "regulation" of sequence, frequency, duration, and pace of immediately experienced events. Clocking and scheduling of events in families is directly related to how the family establishes and maintains priorities. The way that families make decisions about when to start and finish activities or how much time to give to events or whether to do activities separately or together are all at some level decisions that conflate the meaning of time and values. Clocking phenomena are among the most immediate, poignant, and observable influences on family behavior since "every experience is affected in one way or another by the way in which the family regulates its members' clocking - if people are out of phase with one another, they may not even be able to be home together at the same time, much less make love or fight with one another" (Kantor & Lehr, 1976, p. 82). From this perspective, research that seeks to understand the clocking behaviors of families can provide insight into the "deep-seated and persistent attitude" about the family's social and physical world (Reiss, 1981, p. 226). The notion of clocking has received very little attention in the empirical literature. With most of the emphasis on time allocations or how much time is spent in various family and household activities, we have only a limited understanding of how families working nonstandard shifts experience pace, duration, or sequence. As a consequence, we have a poor grasp of how they construct and sustain their family world.

"Scheduling congruity theory" has also been proposed as one way of conceptualizing the degree of synchronization among family members with regard to their schedules (Avery & Stafford, 1991). The temporal organization of activities within a family falls along a continuum that ranges from "simple congruity" where there is minimal daily synchronization of activity and individual members seem to operate on schedules that are independent and parallel, to "complex congruity" where activity schedules are integrated into shared activities and resources. In families where there is a high degree of synchronization, there appears to be "effortless collaboration", patterned routines, and the coordination of interests and agendas (Reiss, 1981, p. 236). In families where there is little synchronization, as we might expect in families working nonstandard schedules, different routines are competing for time and space, there is disagreement about plans, and there is conflict instead of collaboration with respect to activities. In families such as these, individual members may be more likely tend to live in a separate space and time with only marginal reference to the family group as a whole (Reiss, 1981). Although one would expect families working nonstandard schedules to fall on the "simple congruity" end of the continuum, this is a question in need of empirical inquiry.

Control Issues

Underlying all efforts to analyze temporal process in families who work nonstandard schedules, are questions of control. These questions are concerned with the degree of control that individuals have over their personal schedules and the way that schedules are established and managed in families. Accordingly, two issues will be explored in this section: the first has to do with the amount of control that family members working nonstandard shifts have over their work; and the second concerns the dynamics of control over time within families. Within families I am interested in the dynamics between women and men and the dynamics of control between parents and children.

Dynamics of Control between Families and Work

Families who work nonstandard schedules are disproportionately found among those with low incomes. In general these are jobs with low pay and low control. Research has indicated that our time culture is deeply differentiated by social class, with the more educated more concerned about keeping track of and controlling their time and the less educated having a more fatalistic position of powerlessness in relation to time (LeShan, 1957; Pronovost, 1989; Rifkin, 1987; Rubin, 1976). Within the subculture of poverty, there is a strong present time orientation with a strong sense of resignation and fatalism about the future (Cottle & Klineberg, 1974). For people living under the conditions of poverty, it is difficult to imagine the future when there is a preoccupation with daily survival. In her classic study of the working class, Rubin (1976) concluded that inability to control the future most sharply distinguishes the working class from the more privileged classes.

For low-income families working nonstandard schedules, the nature of their work also shapes the degree of control that they have over time. As Presser (this volume) has pointed out, nonstandard shifts are typically concentrated in occupations with low incomes such as cashiers, truck drivers, waitresses, cooks, and janitors and cleaners. These occupations also are characterized by low control over the timing and pace of work. Hence, for people working low-income, nonstandard schedules, there is a kind of bifocal handicap in relation to time: as they look to the future, there is a sense of resignation about their ability to change their position; as they look to the present circumstances of their work, there is a relative powerlessness in relation to employers to do anything to change, manage, or orchestrate their work. In light of the fact that many of our theories and practices about balancing work and family rest on an assumption of individual control, this is a target population for whom control over work and family scheduling is very compromised. As a result, much empirical work needs to be done to understand the ways that this control is undermined and the implications that it has for family life.

Gender Dynamics of Control Within Families

Although the dynamics of control between employed family members and their work has an important bearing on the choices and decisions that are made in families, there is another axis of control-between women and men-that warrants examination in these families. Given that one of the main motivations of nonstandard shifts is to provide childcare within the home without having to go to outside sources, a number of issues arise with respect to parental control. As a fathering researcher, I think one of the most fascinating areas for inquiry is to examine how men father differently when they are on their own. A growing body of literature points to the ways in which women control parenting decisions and activities. This has been referred to as the "responsibility dimension" (Pleck & Steuve, 2001) and "gatekeeping" (Allen & Hawkins, 1999) wherein mothers have been shown to exert primary control over standards of parenting and the organization of everyday activity. The dominant role played by mothers in managing the family is evident in the survey language used to describe fathering activity when mothers work shifts: "resident fathers" are the most likely person to provide "relative care" (Presser, this volume, p. 88). This reflects the "second string" assumption, which is that fathers provide "relative care" when mothers are absent, but mothers would never provide "relative care" when fathers are absent. This asymmetry in our language reflects women's dominant role as mothers.

Looking beyond the language, it would appear that nonstandard schedules may be a good thing for fathering. Differences between women and men in roles and activities seem to diminish in nonstandard families whereby fathers are more likely to look like "good mothers" by carrying out a greater proportion of "traditionally female household tasks" (Presser, this volume, p. 89). Equally interesting from my perspective would be to examine more closely how fathers in these situations become "good fathers" by examining the ways that father involvement changes and deepens. However, what remains unclear is the way that the responsibility dimension is played out in these families. One possibility is that there is a greater sharing of responsibility for decisions about how and when things are done; another possibility is that women continue to carry responsibility and control in these families by delegating, making lists, or calling home at key times.

Parent-Child Dynamics of Control

Although most of the emphasis in the work family literature is on the strategies used by adults to manage work and family, the analysis of families working nonstandard shifts directs us to look at the roles that children play in making these families work. This is consistent with a growing literature that emphasizes the agentic role of children in the orchestration of everyday life (Lollis & Kuczynski, 1997; Thorne, 1994). Given the "tag" nature of the parenting experience, one could argue that children are the unifying force in these families who exert control by virtue of their broader knowledge of how the family works. For example, children who are home more of the time see how it works all the time, whereas many parents have a more piecemeal view of the family. When parents are passing by one another, it is the children who provide the bridges and serve to construct and reconstruct how the last shift went with the other parent. This puts children in a powerful role as narrators of the family story, with parents acting as the story recipients. Hence not only do children function in a way to mediate the orchestration of tasks and activities in the family, but they may also play a more prominent role in the way that the family's reality is shaped and recorded.

In some of my own qualitative research about how parents and children organize time in the family, we used the term "parented time" (Thorpe & Daly, 1999) to describe the pattern we observed of parents organizing the everyday schedules on the basis of children's activities and responsibilities. In the same way that the term "gendered time" shakes time from its neutral position and reflects the different standpoints and values that women and men bring to time, we discovered that parents and children also bring different meanings to time. Although we started with the assumption that parents generally control the organization of time in families, it quickly became apparent to us as we looked closely at the data, that children's wishes, needs, and schedules in large part determined parents' organization of their time. Applying this to nonstandard schedules, the question becomes one of examining the way that children exert power and control over the orchestration of schedules in these families. If we accept that children exert a good deal of control over the organization of time in families, then we need also to look at how children in families with nonstandard schedules carry responsibility and pass on tags to their parents.

The dynamics of time control between parents and children may be particularly interesting to examine within the context of single-mother families who work nonstandard schedules. According to Presser, single mothers are more likely to work nonstandard schedules than married mothers, as well as longer hours. Studies of time control among single-parent families suggest two possible ways of thinking about this control: one portrays single parents as being more fragile in their ability to provide parental coverage to their children because of the absence of a "tag" partner (Hodgson, Dienhart, & Daly, 2000), while other research argues that single mothers may be in a position to exert greater control over scheduling of activities at home with the result that their time at home is happier, more flexible, and relaxed compared to women in dual-earner families (Larson, 2001). Although it is tempting to assume that single mothers working nonstandard schedules are in a more precarious position with respect to controlling their time, it may well be that they have greater control over the scheduling of their work and family lives than do two-parent families. However, we know little about the interactive and dynamic aspects of time control between single parents and their children, but given the prevalence of nonstandard schedules in these families, it is an area in need of exploration.

Conclusion

Presser (this volume), in this and related work on nonstandard schedules, has pioneered our understanding of key trends in nonstandard work schedules and their impact on families who are working nonstandard shifts. Like a good cartographer, she has mapped out the territory in ways that invite guided exploration. As this sector of the economy continues to grow in its demand for employees to work nonstandard schedules, so too will the strains on families continue to grow. As a result, there is urgency in these matters and there is considerable exploration to be done. I thank Dr. Presser for helping us to see the territory so that we can explore, in an informed way, the emerging dynamics and challenges in these families.

References

Allen, S., & Hawkins, A. (1999). Maternal gatekeeping. *Journal of Marriage and the Family, 61*, 199–212.

Arendell, T. (2001). New care work of middle class mothers: Managing childrearing, employment and time. In K. J. Daly (Ed.), *Minding the time in family experience: Emerging issues and perspectives* (pp. 163–204). London: JAI Press.

Avery, R. J., & Stafford, K. (1991). Toward a scheduling congruity theory of resource management. *Lifestyles: Family and Economic Issues, 12*, 325–344.

Cottle, T. J., & Klineberg, S. L. (1974). *The present of things future: Explorations of time in human experience.* New York: Free Press.

Daly, K. J. (1996). *Families and time: Keeping pace in a hurried culture.* Thousand Oaks, CA: Sage.

Daly, K. J. (2001). Deconstructing family time: From ideology to lived experience. *Journal of Marriage and the Family, 63*, 283–294.

Daly, K. J. (2002). Time, gender and the negotiation of family schedules. *Symbolic Interaction, 25*, 323–342.

Hodgson, J., Dienhart, A., & Daly, K. (2001). Time juggling: Single mothers' experience of time-press following divorce. *Journal of Divorce and Remarriage, 35*, 1–28.

Kantor, D., & Lehr, W. (1976). *Inside the family: Toward a theory of family process.* San Francisco: Jossey-Bass.

Larson, R. (2001). Mother's time in two parent and one-parent families: The daily organization of work, time for oneself and parenting of adolescents. In K. J. Daly (Ed.), *Minding the time in family experience: Emerging issues and perspectives* (pp. 111–134). London: JAI Press.

LeShan, L. L. (1957). Time orientation and social class. *Journal of Abnormal and Social Psychology, 47*, 589–592.

Lollis, S., & Kuczynski, L. (1997). Beyond one hand clapping: Seeing bidirectionality in parent-child relations. *Journal of Social and Personal Relationships, 14*, 441–461.

Mederer, H. J. (1993). Division of household labour in two-earner homes: Task accomplishment versus household management as critical variables in perceptions about family work. *Journal of Marriage and the Family, 55*, 133–145.

Pleck, J., & Stueve, J. L. (2001). Time and paternal involvement. In K. J. Daly (Ed.), *Minding the time in family experience: Emerging issues and perspectives* (pp. 205–226). London: JAI Press.

Pronovost, G. (1989). The sociology of time. *Current Sociology, 37*, 1–124.

Reiss, D. (1981). *The family's construction of reality.* Cambridge, MA: Harvard University Press.

Rifkin, J. (1987). *Time wars: The primary conflict in human history.* New York: Henry Holt & Co.

Rubin, L. (1976). *Worlds of pain: Life in the working-class family.* New York: Basic Books.

Thorne, B. (1994). *Gender play: Girls and boys in school.* New Brunswick, NJ: Rutgers University Press.

Thorpe, K., & Daly, K. J. (1999). Children, parents and time: The dialectics of control. In C. Sheehan (Ed.), *Through the eyes of the child: Revisioning children as active agents of family life* (pp. 199–223). Stamford, CT: JAI Press.

8

USING DAILY DIARIES TO ASSESS TEMPORAL FRICTION BETWEEN WORK AND FAMILY

David M. Almeida
University of Arizona

Over the past several decades the temporal nature of work life has undergone a transformation. The movement toward a service economy, combined with an increase in the number of mothers with young children in the labor market and improved technology enabling instant global communication, have created a 24/7 economy (Presser, 1999). Such macro-level changes should most certainly have consequences for workers and their families. This same economy that boosts profits and increases consumer convenience may at the same time push employees to work evenings, nights, and weekends. Presser refers to these non-traditional working hours as nonstandard schedules or "fringe time". In her chapter (this volume), Presser draws our attention to the importance of investigating the impact of fringe time working by carefully elucidating various types of nonstandard schedules (e.g., weekend vs. late hours), documenting the prevalence of these work schedules, and describing their potential consequences for the family.

The timing of work hours has received less attention than the total amount of work hours (Jacobs & Gerson, 2001). In fact, some diary research has indicated that we may be working less for pay. Robinson and Godbey (1997) show that from 1965–1985, employed men and women have decreased the number of hours in the labor market by approximately 7 hours per week and that this decrease in work hours has not been met with a similar increase in time with family. Furthermore, Putnam (2000) argues that this increase in discretionary time is spent primarily on leisure pursuits rather than family and civic engagement. We learn from Presser's work (this volume), however, that simply assessing the number of hours at work does not paint a complete temporal picture of work life. Her chapter clearly documents that *when* a person works has certainly changed over the past twenty years. In 1997, only a slight majority of U.S. workers (54%) worked for pay between the hours of 9–5. At some point during their workweek, 20% of American workers worked during the evening or late night and 40% worked on the weekend. Working during this fringe time may quickly become the norm for certain members of our society, such as single mothers with young children.

What are the potential consequences of nonstandard schedules for family life? According to Presser's review, research unfortunately has not provided a clear answer. Some studies report positive consequences, such as increased income and involvement with children inside the home, while others report decreased extracurricular activities and marital tension. It appears that one key potential consequence of nonstandard work schedules is a reduction in the ability to coordinate family schedules, thus creating a temporal friction between work and family (Mott et al., 1965). To understand this friction, one needs to take into account the temporal nature of family life as well as work life. Work by Crouter and Maguire (1998) and by Larson and Crouter (1998) shows that children's activities follow a weekly schedule typically scripted by school and extracurricular activities. For parents and children with "standard" schedules, weekdays are devoted to work and school and evenings and weekends are available for family time. Crouter and Maguire (1998) refer to this available family time as "windows of socialization". The general question I would like to pose is, to what extent do nonstandard work schedules create temporal friction by disrupting this synchrony between work and family schedules?

Weekly Rhythm of Work and Family Time

One way to assess this temporal friction is to examine work and family experiences on a day-to-day basis. Although Presser's work and the studies she cites go a long way toward establishing a link between work schedules and family life, these studies presume that work schedules are a relatively static phenomenon. In my work I have tried to show how activities fluctuate on a daily, weekly, and seasonal basis to create rhythms of individual and family experiences (Almeida & McDonald, 1998, in press; Almeida et al., 2002). Rhythm is the measured repetition of recurring events happening in a regular, sequential, and predictive pattern over time (Fraenkel, 1994). In music, rhythm is the organizing and energizing structure through which tone and pitch find expression. Notes exist in measured time and space, buttressed by beat and tempo, and are arranged within an infrastructure of measures, phrases, and movements. Musical rhythm, in the form of beats, measures, phrases, and movements, synthesize with notes of tone and pitch to create music. Likewise, social temporal rhythms of days, weeks, months, seasons, and years provide the score for daily life to be performed.

Weekly work schedules are one such temporal rhythm that powerfully influences how we structure our time (Zerubavel, 1985). In a previous set of analyses, I examined how temporal characteristics of the work week (i.e., workdays vs. non-workdays) were associated with time devoted to family and community. On days that respondents did not work, they spent up to twice as much time with children and providing informal help to family members as compared to workdays. Similarly, respondents spent significantly more time giving volunteer and informal help to community members on non-workdays (Almeida & McDonald, in press). It appears that when workers are not working they will spend time fulfilling obligations to those around them. The underlying assumption of this interpretation is that available time outside of work coincides with the available time of others. Presser contends, however, that such synchrony may not be present for workers with nonstandard schedules.

One way to examine this synchrony of work and family activities among standard- and fringe-time workers is to study the ebb and flow of work and family time on a daily basis. The use of innovative research tools such as time diaries and event sampling methodology has permitted researchers to obtain detailed accounts of how people spend their time. This daily approach to examining the work-family interweave affords the researcher several benefits that cannot be easily achieved through the use of standard designs. First, daily measurement helps resolve retrospective recall problems by allowing respondents to report about experiences in various domains of life much nearer to the time that they occur (Robinson & Godbey, 1997). Second, the daily design is especially useful in capturing information about the dynamics of daily experiences that appear static in traditional cross-sectional designs. By establishing within-person covariation of time spent in paid work with time contributing to family over several days, this intra-individual approach allows the researcher to rule out temporally stable personality and environmental variables as third variable explanations for these associations (Larson & Almeida, 1999).

Using data from a U.S. national study of daily experiences, I assess here the impact of nonstandard work schedules, specifically weekend work, on time spent with children by addressing the following questions. First, do weekend workers spend fewer hours taking care of their children than workers with solely weekday schedules? Second, are the weekly rhythms of time devoted to work and childcare different for weekend versus weekday workers? Access to daily information on time use permits us to assess whether individuals spend less time with children on workdays compared to non-workdays. Third, our final analyses then explore whether family demands may cause more work disruptions for weekend workers than weekday workers. The lack of synchrony between work and family schedules may create disruptions at work, especially when family members need assistance.

National Study of Daily Experiences

Data for the present analyses are from the National Study of Daily Experiences (NSDE), one of the in-depth studies that are part of the National Survey of Midlife in the United States Survey (MIDUS) carried out under the auspices of the John D. and Catherine T. MacArthur Foundation Research Network on Successful Midlife (Orville Gilbert Brim, Director). Respondents in the NSDE were randomly selected from the MIDUS sample and received $20 for their participation in the project. Of the 1,242 MIDUS respondents we attempted to contact, 1,031 agreed to participate, yielding a response rate of 83%. Over the course of eight consecutive evenings, respondents completed short telephone interviews about their daily experiences. Respondents completed an average of 7 of the 8 interviews, resulting in a total of 7,221 daily interviews. The present analyses used the 451 respondents (223 men and 229 women) who reported working for pay at least four hours per week and had at least one child in the household. Respondents for the present analysis were on average 43 years old, with 2 children in the household and an average family income between $50,000 and $55,000. Men were slightly older than women but had similar levels of education.

Data collection spanned an entire year (March 1996–March 1997) and consisted of 40 separate flights of interviews with each flight representing the eight-day sequence of interviews from approximately 38 respondents. The initiation of interview flights was staggered across the day of the week to control for the possible confounding between day of study and day of week.

The daily telephone interview included questions about daily experiences in the past 24 hours concerning mood, physical symptoms, productivity, cutbacks, and daily stressors and time use. The following analyses focus primarily on both the time respondents spent each day at paid work and the time spent each day doing things with children. Based on their daily reports of work hours we classified respondents into weekend workers (any work hours on Saturday or Sunday) or weekday workers (work hours solely on weekdays). The prevalence of weekend work in our sample (41%) is very close to that found in Presser's study. Because respondents were interviewed over eight days, we averaged the first and last days of the interviews before computing the mean across the rest of the interviews to eliminate day-of-week bias in the average daily estimate.

Results

The first set of analyses tested differences between weekend workers' and weekday workers' average amount of time spent at work and taking care of their children each day. Table 8.1 shows that male weekend workers spent on average one hour more per day at paid employment and 30 minutes less per day with their children than did male weekday workers. Working weekends did not make a difference in how much time women spent at work or with their children. How does this translate into daily rhythms of work and family time? Figures 8.1 and 8.2 show how work and childcare hours were distributed across the days of the week. Weekday workers show a synchronous crossover rhythm of time devoted to work and children where time with children dramatically increases on the weekend. These workers spent an average of two and one half hours with children on weekdays and four hours on the weekend. A different pattern emerged for weekend workers. Time with children remained relatively constant over the entire week and at no point during the week did parents spend more time with children than they did at work.

Table 8.1

Description of Childcare and Paid Work Hours by Gender and Type of Work Schedule

| | Weekday Workers ($n = 268$) | | Weekend Workers ($n = 184$) | | Work Schedule |
	Mean	(SD)	Mean	(SD)	F
Daily Work Hours					
Total	6.55	(1.50)	7.53	(1.96)	33.5*
Men	6.80	(1.44)	8.02	(1.95)	28.9*
Women	6.34	(1.51)	6.90	(1.79)	3.2
Daily Childcare Hours					
Total	2.78	(2.18)	2.16	(1.95)	9.3*
Men	2.43	(2.01)	1.75	(1.42)	8.8*
Women	3.07	(2.59)	2.69	(2.36)	1.0

$N = 452$.
*$p < .01$.

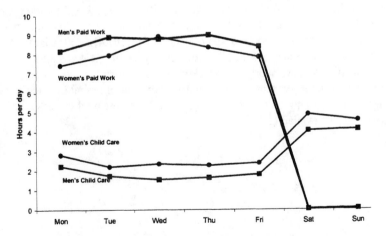

Figure 8.1. Weekly rhythms of paid work and child care hours: Weekday workers.

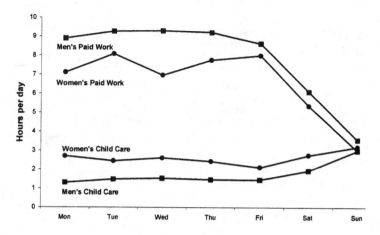

Figure 8.2. Weekly rhythms of paid work and child care hours: Weekend workers.

These findings support Presser's contention that parents' work schedules can create alterations in activities of family life. In our sample, weekend workers spent two fewer hours on the weekend with their children than did weekday workers. Obviously, weekend workers do not have as much available time on the weekend to spend with children. Perhaps these weekend workers are making up child time on days that they are not working. This does not appear to be the case. Figure 8.3 shows the amount of time parents spent with their children on workdays and non-workdays, stratified by work schedule. Results of a 2 X 2 (workday X work schedule) mixed model ANOVA indicated that, on average, parents spent more time with children on non-workdays ($F(1, 440) = 107.4, p < .01$). However, this difference was greater for weekday workers ($F(1, 440) = 4.4, p < .05$). While there was no difference on workdays, weekday workers spent one hour more with children on non-workdays than did weekend workers. One interpretation for these findings is that working on the weekend may limit the time on those days when children are most available.

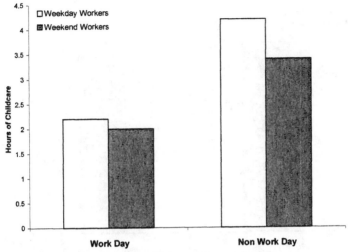

Figure 8.3. Childcare hours on work days and non-work days.

So far these analyses support the contention that weekend work schedules may disrupt rhythms of family life by being out of sync with children's schedules, resulting in decreased time with them. It is possible that lack of synchrony between work schedules and family schedules may also be disruptive to working conditions. Children's structured (e.g., sporting events) or unstructured (e.g., hanging out with friends) activities may create obligations for parents to fulfill, such as attending a game, shuttling children from one activity to another, or tending to minor accidents and/or illness. Fulfilling these obligations may have consequences for work activities.

In my final set of analyses I explore how family demands may disrupt daily work activities and whether such disruptions are more likely to occur for weekend workers. Each day during our study respondents indicated whether they had to "cutback at work because a family member needed their help". Affirmative responses were followed by a series of open-ended probes. The most common reasons for cutting back were child-related schedules followed by family illnesses.

On average, 26% of our respondents reported having to cutback at work at least once during the study week because a family member needed them. Figure 8.4 shows this prevalence broken down by gender and work schedule. Although women were more likely than men to experience family-related disruptions, work schedules were not related to women's work disruption. Among men, weekend workers were almost twice as likely to experience a job disruption as were weekday workers ($x^2 = 4.78, p < .01$). Consider the following week described by a 45-year-old male weekend worker in our study.

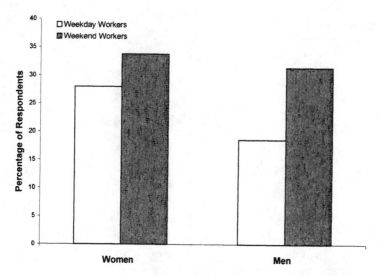

Figure 8.4. Percentage of family-related job disruption by type of work schedule.

Saturday:
   "I had to leave work about an hour earlier because my daughter had a softball game that she had to get to. So I had to drive her there."
Sunday:
   "My daughter left home without my permission and it interfered greatly with my activities. She said she was going to have dinner at a friend's house and I was to pick her up at a certain time and when I called to let her know I was on my way, she said, don't bother I'm not coming home tonight."
Tuesday:
   "For about a half hour I had to leave the office and go over to pick up my daughter from high school and bring her home. Normally I don't have to do that. It was an interruption to my business day. She stayed late to do some extra work in one of her classes and did not take the bus."
Thursday:
   "There was a scheduling conflict with picking my children up from their after-school sports activities so I cut back on my work time."
Friday:
   "My 17-year-old son is on spring break and he was at a party on the river last night and I happened to have on the scanner and I heard that the police were about to go down and check out this party and so I went down there and told them they needed to go home. So, they all came to my house. About 15 boys and 3 or 4 girls were here at my house until 4 o'clock in the morning. I had to get up for work at 7."

These examples suggest that the temporal friction of out-of-sync schedules also may affect work life.

Conclusions

Presser calls on researchers and policy makers to recognize how social trends alter the fabric of our daily lives by seriously considering the import of nonstandard work schedules for family life. The trend of such fringe-time working suggests that most U. S. families will be faced with adapting to this form of work schedule. Therefore, we need to continue to develop new methods to assess how temporal characteristics affect families. The aim of my chapter is to provide an example of how a daily diary design can help inform this agenda. These analyses show that the family-related time deficit that occurs for weekend workers takes place on the weekend and that weekend workers are not able to make up this lost time on their days off. It appears, however, that weekend workers are still attempting to fulfill family obligations. Female weekend workers spent as much time with children as did female weekday workers. Male weekend workers were almost twice as likely to experience some type of work disruption because of family obligations.

The major benefit of a diary approach is that we can better examine the process of temporal friction as it occurs. There are obvious shortcomings in these analyses that are worth mentioning. First, we only assessed one type of nonstandard schedule—weekend work. It would be interesting to assess temporal friction with evening and late-night work as well. Second, nonstandard work has a variety of potential consequences including individual health and well-being. The impacts of sleep disruption, mood, and physical symptoms not only affect the worker but have implications for the quality of family life. Finally, these analyses did not assess the social demography of the effects of weekend work. Presser's chapter shows that single mothers may be at most risk for the effects of a nonstandard schedule. In order to better understand families in a 24/7 economy, we need to address both how and for whom temporal frictions occur.

Acknowledgments

This research was supported by grants from the Alfred P. Sloan Foundation and the National Institute on Aging (AG19239). I am grateful to Joyce Serido, Shevaun Neupert, and Amy Howerter for their helpful comments on a preliminary draft of this paper.

References

Almeida, D. M., & McDonald, D. (1998). Weekly rhythms between parents' work stress, home stress, and parent-adolescent tension. In R. Larson & A. C. Crouter (Eds.), *Temporal rhythms in adolescence: Clocks, calendars, and the coordination of daily life* (New Directions in Child and Adolescent Development No. 82, pp. 53–68). San Francisco: Jossey Bass.

Almeida, D. M., & McDonald, D. (in press). The time Americans spend working for pay, caring for families, and contributing to communities. In J. Heymann (Ed.), *Work, family and democracy*. Princeton: Princeton University Press.

Almeida, D. M., McDonald, D., Havens, J., & Schervish, P. (2001). Temporal patterns in social responsibility. In A. Rossi (Ed.), *Caring and doing for others: Social responsibility in the domains of family, work, and community* (pp. 135–156). Chicago: The University of Chicago Press.

Crouter, A. C., & Maguire, M. C. (1998). Seasonal and weekly rhythms: Windows into variability in family socialization experiences in early adolescence. In R. Larson & A. C. Crouter (Eds.), *Temporal rhythms in adolescence: Clocks, calendars, and the coordination of daily life* (New Directions in Child and Adolescent Development No. 82, pp. 69-82). San Francisco: Jossey Bass.

Fraenkel, P. 1994. Time and rhythm in couples. *Family Process, 33*, 37–51.

Jacobs, J. A., & Gerson, K. (2001). Overworked individuals or overworked families? Explaining trends in work, leisure, and family time. *Work and Occupations, 28*, 40–63.

Larson, R. W. & Crouter, A. C. *Temporal rhythms in adolescence: Clocks, calendars, and the coordination of daily life* (New Directions in Child Development No. 82). San Francisco: Jossey Bass.

Larson, R. W., & Almeida, D. M. (1999). Emotional transmission in the daily lives of families: A new paradigm for studying family process. *Journal of Marriage and the Family, 61*, 5–20.

Mott, P. E., Mann, F. C., McLoughlin, G., & Warwick, D. P. (1965). *Shift work: The social, psychological, and physical consequences*. Ann Arbor, MI: University of Michigan Press.

Presser, H. B. (1999, June 11). Toward a 24-hour economy. *Science, 284*, 1778–1779.

Presser, H. B. (2000). Nonstandard work schedules and marital instability. *Journal of Marriage and the Family, 62*, 93–110.

Putnam, R. D. (2000). *Bowling alone: The collapse and revival of American community*. New York: Simon & Schuster.

Robinson, J. P., & Godbey, G. (1997). *Time for life: The surprising ways Americans use their time*. University Park, PA: The Pennsylvania State University Press.

Zerubavel, E. (1985). *The seven-day cycle*. New York: Free Press.

III

How are the Childcare Needs of Low-Income Families Being Met?

9

CHILDCARE FOR LOW-INCOME FAMILIES: PROBLEMS AND PROMISES

Aletha C. Huston
University of Texas, Austin

Introduction

Childcare serves two functions: support for maternal employment and developmental enrichment for children. Public policies in the United States for these two functions have followed very different paths, in part because their goals are different (Phillips, 1991). For low-income families, subsidies for childcare constitute the major public policy to support maternal employment. Head Start and other early intervention programs represent government efforts to provide developmental enrichment.

In this chapter, I will describe the background of programs in each of these categories. Then I will consider some of the problems and barriers faced by low-income parents who are trying to provide care and opportunities for their children while they are employed. In this context, I will discuss the findings from the Next Generation Project, a collaborative effort to synthesize the findings from numerous experiments testing welfare, employment, and childcare assistance policies. I then consider issues of quality of childcare for low-income children and conclude with some suggestions for current policy and for future consideration.

Two Goals for Childcare

Supporting Maternal Employment

One of the most dramatic shifts in western societies during the last half of the 20th century was entry of women with children into the labor market. As noted in Presser's chapter (this volume), 70% of mothers with children in the U.S. are employed; 51% of them work full-time (U.S. Department of Health and Human Services, 2001). In families with low incomes compared to those with higher incomes, mothers are less likely to be employed, and when they are employed they work fewer hours (although these may more often be irregular and nonstandard hours, as Presser notes). A disproportionate number of low-income families are headed by single mothers, so maternal employment is central to their economic well-being (U.S. Department of Health and Human Services, 2001).

From 1935–1996, the major federal program providing cash support for low-income families with children was Aid to Families with Dependent Children (AFDC). By the early 1980s, however, there was declining political support for paying parents, almost all of whom were single mothers, to stay home with their children. President Ronald Reagan referred to "welfare queens", and policies to move welfare recipients into employment entered the political agenda. One rationale for this change was that mothers at all economic levels were in the labor market, so mothers in the welfare system should be expected to work as well.

This trend culminated in the Personal Responsibility and Work Opportunity Reconciliation Act (PRWORA) of 1996, which ended AFDC as an entitlement program and replaced it with Temporary Assistance for Needy Families (TANF) (Greenberg et al. [2002] for a detailed description of PRWORA). One of the major goals of this legislation was to move families from welfare to work. Indeed, after 1996 the number of people receiving welfare declined dramatically, and employment among single mothers with low incomes increased (Haskins & Primus, 2002; U.S. Department of Health and Human Services, 2001). As a result of these changes in employment among mothers at all income levels, most young children in the United States spend some of their time in childcare—that is, in regular care by someone other than their parents (U.S. Department of Health and Human Services, 2001).

To meet the needs of employed parents, a patchwork of childcare services has evolved in the United States with little public planning. Unlike the public schools, which are intended to provide education for all children at government expense, childcare is largely a market-based system with little centralization. There are few publicly-run childcare facilities for preschool children. Childcare centers are sometimes nonprofit, but for-profit centers, including large national chains, have proliferated in recent years. This strategy is different from that adopted in France, Sweden, and many other European countries (Bergmann, 1996; Waldfogel, 2001). Childcare homes, in which individuals offer care to groups of children in their own homes, constitute another major part of the childcare landscape. Most people operating such homes are individual entrepreneurs, although the profit margin in childcare is usually very small. In addition, informal care is provided by relatives, boyfriends, neighbors, older siblings, and other adults.

The great majority of these facilities, whether officially for-profit or nonprofit, receive their income primarily from parent fees. Some centers are partially subsidized by the sponsoring institutions (e.g., churches, businesses, universities), but these subsidies typically represent a small part of their costs. Although fees often represent a substantial fraction of parents' incomes, childcare workers are paid very low wages (Bloom, 1992; Whitebook, Howes, & Phillips, 1990, 1998). Hence, from an economic point of view, workers are paying part of the costs of care.

Government plays two roles in this system: (a) regulation and (b) financial assistance to parents. Every state has regulations for childcare centers, and most regulate childcare homes, but the requirements vary greatly across states. These regulations are designed to assure minimum levels of safety, health, and quality of care (see, for example, Fiene, 2002). States are required to use a small percent of their federal subsidy funds for quality improvement; they often use these to enforce regulations. Many states have also instituted tiered reimbursement systems that offer higher reimbursement rates for subsidized children to providers who meet higher-than-minimum standards of quality (Greenberg et al., 2002).

The federal government provides financial assistance to parents through childcare tax credits and "flex" accounts, but these are more useful to middle-income than to low-income families. The principal form of assistance to low-income families is payment of subsidies to parents for care they select for their children. Since 1996, federal funding for childcare subsidies has been provided through Childcare Development block grants to states; states are also allowed to use TANF funds for childcare, and they have done so (Fuller et al., 2002).

These government policies are directed entirely at the *demand* or consumer side of childcare—assisting families in paying for individual children's care within the existing array of childcare services. There have been few policy efforts to affect the *supply* of childcare by such means as establishing publicly-run or publicly-financed childcare facilities (Knitzer, 2001). The one form of support to providers is the low-income food program, which provides food assistance to centers and home providers serving low-income children.

In summary, in the U.S., we have evolved a market-based childcare system that is highly decentralized and variable. Childcare is often described as an "industry." Public policy influences this system through regulations designed to assure health, safety, and minimum quality and through assisting some parents in paying fees for available care, but not through providing publicly-supported facilities.

Developmental Enrichment

Since the early 1960s, children in low-income families have also been the target of federal and state government efforts to provide developmental enrichment in the first years of life. Head Start was the first and largest program of this kind, and it was recently expanded to serve very young children in Early Head Start. Some states and localities have also moved in recent years to provide pre-kindergarten programs within the public schools. In Georgia, for example, pre-kindergarten programs are available to all children.

These programs operate very differently than the childcare system. The most obvious difference is that government funds are used to create supply, that is, funding goes to programs, not to families of individual children. Although some programs are run by public schools, many are also run and partially funded by other local agencies. Many have income ceilings for eligibility, and they are typically available without cost or at very low cost to families. Many are part-day programs that run on a school-year schedule, and some (e.g., Head Start) require or at least encourage parent involvement. Their goals are general enrichment for children and their families, and most seek specifically to improve children's school-related skills.

In the late 1990s, after-school enrichment programs for school-age children were also expanded considerably. For example, the 21st Century Learning Centers program went from no funding in the early 1990s to $454 million by fiscal year 2000. Such centers are typically located in schools and can serve children in after-school hours as well as adults.

Changes in Funding for Childcare

Public funds for both childcare and early enrichment increased dramatically during the 1990s. Figure 9.1 (from Fuller et al., 2002) shows the amounts of federal funding for various early childhood programs in 1991 and 2000. Three of the funding streams listed—the Childcare and Development Block Grant, the Childcare Food Program, and TANF transfers to childcare—are used to fund care for children from low-income families. The total amount in these three categories more than doubled in ten years. The number of children served rose from 1.0 million in 1996 to 1.8 million in 1999 (Greenberg et al., 2002). The Dependent Care Tax Credit is a benefit used more by middle-income than by low-income families, and expenditures on it declined. Expenditures on flex accounts (pretax accounts that are earmarked for childcare, medical expenses, and the like) are not included in Figure 9.1.

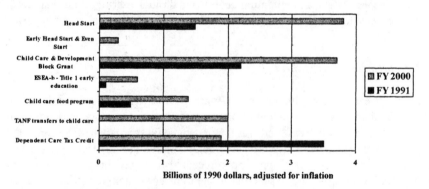

Source: Fuller. B.. Kagan. S., Caspary. G. L.. & Gauthier. C. A. (2002). Welfare reform and child care options for low-income families. *Future of Children. 12*(1). p. 99.

Figure 9.1.   Rising federal commitment to child care & early education.

The remaining three funding streams are for developmental enrichment programs—Head Start, Early Head Start and Even Start, and ESEA – Title 1 Early Education. They, too, increased dramatically in the 1990s.

Integrating Support for Maternal Employment and Developmental Enrichment

As Figure 9.1 makes clear, the funding streams and responsible agencies for childcare as a support to maternal employment and for developmental enrichment are separate. This administrative separation extends to the delivery of the programs. Although they are designed to serve the same children, they run on parallel tracks with little integration. In fact, there is some evidence that these policies not only are not complementary but may actually conflict with one another and force parents to choose between the two types of programs.

The Next Generation Project. Evidence for this statement comes from a comparison of different pilot welfare and employment programs for parents conducted as part of the Next Generation Project. Because I will be citing findings from this study extensively in this paper, I will give a brief description of its overall methods. It is a collaborative endeavor led by Manpower Demonstration Research Corporation (www.mdrc.org), synthesizing the findings from several random-assignment experiments designed to test various welfare, employment, and income policies for low-income parents. All of the projects were designed to increase parental employment, and some were also intended to increase family income. Although none of these experiments was designed specifically to test childcare policies, we have examined variations in their supports for childcare in an effort to determine how such policies affect care for children and barriers to employment for parents.

The programs examined in the Next Generation Project include 9 experimental evaluation studies that tested 21 different welfare and employment programs. These are described in detail in Gennetian, Crosby, Huston, and Lowe (2002). The strategies tested included earnings supplements, mandatory case management and work activities, mandatory job training and educational activities, and time limits on welfare benefits. Each study collected demographic and socioeconomic characteristics at study entry and information about the characteristics of employment, childcare, and other household and personal circumstances (sometimes including child well-being) at a follow-up survey carried out at intervals ranging from 18 months to 4 years after people entered the study. The measures collected are roughly comparable, making a cross-study synthesis of program effects possible.

Nearly all of the studies took place during the early to late 1990s, a time period that included vast changes in welfare policy (i.e., the passage of PWORWA), expansions in the Earned Income Tax Credit, expansions in childcare funding, and stable economic growth with low unemployment rates. Nevertheless, within each study, both program and control group members were exposed to the same changes in welfare and other policies and local or national economic trends, so the comparison between them represents the effects of the experimental policies tested. Overall, the policy approaches tested had effects on employment and income (Bloom & Michalopoulos, 2001) and on achievement and social behavior for children (Gennetian, Duncan et al., 2002; Morris et al., 2001; Zaslow et al., 2002). Because all of the projects are random assignment experiments, we can infer that differences between families in the experimental and control groups are a result of the policies tested, but we cannot be sure which aspects of the policies are responsible for the effects.

Effects on Head Start participation. In one analysis, we examined the impact of 11 of these welfare and employment programs on single mothers' use of Head Start and other types of childcare for their 3- and 4-year-old children (Chang, Huston, Crosby, & Gennetian, 2002). The other 10 programs did not have information about Head Start separately from other forms of childcare in the surveys, so they could not be included in this analysis. All except one of the programs increased maternal employment (i.e., the program group had higher levels of employment than the control group), and almost all of them led to increased use of both center-based and home-based childcare. By contrast, almost all of them led to slight, though nonsignificant declines in children's participation in Head Start. The patterns are shown in Figure 9.2. Each bar represents the *difference* between the program group and the control group in that study. There are panels for each of the 11 studies, and a panel on the far right side showing the weighted means summed across all 11 studies for impacts on Head Start, center care and

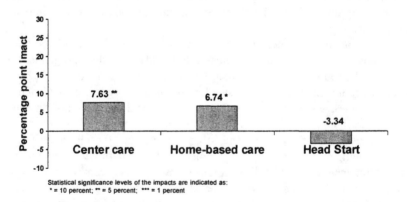

Statistical significance levels of the impacts are indicated as:
* = 10 percent; ** = 5 percent; *** = 1 percent

Figure 9.2. Welfare-to-work programs increased childcare, but not Head Start for preschool-age children.

home-based care.

The findings suggest that two types of policies affecting low-income families—welfare and employment on the one hand, and early childhood intervention on the other—are operating independently, and may actually be in conflict. Women who participate in welfare and employment programs do increase their hours of employment, generating increased use of childcare. They do not, however, increase their use of Head Start along with other types of childcare. There are several possible reasons. Head Start is a part-day, part-year program in most locations so it does not fit most employment schedules. In recent years there have been increasing efforts to provide "wrap-around" childcare services to fill time periods before and after Head Start hours, which may address this issue. Head Start requires parental involvement, which may be difficult for many employed parents. It is also possible that employment increased income, reducing the likelihood that families were eligible for Head Start, but we found no support for this hypothesis. Whatever the reasons, it appears that parents are making choices to place their children in developmental enrichment programs or to increase employment and place their children in other forms of childcare, which may or may not offer developmental enrichment.

Childcare Challenges Faced by Low-Income Families

Current public policies leave low-income parents with little choice about being employed, because cash assistance is no longer guaranteed to poor families. As a result, they must find arrangements for their children that fit their work needs. Childcare is a challenge for almost all employed parents, but parents with little income face additional dilemmas of limited availability, high cost, low quality, and conflicts between providing financial support to their families and providing the best care for their children. In what follows, I will examine some of these challenges using a range of available data, including my own research. Then I will discuss some of the policies that can address these challenges.

Supply—Availability and Access

In many parts of the U.S., the supply of childcare is limited, particularly for parents who live in low-income and rural neighborhoods, lack ready transportation to childcare facilities elsewhere, and have limited ability to pay for care. Analyses by Fuller and his associates show, for example, that in California neighborhoods with low average maternal schooling levels, there were center-based "slots" for 15% of the 2- to 5-year-old children living in the area (Fuller et al., 2002). In a nationwide survey of 100 counties, the supply of early childhood and childcare centers was lower for less wealthy than for more wealthy areas (Fuller & Liang,

1996). Care for infants and toddlers is harder to find than is care for older children, and it is often expensive (Phillips & Adams, 2001). Relative, home-based care is the most commonly used arrangement for infants and toddlers (Capizzano, Adams, & Sonenstein, 2000). Center care is less available for this age group, and many parents worry about whether formal care or nonrelative care will provide the nurturance and attention needed by infants; as well as about safety (Lowe & Weisner, 2002). It is also difficult to find care for children with special needs and during nonstandard and irregular work hours, which characterize the employment of many low-income parents (see Presser, this volume; Raikes, 1998).

Public policies aimed at increasing parental employment typically do not address issues of supply directly. That is, there are few public programs to fund childcare facilities. By contrast, federal and state governments provide large amounts of funding to increase the supply of Head Start, prekindergarten, and other programs to promote early childhood development.

Costs and Subsidies

Childcare is expensive. Although some families can find free care with relatives or through staggering the work schedules of two parents, many low-income families pay for care. When they do pay, the average cost represents 20-25% of their total income (Phillips & Bridgman, 1995). Childcare subsidies are the principal form of assistance provided by federal and state governments. As already noted, the amount of money in subsidy programs has increased substantially over the last 10 years (see Figure 9.1).

Despite these increases, the need for care has increased even more rapidly (Layzer & Collins, 2001). Fewer than 25% of the federally-eligible children in the country receive any subsidies (U.S. Department of Health and Human Services, 1999). For example, the National Study of Childcare for Low-Income Families indicates that 15-20% of eligible children were served in the 17 states surveyed (Layzer & Collins, 2001). When parents do receive subsidies, the average duration is brief. Across five states, the average duration of a subsidy "spell" ranged from three to seven months (Meyers et al., 2002). Parents frequently list childcare problems as a barrier to getting or maintaining employment (Huston, Chang, & Gennetian, in press).

Although everyone agrees that many eligible children are not receiving subsidies, they do not agree about the reasons for this low rate of "take-up." Some eligible parents do not need subsidies because they have unpaid care available from family members. In many states, however, parents can use vouchers for any provider, so they could pay a family member with their subsidy. Moreover, 12 of the 17 states surveyed in the National Study of Childcare for Low-Income Families had waiting lists (Layzer & Collins, 2001), suggesting a considerable amount of unmet need.

Policy Supports for Parent Employment

Barriers to Effective Subsidies

In the Next Generation studies, we identified possible barriers to receiving subsidies and examined policies that might address these barriers. Inadequate reimbursement to providers and high costs to parents represent one set of barriers. More than one half of the states pay providers at less-than-market rates, and many require parent copayments. As a result, providers may limit the number of subsidized children, refuse them altogether, or require the parent to make up the difference (Fuller et al., 2002; Greenberg et al., 2002; Meyers et al., 2002). Although many states now use vouchers, some subsidy systems require parents to pay for care and be reimbursed by an addition to their welfare grant, which might be received as much as two months later. People living on the edge often do not have the cash to make this system work.

Second, the 1996 law encourages states to give priority to families who are receiving cash assistance (TANF) or have recently received it, making it difficult for working parents who have not been on welfare to obtain subsidies. Third, families who are not in the welfare system do not have contact with caseworkers or referral services who might inform them about subsidies and help them to apply. Ethnographic data suggest that many parents are unaware that they might be eligible for subsidies or do not know how to obtain them (see Clampet-Lundquist et al., this volume).

Fourth, in many places, there are formidable administrative barriers to acquiring and maintaining eligibility. Parents often have to spend several hours visiting different offices, often including the welfare office, to apply initially or to be recertified for eligibility (Adams, Snyder, & Sandfort, 2002). Caseworkers deny benefits or provide inaccurate information about eligibility (Clampet-Lundquist et al., this volume). Once eligible, parents have to be recertified often. In a survey of five states, the time spans for recertification ranged from every month to one year. States requiring more frequent recertification had shorter average durations of subsidy spells, possibly indicating that some eligible parents were not completing the recertification process (Meyers et al., 2002). People with irregular and unstable employment may find it difficult to maintain eligibility requirements for continuous employment.

Conversely, there are "eligibility cliffs", that is, small increases in income can move them above a threshold, leading to a sudden loss of eligibility (Lowe & Weisner, in press). The following case comes from ethnographic interviews in the New Hope Project, one of the Next Generation studies:

Michol, who worked during the day to support her family, enrolled her daughter in an after-school care program where she could be supervised until her mother picked her up after work. Michol was able to pay for this care with help from the state childcare assistance program. On being informed unexpectedly that she would no longer receive a childcare subsidy because her income had risen slightly above the eligibility limit, Michol had to make new childcare arrangements on short notice. She enrolled her daughter in a daycare center operated by her sister for a while and later switched to a more affordable center run by her daughter's godmother. It would have been virtually impossible for Michol to have anticipated passing the eligibility threshold because her income fluctuated considerably from month to month (Lowe & Weisner, in press, p. 2).

Finally, although the Childcare Development Fund consolidated four federal funding streams into one fund, many states still have different funding streams for people on welfare or leaving welfare and for those outside the welfare system. For example, a parent leaving welfare may receive transitional childcare assistance that expires after a certain period; she must then reapply for ordinary low-income assistance, often from a different agency.

Expanded childcare assistance. As noted earlier, in the Next Generation Project, we compared welfare and anti-poverty programs designed to increase employment and reduce welfare receipt. In five studies testing a total of seven programs (New Chance, New Hope, Florida's Family Transition Program, two programs in the Minnesota Family Investment Study, and two programs in Vermont's Welfare Restructuring Project), participants were offered some forms of "expanded assistance for childcare", that is, supports for childcare over and above that available to control group members. These expanded supports addressed some of the problems in the subsidy system described above (Gennetian, Huston, et al., 2002). "Expanded assistance for childcare" included some or all of the following:

1. Programmatic promotion of formal care. For example, the New Chance program encouraged the use of formal care directly by providing free center care for participants. The Milwaukee New Hope program reimbursed the full cost of care after a co-payment based on participant earnings and number of children, and caseworkers encouraged people to use center care because it was more reliable. Case management/support services for childcare. For example,

the Florida Family Transition Project program provided childcare resource and referral agents at the site of the welfare office.

2. Efficient reimbursement. For example, in the two Minnesota programs, childcare payments were made directly to childcare providers (versus reimbursing parents two months later via the welfare grant).

3. Restriction of subsidy to regulated care. For example, the childcare subsidies in the New Hope program could be used only for licensed center or home-based care.

4. Reduced bureaucratic hassles. Some programs provided a seamless subsidy system for transitions on and off welfare or combined application and eligibility determination with other programs. The Florida and Vermont programs extended the time limit for use of transitional childcare benefits, and New Hope determined eligibility for childcare along with that for other benefits.

In each study, parents in both the program and control groups were eligible for whatever low-income childcare assistance programs were available in their region. In the remaining 14 programs, there was no added childcare component, so the childcare assistance policies were essentially the same for program and control group members. That is, all participants were officially offered the same level of childcare assistance via subsidies, referrals, and other services irrespective of their research group status. It is important to note that although there was substantial variation in the absolute level of support available across locales and states, our analysis was focused solely on program-control group *differences* in childcare policy and practice *within* studies.

Effects of Expanded Childcare Assistance

Effects on childcare use. Almost all of these pilot welfare and employment programs increased employment and led to concomitant increases in the use of childcare, especially paid childcare. Expanded childcare assistance polices affected the *types* of care chosen by families. Programs that offered more comprehensive, more efficient, or more generous assistance to families increased the use of formal center-based care rather than home-based care, particularly for very young children. The average impacts across programs are summarized in Figure 9.3. Programs with expanded assistance also increased the duration and stability of care for all age groups studied (Crosby, Gennetian, & Huston, 2002). These findings are consistent with other studies showing that many low-income parents choose center-based care when it is available and affordable (Fuller et al., 2002).

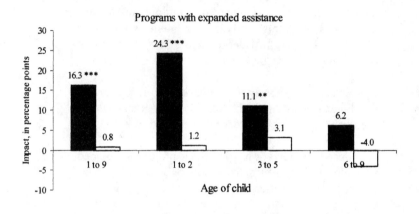

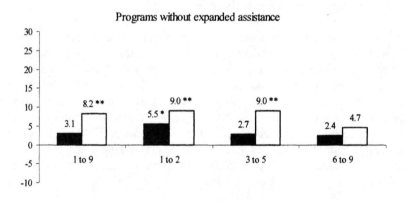

Note. Statistical significance levels of the impacts are indicated as: * = 10 percent; ** = 5 percent; *** = 1 percent (two-tailed)
† indictates that the differences between the impacts of the two types of programs is statistically significant at the p< .01 level (two-tailed).
Age subgroups are defined by age at study entry

Source: Crosby, D. A., & Gennetian. L. A., & Huston, A. C. (2002). Child Care Assistance Policies Can Affect the Use of Formal Care for Children in Low-Income Families. The Next Generation Project.

Figure 9.3. Average impacts on formal and home-based care for programs with and without expanded child care assistance.

Effects on cost, subsidy receipt, and childcare barriers to employment.
Programs with expanded childcare assistance increased access to subsidies and
reduced out-of-pocket costs to parents. Impacts on the proportion of parents
receiving subsidies are shown in Figure 9.4. Those in programs with expanded
assistance were significantly more likely to be receiving subsidies, especially for
care of very young children. Despite the fact that parents in programs with expanded
assistance were using more childcare and more expensive center-based care, they
paid slightly less than did control parents; parents in programs without enhanced
childcare services paid more than controls (see Figure 9.5). Finally, parents were
asked whether they had experienced childcare problems that interfered with
employment (e.g., had to quit a job because of childcare problems). Overall, parents
in programs with enhanced childcare assistance reported fewer childcare problems
than did their control group counterparts; programs without enhanced assistance
tended to increase reports of childcare problems (Gennetian et al., 2002).

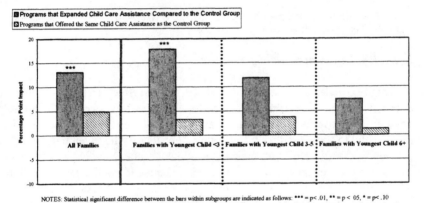

NOTES: Statistical significant difference between the bars within subgroups are indicated as follows: *** = p< .01, ** = p < 05, * = p< .10

Source: Gennetian L A., Crosby, D. A., Huston, A C., & Lowe, T. (2002) How Child Care Assistance in Welfare and Employment Programs Can Support the Employment of Low-Income Families The Next Generation Project.

Figure 9.4. Comparison of average impacts on subsidy use for programs with and without
program differences in child care policy.

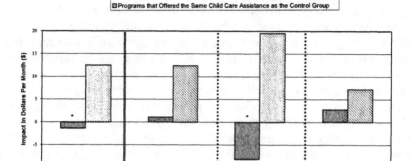

NOTES: Statistical significant difference between the bars within subgroups are indicated as follows: *** = p< .01, ** = p < .05, * = p< .10
Source: Gennetian L. A., Crosby, D A., Huston, A C., & Lowe, T. (2002) How Child Care Assistance in Welfare and Employment Programs Can Support the Employment of Low-Income Families The Next Generation Project.

Figure 9.5. Comparison of average impacts on monthly child care costs for programs with and without program differences in child care policy.

Individual Differences Among Families

Although expanded childcare assistance led to average effects on parents' childcare decisions and the support they received for childcare, the effects were certainly not universal. It seemed likely that the assistance policies we examined would be more useful to some families than to others. For four of the seven programs that provided expanded childcare assistance—New Chance, New Hope, and two in Minnesota—we examined family structure, parents' education and work skills, ethnic group, and beliefs about family and work, all measured before parents experienced the program, as predictors of their childcare decisions. The characteristics that mattered most, particularly for use of center-based care, were family structure (ages and number of children), parents' education, and personal beliefs about family and work. Childcare subsidies and other policies designed to reduce the cost of care and to increase parents' employment appeared to meet the needs associated with caring for very young children and for large families. They were most effective in reaching parents with relatively less consistent prior employment experience. Parents whose education and personal beliefs were consistent with preference for center-based care were most likely to take advantage of the opportunity to choose that option and to use subsidies (Huston, Chang, & Gennetian, 2002).

Implications

Even the rather modest enhancements to childcare supports in most of the Next Generation studies affected parents' childcare decisions, use of subsidies, cost, and conflicts with work. These findings make it clear that most parents must use paid care and need childcare assistance. The notion promoted by some policy makers that low-income parents prefer and can find relatives and others to do unpaid care is not supported. This is especially true as parents work more hours. We compared program impacts on the amount of parent employment with their impacts on use of paid childcare. The results are shown in Figure 9.6. The larger the impact on employment, the more likely people were to use paid care, probably because it is more difficult to arrange unpaid care for full-time work than for occasional or part-time employment. In recent discussions of reauthorization of the federal welfare legislation, the President and others have advocated raising the definition of full-time work from 30 to 40 hours a week. Clearly, the policy goal is full-time employment, which requires paid childcare for most single-mother families.

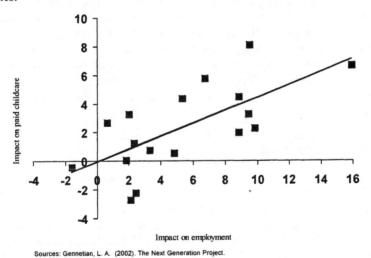

Sources: Gennetian, L. A. (2002). The Next Generation Project.

Figure 9.6. Impact on employment and on use of paid childcare.

The modest improvements tested in these studies suggest that subsidies paying market costs of care, free care, good referral and casework services, and reduced bureaucratic hassles can make a difference by increasing access to subsidies and reducing cost of care. They increase the use of formal care, which may serve the goal of enabling maternal employment better than home-based care because it is more reliable. On the other hand, it is less flexible with respect to the number of hours per week that children can attend, and little center-based care is available outside weekday work hours. Moreover, low-income parents, like other parents, vary in how comfortable they feel about placing their children in center care. Nonetheless, these policies appear to serve the goal of supporting maternal employment better than the policies generally available to control families.

Do they, however, contribute to developmental enrichment for children? They do not lead parents to use Head Start more, but they do increase use of formal, center-based care. There is some evidence that center care, on average, leads to better cognitive and language development than home-based care (NICHD Early Childcare Research Network, 2000b, 2002a), but most people assume that the effects of either type of care depend on its quality. I turn now to issues of quality of care for low-income families.

Quality of Childcare

The overall quality of childcare in the United States is highly variable, and, not surprisingly, low-income children tend to be in lower quality care than do middle-income children. Some of the reasons have to do with the issues of cost and access that I have already addressed. Low-income families are more likely than other families to use home-based care, including unregulated care by relatives and others (Capizzano, Adams, & Sonenstein, 2000). Such care is less expensive than regulated care, and it may be all that is available to people with nonstandard and irregular work hours.

What is Quality Care?

Quality is typically defined in two ways: (1) structural features that can be regulated, including low child-to-adult ratio, low group size, caregiver training in child development, and stability of caregivers within a setting, and (2) process features, including sensitive, responsive caregiving, intellectual and language stimulation, an orderly and enriched physical environment, and caregiver involvement (Lamb, 1997).

Structural features. In a recent research brief published by the U.S. Department of Health and Human Services, 13 criteria for evaluating quality are described along with research documenting their importance. Several of these criteria concern health and safety (e.g., immunizations, fire drills, toxic substances, hand-washing). They also specify training for caregivers and standards of discipline and supervision. For infants, a child-to-adult ratio of 3:1 with a maximum group size of 6 is recommended; for 3-year-olds, the report recommends a ratio of 7:1, with a maximum 14 children in a group (Fiene, 2002). The National Association for the Education of Young Children has an extensive system of accreditation, which requires higher quality standards than those needed for licensing in most states (http://www.naeyc.org).

Process. Structural features of childcare are distal indicators intended to reflect proximal processes of caregiver-child interaction, the types of activities in which children are involved, intellectual and language stimulation, and the quality of the physical environment. Process is best evaluated by direct observation, and there are several widely used systems to quantify observations (e.g., ECRS). My own involvement in this type of research has occurred in the NICHD Study of Early Childcare and Youth Development, a longitudinal multisite study following a large sample (N=1364) of children from their births in 1991 through the school years (NICHD Early Childcare Research Network, 2001b). The study has detailed information about families and childcare experiences, including frequent observations of mother-child interaction and childcare settings.

We conducted observations of both home and center-based childcare settings attended by the sample children when they were 6, 15, 24, 36, and 54 months old. During several hours in the setting, trained observers made periodic ratings of the caregiving that the focal child was receiving, using the Observational Record of the Caregiving Environment (ORCE). On a scale of 1 to 4, observers rated caregiver sensitivity, responsiveness, cognitive stimulation (particularly language), and detachment (reverse coded). The specific scales changed with child age, but the ratings were sufficiently highly correlated that they could be combined into a summary score labeled "positive caregiving". The rating system was designed to be equally appropriate in home-based or center-based settings. A second indicator of quality in all home-based settings was obtained by completing a version of the Home Observation Measure of the Environment (HOME) adapted for a childcare setting. The details of these observations are presented in (NICHD Early Childcare Research Network, 2000a).

Type and Quality of Care Used by Low-Income Parents

National survey data indicate that low-income families use more home-based care and less center care than do middle and upper income families (Cappizzano et al., 2000). In the Three Cities Study, a recent investigation of low-income single mothers in Boston, Chicago, and San Antonio, childcare for 3-year-old children was assessed by observation in the childcare settings. Most of the children were either in centers (44%) or unregulated home care, primarily with relatives (45%). The remaining 11% were in regulated home care (Coley, Chase-Lansdale, & Li Grining, 2001). In the NICHD sample, low-income families used more care by partners (split-shift parent care) and by grandmothers than did more affluent families (NICHD Early Childcare Research Network, 2001a).

For some structural indicators of quality (e.g., child-to-adult ratio), relative and home-based care rates higher than center care. That is, there are fewer children per adult in care by grandparents and relatives than in childcare centers. Nevertheless, observational measures indicate that when children are cared for by grandparents, relatives, or other informal arrangements, the overall quality for low-income children tends to be low (Phillips & Adams, 2001). In the Three Cities Study, for example, observational measures indicated that centers had significantly higher ratings of developmental appropriateness and warmer provider-child relationships than did home-based settings. Eighty percent of the centers were rated as "good" compared to 11% of the unregulated home settings; 6% of centers and 45% of unregulated home settings were rated "inadequate". It is noteworthy, however, that mothers were more satisfied with unregulated home care, finding it more flexible and convenient than center care, possibly because it met their needs for care during unpredictable and nonstandard employment hours (Coley, Chase-Lansdale, & Li Grining, 2001).

In the NICHD study, 235 (18%) of the families had average incomes below the federal poverty level, and another 180 (13%) had incomes between 100% and 180% of the poverty threshold during the first three years of the children's lives (NICHD Early Childcare Research Network, 2001a). We analyzed income differences in quality within each of five types of care: fathers, grandparents, providers in the child's home (e.g., nannies), childcare homes (many of which were regulated), and childcare centers. Children in low-income families received lower quality care than did children from higher income families in home-based settings, but not in centers (NICHD Early Childcare Research Network, 1997). It was particularly interesting that infants in near-poor families (those with incomes between 100% and 200% of the federal poverty threshold) received even lower quality center care than did children in families with incomes below the poverty threshold. Although numbers were small, it appeared that the very poor children were more likely to receive subsidized center care than were those in near-poor families (NICHD Early Childcare Research Network, 1997).

Childcare and Children's Development

Quality. The quality of childcare can make an important difference in children's language development, overall cognitive development, and acquisition of academic skills. A large body of literature, both longitudinal and experimental, demonstrates that high-quality early education and childcare can contribute to intellectual skills and school readiness, particularly for children from economically disadvantaged homes (Vandell & Wolfe, 2000). In the NICHD study, we evaluated the relations of the average quality of childcare received from infancy through early childhood to children's intellectual functioning and social behavior at several ages. Even with many controls for selection effects, high-quality care predicted better language, memory, and school readiness by the time children in the preschool years (NICHD Early Childcare Research Network, 1999, 2000b, 2002a, 2002b). When low-income children were analyzed separately, similar findings emerged. Those who had received high-quality care for at least 20 hours a week had better language and cognitive skills than those who received low-quality care (NICHD Early Childcare Research Network, 2001a). Our research and other studies (e.g., Peisner-Feinberg et al., 1999) also found that high-quality care was associated with positive social skills and low levels of externalizing behavior (disobedience, aggression, assertiveness) (NICHD Early Childcare Research Network, in press).

Type of care. Childcare centers may offer more opportunities for early education, on average, than do home settings. In the Study of Early Childcare, children who had been cared for in childcare centers performed better on language and cognitive measures than did children who had spent comparable amounts of time in home-based care. The superiority of centers held even when quality was controlled (NICHD Early Childcare Research Network, 2000b; 2002a). This finding suggests that the shift to center-based care found in the Next Generation studies may be a positive influence on children's academic development. The picture is more mixed, however, with respect to children's social behavior. Children with more center care experience were rated by caregivers as less socially competent and as showing higher levels of externalizing behavior than children with home-based histories (NICHD Early Childcare Research Network, in press), suggesting possible negative effects of center care experience on children's social behavior.

Costs of Quality

Although price and quality are not perfectly correlated, high-quality care generally costs more than low-quality care, largely because personnel costs constitute the bulk of childcare costs. The Childcare Staffing Study was an investigation of 227 childcare centers in 1988 with a follow-up for those still operating in the late 1990s. The most striking finding is the very low wages paid to childcare teachers and providers. The average childcare worker earned about half of the median wage for women with comparable levels of education and one third of the median for the entire civilian labor force. Not surprisingly, there is high turnover among personnel in childcare centers (an average of 41% in 1988 and 31% in 1998), and the rate of turnover was higher in centers that paid lower wages (Whitebook et al., 1990, 1998). Observations in the classrooms also indicated that centers paying better wages with lower turnover provided higher quality care than did other centers (Phillips et al., 1994).

Policies to Improve Quality

Officials who administer childcare subsidies face a constant dilemma—whether to pay for higher quality for fewer children or to pay lower rates and serve more children. Federal legislation requires states to spend at least 4% of the federal childcare funds on quality enhancement, and recent evidence indicates that they spend closer to 6% (Greenberg et al., 2002). Many states have adopted a tiered reimbursement system, paying higher rates to centers and home providers who meet criteria for higher-than-minimum quality. A recent observational study demonstrated that centers in the highest reimbursement level in Oklahoma provided higher quality care than did centers at lower levels, but it is not clear whether the policy led to improved quality or merely rewarded what was already in place (Norris & Dunn, 2001). One survey of several states offering tiered reimbursements demonstrated an increase in the number of providers applying for accreditation from the National Association for the Education of Young Children, a credential that qualifies a center for the highest tier (Gormley & Lucas, 2000).

On the other hand, many policy analysts argue that high quality does not offer sufficient benefits to be worth the extra money. They assert that the differences associated with variations in quality in existing childcare settings are small and do not endure into later childhood (Blau, 2000; Scarr, 1998). Hence, "good enough" childcare, meeting minimum health and safety standards, will suffice. Others counter that existing childcare settings do not represent optimal levels of quality well, and longitudinal data show that effects do endure at least into early elementary school (Peisner-Feinberg et al. 1999; Vandell & Wolfe, 2000). Tests of high-quality early interventions, tested with random assignment designs, do show large and lasting benefits for academic and occupational achievement and for lower levels of delinquent and criminal behavior (Barnett, 1995; Ramey et al., 2000; Yoshikawa, 1995). However, policy makers question the feasibility and cost of expanding such programs on a large scale. Haskins (1989), for example, suggested that the long-term benefits of Head Start are of questionable benefit given the cost of the program.

Summary

In summary, children from low-income families receive lower-quality care and are more often in unregulated home-based settings than are more affluent children. High-quality care can contribute to their intellectual development and school readiness. In recognition of these facts, government at many levels has instituted a range of early interventions and policies to improve subsidized childcare quality. Paying for high quality childcare with public funds would be expensive, and policy makers do not agree about whether the benefits obtained would be sufficient to justify the cost.

Another set of policies and programs are designed specifically to provide developmental enrichment and improve educational attainment among children from low-income families. There has been widespread support for investment of public funds in these programs.

Conclusion

The United States has evolved two systems for providing care and education to young children. One is a market-based system of childcare designed to support parental employment. It is funded primarily with parent fees and low wages to workers. Public funding is contributed through subsidies to families, but with the exception of the low-income food program, not through direct funding to subsidize programs or providers. This system is different from that in many European countries, and it now has a political constituency of national for-profit centers and individual entrepreneurs providing home-based care.

The second system is designed to provide early education and enrichment to children who are at risk of low school performance. It is generally free or very low cost to parents, and programs are funded directly by federal and state public funds as well as by community organizations.

Despite large increases in federal and state expenditures for both types of programs in the 1990s, problems remain. First, childcare and early enrichment programs tend to run on parallel tracks with little coordination, making it difficult for parents to use both. Second, most low-income families receive no public help in paying for childcare. There are also not enough Head Start slots for all eligible children. The reasons are numerous, but some of the unmet need is a result of flaws in the subsidy system. Third, low-income parents often face very limited options for childcare, and many of their children receive low-quality care. Given a finite number of dollars, there are inherent conflicts between offering high quality, which generally is more costly, and serving a large number of children with lower quality care.

What do we know? The evidence from the Next Generation study indicates that improvements within our current system of childcare supports for low-income parents can open the door to center-based care for some of them and can increase access to subsidies while reducing parents' costs. We know that high-quality center-based childcare can make a difference for children's intellectual development and readiness for school, though it is difficult to estimate the magnitude of potential effects. Public policy can probably improve quality by regulation and standards, by increasing funding, and by increasing supply, but there is little direct evidence about the effects of these various policy options.

Because the research and policy conversations about childcare are constrained by the options currently available for study, they do not lead policy makers to entertain a more radical restructuring of our system of early care and education. In France and Sweden, for example, there are universally available full-day preschool programs for which parents pay a small portion of the costs (Waldfogel, 2001). In a recent book, two economists, Helburn and Bergmann (2002), examined three possible plans for childcare for children ages 1–12 in the United States, providing cost estimates for each. The most modest was full funding for the current system of subsidies, i.e., making them available to all who qualify, which they estimated would require $25.8 billion, or $12.8 billion more than current expenditures. The second is a proposal to provide reasonable quality care and to reimburse all families for costs exceeding 20% of their above-poverty threshold income, estimated to cost $46.4 billion ($26.4 billion above current spending). Neither of these proposals includes expansion of Head Start or universal prekindergarten. The third is a system of universal free care, estimated at $122.5 billion ($102.5 billion above current levels). Economists make widely varying cost estimates, so these figures can be taken as approximate at best. The point here is that we should be thinking outside the parameters of the existing system.

Expansion of the public education system to provide both preschool education and childcare is still another direction to consider. Zigler and Gilman (1996), for example, proposed the School of the Twenty-first Century, which would provide optional full-day, full-year programs for children as young as 3 years old within the public school system. Care and education for children under 3 would be provided in licensed home-based settings. One advantage of linking preschool programs to the public schools is professional benefits for teachers, who would be on the same pay schedule as other public school teachers. No specific cost estimates for this proposal were provided, but it resembles the universal program described by Helburn and Bergman (2002), and it would undoubtedly be much more expensive than our current system.

These two systems of early care—childcare and early enrichment—are dealing with the same children in similar settings, but they are rarely considered jointly. Our national debate on welfare reform has led to an apparent consensus that it is desirable to promote employment among poor, single mothers. The current discussions surrounding reauthorization of the 1996 legislation revolve around increasing the number of hours that parents are required to work, and supports for nonworking mothers have declined dramatically (Greenberg et al., 2002). Childcare is critical to achieving these employment goals.

At the same time, new education legislation has been enacted to improve the quality of education—often dubbed the "Leave no child behind" bill. We have adopted a national priority for increasing literacy among children in the first few years of school. Achieving that goal depends heavily on improving development of language and literacy skills in the preschool years, a major goal of developmental enrichment programs.

The same children are subject to policies intended to support parental employment and to provide developmental enrichment, but the two sets of policies are not only poorly coordinated but sometimes in conflict with one another. We have expanded funding for both types of programs dramatically in the last ten years, but efforts to provide care for young children will continue to be piecemeal unless we plan more carefully to meet these dual goals. Childcare settings can provide opportunities for children to learn literacy, academic skills, and social skills, but they are not usually considered "early education". Enrichment programs can provide care while parents are at work, but they are not usually designed to be "childcare". We are missing an important opportunity to improve the lives and prospects of our most deprived citizens by making it difficult for parents to find the best educational opportunities for their children and to fulfill their obligation to earn a living for their families. Better coordination of policies to promote parental employment and children's development could have dual benefits, not only for low-income parents and children, but for society at large, allowing parents to earn a living for their families and increasing the likelihood that children will succeed as they move through the educational system.

Acknowledgments

The Next Generation Project is a collaborative effort led by Manpower Demonstration Research Corporation. Funding is provided by the David and Lucile Packard Foundation, William T. Grant Foundation, and the John D. and Catherine T. MacArthur Foundation. The NICHD Study of Early Child Care and Youth Development is a multi-site longitudinal study of early childcare. Funding is provided by cooperative agreement NICHD U10 HD 25430.

References

Adams, G., Snyder, K., & Sandfort, J. (2002, March). *Getting and retaining childcare assistance: How policy and practice influence parents' experiences.* (Assessing the New Federalism Occasional Paper No. 55). Washington, DC: Urban Institute.

Barnett, W. S. (1995). Long-term effects of early childhood education programs on cognitive and school outcomes. *The Future of Children, 5,* 25–50.

Bergmann, B. (1996). *Saving our children from poverty: What the United States can learn from France.* New York: Russell Sage Foundation.

Blau, D. M. (2000). The effect of childcare characteristics on child development. *The Journal of Human Resources, 34,* 786–822.

Bloom, D., & Michalopoulos, C. (2001). *How welfare and work policies affect employment and income: A synthesis of research.* New York: Manpower Demonstration Research Corporation.

Bloom, P. J. (1992). Staffing issues in childcare. In B. Spodek & O. N. Saracho (Eds.), *Issues in childcare: Yearbook in early childhood education. Vol. 3.* New York: Teachers College Press.

Capizzano, J., Adams, G., & Sonenstein, F. (2000). *Childcare arrangements for children under five: Variation across states.* Assessing the New Federalism. Washington, DC: The Urban Institute Press.

Chang, Y. E., Huston, A. C., Crosby, D. A., & Gennetian. L. A. (2002). *The effects of welfare and employment programs on children's participation in head start* (The Next Generation Project Working Paper). New York: Manpower Demonstration Research Corporation.

Coley, R. L., Chase-Lansdale, P. L., & Li Grining, C. P. (2001, April). *Low-income families and childcare: Quality, options and choices.* Paper presented at the Biennial Meeting of the Society for Research in Child Development, Minneapolis, MN.

Crosby, D. A., Gennetian, L. A., & Huston, A. C. (2001, September). *Does childcare assistance matter? The effects of welfare and employment programs on childcare for preschool and young school aged children* (Next Generation Working Paper No. 3). New York: Manpower Demonstration Research Corporation.

Fiene, R. (2002). *13 Indicators of quality childcare: Research update.* Washington, DC: Office of the Assistant Secretary for Planning and Evaluation and Health Resources and Services Administration/Maternal and Child Health Bureau, U.S. Department of Health and Human Services.

Fuller, B., Kagan, S., Caspary, G. L., & Gauthier, C. A. (2002). Welfare reform and childcare options for low-income families. *Future of Children, 12,* 97–119.

Fuller, B., & Liang, X. (1996). Market failure? Estimating inequality in preschool availability. *Educational Evaluation and Policy Analysis, 18,* 31–49.

Gennetian, L. A., Duncan, G. J., Knox, V. W., Vargas, W. G., Clark-Kauffman, E., & London, A. S. (2002). *How welfare and work policies for parents affect adolescents: A synthesis of research.* New York: Manpower Demonstration Research Corporation.

Gennetian, L., Huston, A. C., Crosby, D. A., Chang, Y. E., & Lowe, E. (2002). *Making childcare choices: How welfare and work policies influence parents' decisions* (Policy Brief). New York: Manpower Demonstration Research Corporation.

Gennetian, L. A., Crosby, D. A., Huston, A. C., & Lowe, T. (2002). *How childcare assistance in welfare and employment programs can support the employment of low-income families* (The Next Generation Project Working Paper). New York: Manpower Demonstration Research Corporation.

Gormley, W. T., Jr., & Lucas, J. K. (2000). *Money, accreditation, and childcare center quality* (Working Paper). New York: Foundation for Child Development.

Greenberg, M., et al. (2002). The 1996 welfare law: Key elements and reauthorization issues affecting children. *Future of Children, 12,* 27–57.

Haskins, R. (1989). Beyond metaphor: The efficacy of early childhood education. *American Psychologist, 44,* 266–273.

Haskins, R., & Primus, W. (2002). Welfare reform and poverty. In I. Sawhill et al. (Eds.), *Welfare reform and beyond* (pp. 59–70). Washington, DC: Brookings Institution.

Helburn, S. W., & Bergmann, B. R. (2002). *America's childcare problem: The way out.* New York: Palgrave.

Huston, A. C., Chang, Y. E., & Gennetian, L. A. (2002). Family and individual predictors of childcare use by low-income families in different policy contexts. *Early Childhood Research Quarterly, 17,* 441–469.

Kamerman, S. (1996). Child and family policies: An international overview. In Zigler et al. (Eds.), *Children, families, and government* (2nd ed., pp. 31–48). New York: Cambridge University Press.

Knitzer, J. (2001). Federal and state efforts to improve childcare for infants and toddlers. *Future of Children, 11*, 79–98.

Lamb, M. E. (1997). Nonparental childcare: Context, quality, correlates, and consequences. In I. Sigel & K. A. Renninger (Eds.), *Child psychology in practice* (5th ed., pp. 73–134). New York: John Wiley.

Layzer, J. I., & Collins, A. (2001). *Access to childcare for low-income working families report.* Washington, DC: U.S. Department of Health and Human Services.

Lowe, E. D., & Weisner, T. S. (in press). You have to push it — who's gonna raise your kids?: Situating childcare and childcare subsidy use in the daily routines of lower income families. *Children and Youth Services Review.*

Meyers, M. K., Peck, L. R., Davis, E. E., Collins, A., Kreader, J. L., Georges, A., Wever, R., Schexnayder, D. T., Schroeder, D. G., & Olson, J. A. (2002). *The dynamics of childcare subsidy use: A collaborative study of five states.* New York: National Center for Children in Poverty.

Morris, P. A., Huston, A. C., Duncan, G. J., Crosby, D., & Bos, J. M. (2001). *How welfare and work policies affect children: A synthesis of research.* New York: Manpower Demonstration Research Corporation.

NICHD Early Childcare Research Network. (1997). Poverty and patterns of childcare. In J. Brooks-Gunn & G. Duncan (Eds.), *Consequences of growing up poor* (pp. 100–131). New York: Russell Sage Foundation.

NICHD Early Childcare Research Network. (1999). Child outcomes when childcare center classes meet recommended standards for quality. *American Journal of Public Health, 89*, 1072–1077.

NICHD Early Childcare Research Network. (2000a). Characteristics and quality of childcare for toddlers and preschoolers. *Applied Developmental Science, 4*, 116–135.

NICHD Early Childcare Research Network. (2000b). The relation of childcare to cognitive and language development. *Child Development, 71*, 960–980.

NICHD Early Childcare Research Network. (2001a). Before Head Start: Income and ethnicity, family characteristics, childcare experiences, and child development. *Early Education and Development, 12*, 545–576.

NICHD Early Childcare Research Network (2001b). Nonmaternal care and family factors in early development: An overview of the NICHD study of early childcare. *Journal of Applied Developmental Psychology, 22*, 457–492.

NICHD Early Childcare Research Network. (2002a). Early childcare and children's development prior to school entry: Results from the NICHD study of early childcare. *American Educational Research Journal, 39*, 133–164.

NICHD Early Childcare Research Network. (2002b). Structure>Process>Outcome: Direct and indirect effects of caregiving quality on young children's development. *Psychological Science, 13*, 199–206.

NICHD Early Childcare Research Network. (in press). Does amount of time spent in childcare predict socioemotional adjustment during the transition to kindergarten? *Child Development.*

Norris, D. J., & Dunn, L. (2001). *Tiered childcare licensing and children's experiences.* Paper presented at the Biennial Meeting of the Society for Research in Child Development, Minneapolis, MN.

Peisner-Feinberg, E. S., Burchinal, M. R., Clifford, R. M., Culkin, M. L., Howes, C., Kagan, S. L., & Yazejian, N. (2001). The relation of preschool childcare quality to children's cognitive and social developmental trajectories through second grade. *Child Development, 72*, 1534–1553.

Phillips, D. A. (1991). With a little help: Children in poverty and childcare. In A. C. Huston (Ed.), *Children in poverty: Child development and public policy* (pp. 158–189). New York: Cambridge University Press.

Phillips, D., & Adams, G. (2001). Childcare for our youngest children. *Future of Children, 11*, 35–52.

Phillips, D. A., Voran, M., Kisker, E., Howes, C., & Whitebook, M. (1994). Childcare for children in poverty: Opportunity or inequity? *Child Development, 65*, 472–492.

Phillips, D. A., & Bridgmann, A. (1995). *Childcare for low-income families: Summary of two workshops.* Washington, DC: National Academy Press.

Raikes, H. (1998). Investigating childcare subsidy: What are we buying? *Social Policy Report: Society for Research in Child Development, 12*, 1–18.

Ramey, C. T., Campbell, F. A., Burchinal, M. R., Skinner, M. L., Gardner, D. M., & Ramey, S. L. (2000). Persistent effects of early childhood education on high-risk children and their mothers. *Applied Developmental Science, 4*, 2–14.

Scarr, S. (1998). American childcare today. *American Psychologist, 53*, 95–108.

U.S. Department of Health and Human Services. (1999). *Access to childcare for low-income families.* Retrieved from http://www.acf.dhhs.gov/news/press/ccreport.htm

U. S. Department of Health and Human Services. (2001). *Trends in the well-being of children and youth, 2001.* Retrieved from www.aspe.hhs.gov/hsp/01trends

Vandell, D., & Wolfe, B. (2000). *Childcare quality: Does it matter and does it need to be improved?* Washington, DC: Office of the Assistant Secretary for Planning and Evaluation, U. S. Department of Health and Human Services.

Waldfogel, J. (2001). International policies toward parental leave and childcare. *Future of Children, 11*, 99–111.

Whitebook, M., Howes, C., & Phillips, D. (1990). *Who cares: Childcare teachers and the quality of care in America.* Oakland, CA: Childcare Employee Project.

Whitebook, M., Howes, C., & Phillips, D. (1998). *Worthy work, unlivable wages. The National Childcare Staffing Study, 1988-1997.* Washington, DC: Center for the Childcare Workforce.

Yoshikawa, H. (1995). Long-term effects of early childhood programs on social outcomes and delinquency. *Future of Children, 5*, 51–75.

Zaslow, M. J., Moore, K. A., Brooks, J. L., Morris, P. A., Tout, K., Redd, Z. A., & Emig, C. A. (2002). Experimental studies of welfare reform and children. *Future of Children, 12*, 79–98.

Zigler, E. F., & Gilman, E. (1996). Not just any care: Shaping a coherent childcare policy. In E. F. Zigler, S. L. Kagan, & N. W. Hall (Eds.), *Children, families, and government: Preparing for the twenty-first century* (pp. 94–116). New York: Cambridge University Press.

10
THE CRISIS OF CARE

Barrie Thorne
University of California, Berkeley

Introduction

How could any affluent country, if only out of long-term self-interest, allow so many of its children to grow up in nightmare childhoods? Ten years ago a visiting Norwegian sociologist asked me that question in an urgent and genuinely puzzled way. She had just come from a conference in San Francisco on U.S. public policy and family poverty, and she was reeling from the human import of the statistics about child poverty that she had heard. I have never forgotten her question and its stark perspective on the irrationality and injustice of U.S. policies relating to children and families. Aletha Huston's excellent analysis of the U.S. childcare system and the needs of low-income parents (in this volume) sticks close to the empirical ground, but she also alludes to irrationality and injustice and she pauses at several points to call for radical rethinking. In these comments I will pick up on that call.

Before turning to the larger political context, I will report from recent ethnographic research that illuminates the complex ways in which families in California are trying to cope with gaps of provisioning for the care of their children. These case studies bring lived experiences into conjunction with statistical profiles of widening and racialized social class divides. The case studies also illustrate varied and sometimes contested cultural framings of "care," "need," and "obligation." My discussion draws upon feminist theories of care, which are useful in interrogating the dramatic inequalities and the market logic that, as Huston observes, characterize the current U.S. childcare system. I will conclude by sketching an alternative vision that frames caring as a collective responsibility, and children as a social rather than privatized good.

Qualitative Case Studies of the Contemporary U.S. Childcare System

Skocpol (2000) has observed that public programs in other industrial democracies *correct* for difficulties and inequities in the private wage market. However, especially since the 1980s, U.S. public policies have tended to *exacerbate* market

165

disparities. Huston's analysis of U.S. childcare policies illustrates this point. The federal welfare reform legislation of 1996 forced impoverished single mothers to take on full-time jobs, mostly at and sometimes below minimum wage. But the legislation did not provide adequate support for the care of these mothers' children. Over the last two decades the ability of low- and middle-income U.S. families to provide care has been eroded not only by cut-backs in state provisioning, but also by heightened job insecurity and the intensification of wage work (Hochschild, 1997; Wallulis, 1998). There is, in short, a growing crisis of care.

As Huston notes, the U.S. has a "market-based child care system that is highly decentralized and variable," and in the absence of adequate public subsidies, access to and the quality of paid care strongly correlate with income. The affluent have multiple market options that are flagged, like products on a supermarket shelf, by a nuanced array of labels—nannies, babysitters, housekeepers, au pairs, preschools, day care—and for school-aged children, fee-based after-school programs, lessons, and other specialized activities focused on sports, music, drama, dance, computers, and science. The result, especially among upper middle-class families in metropolitan areas, is a trend, in effect, toward gated childhoods, with children's out-of-home time organized almost entirely through markets that exclude those without the means to pay. In these privatized and relatively homogeneous enclaves, kids often have little contact with those who are less privileged in racialized hierarchies of social class.

At the other end of the class spectrum, parents from lower (and even middle) incomes lack the means to purchase quality paid care. Even if they qualify for government subsidies, they often confront long waiting lists. Low-income solo mothers and their children who are without kin or friends able to lend a daily hand lead especially pressed lives. Furthermore, low-income workers are the least likely to receive "family-friendly" benefits from employers, such as paid sick leave, vacation leave, and job flexibility, and they are much more likely to have to work evenings or nights (Heymann, 2000). Deterioration in the quality of public schools and in services like public transportation, parks, and libraries compounds the problems.

The California Childhoods Project

How do employed lower-income parents provide for the care of their children? Between 1996 and 1999, Faulstich Orellana and I worked with multilingual teams of graduate and undergraduate students to gather data about the daily lives of children, ages 5-12, who are growing up in a varied social class and racial ethnic circumstances in urban California. We set out to trace the local effects of a series of large-scale trends that are reconfiguring the landscape of U.S. childhoods.

(1) *High rates of immigration,* the result of economic restructuring and 1965 changes in federal immigration laws. California has received more immigrants than any other state; in 2000, 46% of the state's children had at least one immigrant parent, and 40% spoke a language other than English at home (Palmer, Younghwan, & Lu, 2000).

(2) *Widening social class divides,* especially in the wake of political and economic changes of the 1980s. California's rates of child poverty have increased by more than 10% over the last two decades, to the current figure of 22%; the state also has an unusually high proportion of households with annual incomes over $200,000, while the middle-class is shrinking (Palmer et al, 2000). In Oakland, 25% of children now live below the poverty line; the median income of white households is nearly twice that of African Americans, Latinos, and Asian Americans (Gammon & Marcucci, 2002). Half of white children in Oakland now attend private rather than public schools, a figure much higher than among families of other racial ethnic backgrounds (Tucker & Katz, 2002).

(3) *Cuts in state provisioning for families and children,* with dramatic deterioration in the quality of public schools, parks, and recreation programs. In the 1950s and early 1960s, California had one of the best public school systems in the country, although resources diverged along lines related to race and class. In 1996, when our research began, the state ranked 41st in per-pupil school funding.

(4) *The expansion of market-based infrastructures of services for families and children,* such as private schools and fee-based after-school programs, which are available only to those with the means to pay. Affluent childhoods have become more commodified and privatized; middle- and low-income families rely more on public institutions, although forces of commercialization exert a strong influence on children's lives across lines of class and culture.

(5) *The speed-up of family change*, with high rates of
maternal employment, a growing care deficit, and the
juxtaposition of many different family forms and
childrearing practices in crowded urban areas. The
forces of globalization have unsettled previously
dominant ideals of and assumptions about childhood
(Stephens, 1995).

These structural shifts are transforming childhoods in urban California as
dramatically as the changes of the Progressive Era a century ago, when the passage
of laws against child labor and requiring comprehensive public schooling
consolidated a normative ideal of the domesticated and schooled child (Zelizer,
1985). Children's lives are still organized through families and schools, but social
class divides are wider than at any time in U.S. history. In urban California, these
divides are increasingly institutionalized and heavily racialized.

To explore the changing contours of urban childhoods, my co-researchers
and I did three years of fieldwork and interviewing in two geographic areas. I
guided data-gathering in a mixed-income, ethnically diverse part of Oakland, where
the children of immigrants from Mexico, Central America, China, Vietnam, Laos,
Yemen, and other countries, as well as African American and white children
converge in the public school. Faulstich Orellana organized research in the Pico
Union area of Los Angeles, a low-income, inner-city enclave of transmigrants
from Mexico and Central America. How, our project asks, do parents and children
from different economic and cultural circumstances perceive and negotiate the
demographic and cultural shifts related to immigration, widening income gaps,
increases in maternal employment, the decline of public responsibility for children,
and the commercialization of childhoods? How do kids and "their adults" organize
children's uses of time and space, the company they keep, and the process of
growing older?

In mapping the daily lives of children from varied cultural and class
backgrounds, we discovered an astounding array of care arrangements, some as
complex and contingent as Rube Goldberg machines—and as prone to falling
apart, with children often pressed to pick up the pieces (Thorne, 2001). For example,
we interviewed Betty Jones, a low-income solo African American mother who
worked the late afternoon and evening shift as a custodian in an Oakland hospital.
Her car had broken down months before and she couldn't afford repairs, so her
11-year-old son Tyrone (all names have been changed) took responsibility for
bringing himself and his 6-year-old sister to school on a city bus. After school,
Tyrone picked up his younger sister and they walked to a bus stop to begin an
hour-long daily ride, including a transfer, from Oakland to San Leandro where
their grandmother lived. The grandmother took them with her to her evening job
as a custodian in an office building. After she got off work at 10 or 11 p.m., she
drove the kids back to their apartment in a low-income area of Oakland.

This scheduling exhausted all of them, and Betty, the children's mother, was concerned about her own mother's willingness to continue watching after grandchildren while cleaning offices at night. Like others we interviewed with very tight budgets, Betty wanted to send her kids to the after-school program located at the public school but she found the fees exorbitant; her income was more than used up by basics like food, rent, and utilities. Betty's swing shift job as a hospital custodian precluded the presence of her children, unlike the hospital job of another solo African American mother in our study. Deborah Payson worked regular hours in a clerical position in a different Oakland hospital, which was near the public school. Her daughter, Sheila, who was one of Tyrone's classmates, walked to the hospital after school and hung out until 5 p.m., when her mother got off work. While she waited, Sheila did her homework and sometimes helped with filing. Deborah was grateful that her co-workers didn't mind having Sheila around. Child-friendly worksites may become valuable resources for working parents, especially if kids can get there by themselves after school.

Dropping off and picking up kids from school has become a named chunk of daily labor in contemporary households (Thorne, 2001). Many kids in Oakland live at some distance from their schools (the public school district has never had its own bus system, except for disabled students), and there is widespread anxiety about the safety of kids walking to school alone. When transportation to and from school is an issue, caregivers especially value temporal and spatial flexibility at places of employment. For example, Xiaoying Lie, a Chinese immigrant mother, was employed in a garment factory in Oakland; her husband, who worked a double shift in a restaurant an hour away from their house, was unavailable to help transport their children to and from school. Xiaoying spoke with her boss, who was also from China, and got permission to take a mid-afternoon break to pick up her fifth- and sixth-grade daughters from the public school and drive them home. After dropping them off, Xiaoying returned to the factory until 7 p.m. The girls took care of themselves and had dinner waiting when their mother returned for the evening.

Rhonda Franklin, an African American who drove a delivery truck, maneuvered her work schedule so that she could help out her sister, who had almost no flexibility in her daytime shift at K-Mart. Rhonda planned ahead so that she could interrupt deliveries and make it to the public school by 3:30, pick up her 7-year-old niece, Jessie, and drop her off at a neighbor's house. When Rhonda couldn't get to the school and Jessie stood waiting beyond the span of time the school staff deemed acceptable, Jessie or a staff member would try to reach the aunt or mother by phone. There were also crises when the neighbor couldn't be at home. Jessie sometimes ended up staying home by herself, although she found it scary.

School schedules and work schedules often collide and can easily move out of sync.[1] For example, Pedro Ramirez, a Mexican immigrant father who worked for an Oakland delivery service, had scheduled a late lunch break to coincide with his 7-year-old daughter Rosalia's school dismissal time. Several months before, Rosalia had been switched from a late to an early morning reading group, which meant she had to be picked up at 3 p.m. instead of 4 p.m. Pedro negotiated a change in his work schedule so that he could continue to pick up Rosalia after school and drive her to the restaurant where her mother was employed as a food server. The mother had little flexibility during her work shift, which ended at 4. But her job site was a fixed and safe location, with leeway for the temporary presence of a child. Knowing that this makeshift arrangement depended on the goodwill of the restaurant owner and that her parents had few other options, the daughter sat unobtrusively on a chair near the kitchen, doing a bit of homework and watching the restaurant scene while she waited for her mother to get off work.

Compared with families with few children and with minimal ties to local relatives (a situation more typical of middle- and upper middle-class white households in Oakland), immigrant and other families who are embedded in thick networks of kin tend to have extra flexibility in organizing children's out-of-school time. Children from two large Yemeni immigrant families attended the public school that anchors our Oakland fieldsite. In both extended families, older siblings and cousins took responsibility for walking with younger kids to and from school, and older girls did a great deal of childcare and housework at home. Aunts and uncles could also be mobilized. The domestic demands of immigrant parents who are working long hours may spur other relatives to migrate in order to help with housework and childcare, as in the case of grandparents who came from Hong Kong to live with their son (who had a manufacturing job) and his wife (who was employed in a garment factory). The grandmother cooked, shopped for groceries, cleaned, and did childcare; the grandfather routinely took a city bus to the public school and waited for their two young grandchildren (an "early bird" and a "late bird" reader; they got out an hour apart) and escorted them home from school.

---

[1] In our Pico Union research site, a densely populated, extremely low-income enclave of immigrants from Mexico and Central America, the adults (many of them undocumented) have high rates of employment and also a great deal of job instability. The men work as day laborers, janitors, or gardeners, or in restaurants. Women also work in restaurants or the garment industry, or as paid domestic workers. Marjorie Orellana surveyed all of the fourth- and fifth-grade students in the large year-round public elementary school that anchors the site and asked how they spent time when their school track was not in session (the three tracks rotate through two months of school and a one-month break). Only 10% of the kids participated in a formal, off-track program such as one organized by the YMCA. Many city programs for kids were geared to conventional summer vacations, not to month-long breaks every two months. No programs for school-age-children provided free or low-cost all-day care (Orellana & Thorne, 1998). As with immigrant families in Oakland, these families relied on networks of kin, older siblings, and children's self-care; and children sometimes accompanied parents to their places of work. In a recent paper, Orellana (2001) documents the extensive labor contributions that immigrant children make to families, schools, and communities, often under the rubric of being "helpers."

The friendships children make in school may become conduits to the care resources of other households. For example, at the end of each school day, two close fifth-grade friends—Julie, from a white, working-class family, and Faria, from a Pakistani immigrant family—walked together to a video store owned by a friend of Faria's father, who had migrated from the same village. The store provided a safe, loosely adult-supervised way-station where the girls could wait to be picked up. Other families used the public library as a way-station, to the consternation of librarians who announced that the facility was *not* a "day care center." A third-grader told us that after school let out, he walked to the nearby home of a "lady from church"; his mother, who was employed in a low-wage job, mobilized help through the Pentecostal Church they attended.

Conceptualizing "Cultures of Care"

My efforts to grasp the dynamics of these varied, contingent, and shifting arrangements for the out-of-school care of elementary school children have been enriched by workshops and discussions at the Berkeley Center for Working Families (CWF), which Arlie Hochschild and I co-directed between 1998 and 2002.[2] The CWF intellectual community focused on work, family, and "cultures of care", that is, the varied resources, beliefs, and practices that shape the care that working families give, receive, and all too often might like to have but fail to acquire. We took a holistic and contextual approach, seeking to illuminate different "ecologies of care", that is, relationships, transfers, and trajectories of care that may extend beyond households to include extended kin, paid caregivers, and an open-ended array of helping "kith", such as friends, neighbors, paid caregivers, co-workers, and acquaintances made through religious and civic organizations. Networks of care may even extend across national borders, as when immigrant parents leave their children behind or send them back to be cared for by relatives or friends "back home" in Guatemala or the Philippines (Orellana et al., 2001; Thorne et al., in press).

Using an innovative methodological strategy, CWF researcher Karen Hansen (2001) developed a detailed case study of the networks that four different white working families, from across the class spectrum, organized for the care of their school-aged children. She interviewed all of the people (relatives, friends, paid caregivers of various kinds) who were directly involved in caring for the children at the center of each network. Hansen discovered that care was variously constructed as a diffuse obligation, a favor, a gift, and a tit-for-tat exchange. Her analysis highlights the fact that care is not only a form of work but is also deeply embedded in relationships (Ruddick, 1998). Contractual arrangements, where money is involved, work through a somewhat different logic than helping relationships among

---

[2] The Berkeley Center for Working Families archival web site, including on-line working papers, can be accessed at <http://www.bc.edu/bc_org/avp/wfnetwork/Berkeley/.>

kin or friends. Each logic has characteristic tensions and dynamics of reciprocity. The networks that Hansen studied, and the ones I have briefly sketched, varied in size and elasticity; some, in Hansen's terms, were more "robust and pliable", and others "thin and brittle". The contours, as Hansen argues, reflect and are shaped by particular constellations of resources (time, money, people, transportation), which are connected to but not in any simple way determined by social class.

A fuller account of the case studies I presented earlier would examine the ways in which child-care help was mobilized, sustained, and/or withdrawn in ongoing relationships between parents and relatives, friends, neighbors, co-workers, or fellow church members. Issues of reciprocity (should one offer a bit of payment or bring gifts of food to "the lady from church"?), trust (can one rely on a fellow villager of the father of one's daughter's friend?) and control (is it acceptable for the staff to discipline kids who come to the library on their own?) often emerge. One can more easily terminate relationships with a paid caregiver than, say, with a grandmother or an aunt. Differences over questions of discipline, television watching, and food (is candy allowed?) often create tensions between parents and other caregivers.

These case studies of cultures of care allude to a process that Fraser (1989) has termed "the politics of needs assessment." Conceptions of needs and how they should be met (from minimally acceptable to "good enough" to "high quality") are culturally framed, and often contested. In assessing issues of child-care quality, Huston draws upon research by experts in child development. But these ideas about and measures of the needs, say, of 4-year-old or a 10-year-old (gender may also enter into the framing) are sometimes at odds with other belief systems, especially when notions of "desirable outcome" extend beyond core matters like physical safety, basic nutrition, and literacy acquisition. In our research on childhoods in Oakland, we've found that various caregiving adults, including parents and teachers, may have quite divergent ideas about issues such as the desirability of older children taking responsibility for younger siblings, the age at which a child—or a girl or a boy—should be allowed to walk to school or to stay home alone, and when and how kids should be disciplined (Thorne et al., in press). Divergent assumptions sometimes boil up into open conflict.

Children, of course, have their own ideas about needs and rights; and in formal interviews and informal conversations they reported arguing with their parents and other caregivers about what they should eat, when they should go to bed, how much and what sort of television they could watch, and whether or not leaving elementary school means that they have also outgrown after-school programs (also see CWF research by Kaplan [2001] and Polatnick [2001]). Raising children (an adult-centered framing) and growing up (a term more in line with children's perspectives) are complex and relational processes, marked by continual negotiation and struggles over power and autonomy (Haavind, forthcoming; Thorne, 2001).

In mainstream American culture, the negotiation of increased individual autonomy and freedom (e.g., making one's own choices about what to wear and how to spend free time) symbolically marks the process of growing older. But immigrants from rural areas of Asia, Mexico, Central America, and the Middle East tend to be deeply ambivalent about this emphasis on individual autonomy. Many of these families migrated to the U.S. in search of educational and employment opportunities unavailable in their countries of origin; they want their children to learn English, do well in school, and engage in life in this country. But immigrant parents also fear that their children will pull away from family obligations and cultural roots and succumb to the individualized excesses of "doing what you want." Non-immigrant teachers, parents, and experts in child development are sometimes troubled when they learn that immigrant kids are making significant labor contributions to their households by caring for siblings, doing housework, and working in family stores (Orellana, 2001; Thorne et al., in press). To middle-class American eyes these kids may look "adultified" and "parentified." But through the lenses of other cultural traditions, the early assumption of responsibility is a mark of growing older, and sheer necessity may press parents to rely on the labor of their children.

I have reported from a potpourri of qualitative studies to add contextual nuance to Huston's description of the childcare arrangements and challenges of low-income U.S. families. Our research highlights the value of linking the study of material resources with attention to cultural beliefs and practices. We have studied the experiences and practices of adult caregivers in conjunction with the perspectives and actions of children who, as I have indicated, not only receive but also may give and negotiate care.[3] We have tried to grapple with complex connections among structures of class, racial-ethnicity, gender, and age.

Social class is best understood through a relational lens, and focusing on only one stratum—such as middle-class working families or low-income single-mother families—obscures a sense of the whole. (Although research on paid work and family life has flourished over the last two decades, it is much too sliced up; for example, the literature on dual-earner middle-class families tends to be set apart from studies of working-class and impoverished families.) A relational perspective broadens research on affluent working parents, for example, to include the family lives and experiences of the nannies and housekeepers whom they employ. Many of these low-income careworkers in the U.S. are immigrants who left children behind in Mexico, El Salvador, or the Philippines, to be cared for by relatives who may or may not be able to meet their needs. "Chains of care" (to use Arlie

---

[3] In my writing on contemporary childhoods I am trying to bridge a striking gap between research on adult caregivers and research on children as social actors, including their contributions as givers of care. Theoretical and empirical research on parenting/mothering/fathering/childrearing tends to efface the perspectives and agency of children. In contrast, sociologists of childhood emphasize children's standpoints and agency, but often in ways that obscure their connections with caregiving adults. Attention to the standpoints of both children and adults, and a more relational understanding of agency, can help bridge this gap (Thorne, 2000).

Hochschild's term) and transnational migration streams, as well as dramatic—and interrelated—patterns of global and domestic inequality should be included in any portrait of the U.S. landscape of childcare (Ehrenreich & Hochschild, 2003; Glenn, 1992; Hondagneu-Sotelo, 2001; Parrenas, 2001).

From Market Logic to an Ethic of Care

I will now step back from the situated specifics of the U.S. crisis of care and pick up on Huston's call for us to think "outside the parameters of the existing system." My critical perspective is anchored in the work of feminist theorists such as Joan Tronto (1994), Sara Ruddick (1998), and Evelyn Nakano Glenn (2000), who have developed *care* as a category of analysis and as a framework for moral and political thought. As Huston observes, European welfare states have been far more generous than the U.S. in social provisioning for families and children; indeed, Scandinavians refer matter-of-factly to "the caring state," an idea that sounds like an oxymoron to contemporary U.S. ears.

Cross-national comparisons can help us grasp our own cultural assumptions, as can reflections on earlier times in U.S. history when national social provision was seen as more legitimate than it is today. For example, in the Progressive Era comprehensive public schooling was introduced in every state; in the 1930s Congress established Social Security as a general entitlement (at least for workers), and in the late1940s the Oakland Parks and Recreation Department established free after-school programs at every elementary school in the city, a form of government provisioning that ended in the 1960s, ironically in a period when rates of maternal employment were rising. Although it was framed as a means-tested rather than entitlement tier of Social Security legislation, AFDC was originally framed as a *childcare* program rooted in a discourse of maternalism. Somehow, over the ensuing decades, it got reframed as a program for "free-loading" women, disparaging their needs and contributions as mothers (Mink, 1998). CWF researcher Anita Garey (2002) has highlighted another discursive sign of the increased devaluing and privatization of care in the U.S.: current legislative moves to subsidize after-school programs carefully avoid the language of "care." Instead, advocates of state subsidies emphasize the need to promote academic achievement and to keep kids off of drugs and away from crime (as potential victims and perpetrators). On the other hand, corporations make ample use of the language of care, for example, by touting their "customer care representatives." Luxury hotels take care of "needs" (e.g., for personalized massages or for an orchid leaf presented with tissue-wrapped laundry) that guests are not even aware they have (Sherman, 2002). These strange twists of discourse reflect the delegitimation of state provisioning, the power of the capitalist market, and striking inequalities in the distribution of care.

Instituting comprehensive as opposed to means-tested and stigmatized public support for children, the sick, or the elderly now feels virtually impossible in the U.S. Indeed, in this mean-spirited time, the rich are getting richer with hidden transfers from the state, such as tax cuts, mortgage write-offs, and corporate bail-outs—subsidies framed as entitlements and obscured by the imagery of self-sufficient families. Those with more power are able to command resources and care, under conditions favorable to them. Many of the poor, on the other hand, are getting poorer and the public subsidies they receive are not only heavily means tested, but also highly stigmatized.

How did a sense of collective responsibility for the vulnerable and dependent become so eroded? As capitalist markets have expanded, so has the fiction of the autonomous individual who acts primarily out of self-interest and whose needs are sustained by a self-sufficient, privatized family (Fineman, 2000). The masculine ideal of a worker unencumbered by caregiving obligations is built into workplace structures and patterns of reward, which strongly disadvantages workers, the majority of them women, who have primary responsibilities for care (Williams, 1998). Dependence and needs for care have been increasingly privatized and thus depoliticized.

An alternative vision starts not with an assumption of individual and household autonomy and the devaluing of dependency and care, but rather with a recognition of human interdependence and of *collective* rather than privatized responsibility for care. We should push for the state to exercise its redistributive powers and offer more generous programs of public assistance for families raising children. Care should be given greater recognition and value. Institutions should be redesigned so that breadwinning and caregiving are organized in more compatible and less gender unequal ways. As Nancy Fraser (1997) has written:

> Women today often combined breadwinning and caregiving,
> albeit with great difficulty and strain. A postindustrial
> welfare state must ensure that men do the same, while
> redesigning institutions so as to eliminate the difficulty and
> strain. We might call this vision Universal Caregiver
> (p. 61).

Folbre (2000) has outlined a series of political strategies that would help us ameliorate the crisis in care. For example, she highlights the need for linking two social movements already underway: political mobilization by *those who need help with care* (parents, advocates for the disabled, the frail elderly, and the chronically ill; healthcare consumers) and movements by underpaid *careworkers* who, often through unions, are organizing "living wage," "worthy wage," and "comparable worth" campaigns. Scholars can also help spur recognition that change is possible. For example, when we write about "robust" empirical trends, we should avoid the language of inevitability, as in statements like "low-wage work is here to stay." The irrationalities and injustices of poverty were made, and they can be changed by collective human action.

Acknowledgments

The California Childhoods Project, which provided most of the qualitative data reported in this chapter, was sponsored and funded by the John D. and Catherine T. MacArthur Foundation Research Network on Successful Pathways through Middle Childhood, with additional support from the University of California, Berkeley, Institute of Human Development and from the Berkeley Center for Working Families, funded by the Alfred P. Sloan Foundation. Special thanks to the colleagues who helped gather and analyze the data: Marjorie Faulstich Orellana, Wan Shun Eva Lam, Hung Thai, Eréndira Rueda, Nadine Chabrier, Allison Pugh, Anna Chee, Eileen Mears, Ana Gonzales, and Gladys Ocampo. The intellectual community at the Center for Working Families, especially Arlie Hochschild, helped me think more deeply about families, communities, work, cultures of care, and the problems of contemporary U.S. society.

References

Ehrenreich, B., & Hochschild, A. (Eds.). (2003). *Global woman: Nannies, maids, and sex workers in the new economy*. New York: Metropolitan Books.

Fineman, M. A. (2000). Cracking the foundational myths: Independence, autonomy, and self-sufficiency. American University Journal of Gender, Social Policy and Law, 8, 13–30.

Folbre, N. (2001). *The invisible heart: Economics and family values*. New York: New Press.

Fraser, N. (1989). *Unruly practices*. Minneapolis: University of Minnesota Press.

Fraser, N. (1997). *Justice interruptus: Critical reflections on the 'postsocialist' condition*. New York: Routledge.

Gammon, R., & Marcucci, M. R. (2002, August 27). Census: Racial income disparities abound. *Oakland Tribune*, pp. News-1, 7.

Garey, A. (2002). *Concepts of care in after-school programs: Protection, instruction, and containment* (Berkeley Center for Working Families Working Paper No. 48). Retrieved from http://www.bc.edu/bc_org/avp/wfnetwork/Berkeley/

Glenn, E. N. (1992). From servitude to service work: Historical continuities in the racial division of paid reproductive labor. *Signs, 18*, 1–43.

Glenn, E. N. (2000). Creating a caring society. *Contemporary Sociology, 29*, 84–94.

Haavind, H. (in press). Contesting and recognizing historical changes and selves in development: Methodological changes. In T. Weisner (Ed.), *Discovering successful pathways in children's development.*

Hansen, K. (2001). *Class contingencies and networks of care for school-aged children* (Berkeley Center for Working Families Working Paper No. 27). Retrieved from http://www.bc.edu/bc_org/avp/wfnetwork/Berkeley/

Heymann, J. (2000). *The widening gap: Why America's working families are in jeopardy—and what can be done about it.* New York: Basic Books.

Hochschild, A. R. (1997). *The time bind.* New York: Metropolitan Books.

Hondagneu-Sotelo, P. (2001). *Doméstica: Immigrant workers cleaning and caring in the shadows of affluence.* Berkeley: University of California Press.

Kaplan, E. B. (2001). Using food as a metaphor for care: Middle-school kids talk about family, school, and class relationship. *Journal of Contemporary Ethnography, 29,* 474–509.

Mink, G. (1998). *Welfare's end.* Ithaca, NY: Cornell University Press.

Orellana, M. F. (2001). The work kids do: Mexican and Central American immigrant children's contributions to households and schools in California. *Harvard Educational Review, 71,* 366–389.

Orellana, M. F., & Thorne, B. (1998). Year-round schools and the politics of time. *Anthropology and Education Quarterly, 29,* 446–472.

Orellana, M. F., Thorne, B., Chee, A., & Lam, W. S. E. (2001). Transnational childhoods: The participation of children in processes of family migration. *Social Problems, 48,* 572–591.

Palmer, J. S., Younghwan, S., & Lu, H. (2002). *The changing face of child poverty in California. State child poverty update.* New York: National Center for Children in Poverty, Millman School of Public Health, Columbia University.

Parrenas, R. (2001) *Servants of globalization: Women, migration, and domestic work.* Stanford, CA: Stanford University Press.

Polatnick, M. R. (2002). Too old for child care? Too young for self-care?: Negotiating after-school arrangements for middle school. *Journal of Family Issues, 23,* 728–747.

Ruddick, S. (1998). Care as labor and relationship. In J. C. Haber & M. S. Halfon (Eds.), *Norms and values* (pp. 3–25). Totowa, NJ: Rowman and Littlefield.

Sherman, R. (2002). *'Better than your mother': Caring labor in luxury hotels* (Berkeley Center for Working Families Working Paper No. 53). Retrieved from http://www.bc.edu/bc_org/avp/wfnetwork/Berkeley/

Skocpol, T. (2000). *The missing middle: Working families and the future of American social policy.* New York: W. W. Norton.

Stephens, S. (Ed.). (1995). *Children and the politics of culture.* Princeton, NJ: Princeton University Press.

Thorne, B. (2001). Pick-up time at Oakdale Elementary School: Work and family from the vantage points of children. In R. Hertz & N. Marshall (Eds.), *Working families* (pp. 354–376). Berkeley: University of California Press.

Thorne, B. (2000, August). *Children's agency and theories of care.* Paper presented at the annual meetings of the American Sociological Association, Washington, DC.

Thorne, B., Orellana, M. F., Lan, W. S. E., & Chee, A. (in press). Raising children, and growing up, across national borders: Comparative perspectives on age, gender, and migration. In P. Hondagneu-Sotelo (Ed.), *Gender and U.S. immigration*. Berkeley: University of California Press.

Tronto, J. (1994) *Moral boundaries: A political argument for an ethic of care*. New York: Routledge.

Tucker, J., & Katz, A. (2002, August 27). Whites shun public schools: Census shows nearly 50% of Caucasians don't use city education system, *Oakland Tribune*, pp. News-1, 7.

Wallulis, J. (1998). *The new insecurity*. Albany, NY: SUNY Press.

Williams, J. (1998). *Unbending gender: Why family and work conflict and what to do about it*. New York: Oxford Press.

Zelizer, V. (1985). *Pricing the priceless child*. New York: Basic Books

11

CHILDCARE AS A WORK SUPPORT, A CHILD-FOCUSED INTERVENTION, AND A JOB

C. Cybele Raver
University of Chicago

Introduction

Huston's chapter (this volume) is critical to our understanding of the ways that low-income families manage the demands of employment and rearing their children. Women who are trying to meet welfare reform mandates to employment are faced with a harsh set of childcare choices. Specifically, these mothers face a market-based system that is unlikely to adequately meet the needs of their children at the subsidy price that the government is likely to pay. Huston underscores a central theme in work by Edin and Lein (1995), that poor women receive too low a wage to be able to afford the high cost of high-quality care on their own. The implications of this substandard care for children's outcomes are grave indeed.

Potential Costs of Low-Quality Childcare to Young Children

Huston raises concern about the quality of childcare faced by many low-income children. While some researchers suggest that the effect sizes of childcare quality for children's outcomes are relatively modest (Scarr & Eisenburg, 1993), others suggest that effect sizes are substantially larger when the associations between low-quality childcare and low-income children's outcomes are examined. Specifically, Burchinal and colleagues (2000) suggest that low versus high quality of care is associated with substantially larger effects for low-income children's language and cognitive outcomes, with 1-point improvement on the ECERS measure of childcare quality associated with a 6-point (or .4 SD) increase on a commonly used measure of cognitive development (MDI). These estimates are net of demographic characteristics that might influence some families to be more likely than others to select one type of care over another. The effects are similar in magnitude to those obtained in intensive early educational interventions such as the Abecedarian Project, where children who were randomly assigned to an experimental group provided with high-quality care throughout infancy and early childhood were doing substantially better cognitively than children randomly assigned to a control group (see Burchinal et al. [2000] for further discussion). Both sets of estimates give us a clear indication that there are few inexpensive solutions to the problem of quality of care.

While I've just mentioned the association between childcare quality and children's cognitive outcomes, I am particularly interested in the impact of care on children's social and emotional outcomes. In my *Social Policy Reports* review of the effectiveness of interventions aimed at reducing children's behavioral difficulties and strengthening their chances for early school success, the high prevalence of behavioral difficulties among low-income children in preschool environments is particularly striking (Raver, 2002a). Approximately 2–7% of preschool-aged children manifest such high levels of acting out and aggressive behavior that they exceed a threshold of clinical severity. However, a number of researchers and practitioners in early childhood education and care suggest that the number of children exhibiting elevated levels of behavior problems, particularly in high-risk, low-income contexts, is quite a bit higher, and may represent between 25–30% of the children in a given preschool classroom (see Campbell, Shaw, & Gilliom, 2000; Raver & Knitzer, 2002, for reviews). Observational research by Arnold, McWilliams, and Arnold (1998) suggests that some low-income preschool classrooms are characterized by a chaotic and emotionally negative tone on both teachers' and children's parts, with children exhibiting high rates of behavioral difficulty and teachers growing increasingly exasperated.

Interestingly, most research in developmental psychology that focuses on children's ability to regulate their negative emotions and behaviors examines family processes in emotion socialization (see Eisenberg, Cumberland, & Spinrad, 1998, for a review). Specifically, models often focus on ways that parents and children can get caught up in coercive cycles of negative mutual reinforcement that lead to a greater likelihood of behavioral problems among children. Fewer frameworks are available for considering emotional development in the context of nonparental childcare.

In early education, teachers' nurturance and sensitivity has been considered from the attachment-oriented framework (Pianta, 1999), and there has recently been some excellent intervention research on ways that teachers can foster an orderly, emotionally positive environment (Webster-Stratton, Reid, & Hammond, 2001), but fewer investigators have considered the childcare classroom as an important ecological context in which infants and young children learn how to regulate their behavior and emotions. In short, we know less about the mechanisms that support or undermine paid caregivers' socialization of children's emotional and behavioral competence.

Reconceptualizing Quality of Care

What does the extant literature tell us about classroom mechanisms that might influence children's emotional and behavioral development? Obviously, quality of care is a critical component of the classroom to examine. As Huston points out, scholars generally measure two dimensions of quality: structural features (including teacher education and training, class size, wages paid to workers) and two dimensions of process (including whether caregivers and environments are cognitively stimulating and whether caregivers are warm, responsive, and sensitive in their interactions with the children in their care). It is unclear how malleable these variables are to intervention. Interestingly, attempts to improve quality through generalized staff training programs have raised the extent to which caregivers provide greater cognitive stimulation, but have not had an impact on the emotional warmth, sensitivity, or "acceptance" dimensions of caregivers' quality of care (Kontos, Howes, & Galinsky, 1996). This suggests that generalized early childhood training and education may have good prospects for raising the material, cognitive stimulation dimensions of the HOME score, but may be less likely to improve the acceptance and sensitivity domains of the HOME. From the field of early clinical intervention, some solid empirical evidence suggests that specific emotionally- and behaviorally-oriented training programs can generate modest to moderate improvements in caregivers' provision of more emotionally positive, well-regulated classrooms (see Raver, 2002a, for a review). Additionally, structural features such as wages and smaller group size have been associated with higher levels of caregivers' cognitive stimulation *and* with higher levels of responsiveness and sensitivity for the children in their care (Phillips et al., 2000).

What other avenues of intervention might we pursue in improving childcare quality in ways that foster children's behavioral and emotional development? One theoretical model that might be helpful is that of parenting in the stressful context of material hardship. McLoyd and colleagues' (1994) model offers us a new lens through which to see childcare quality: childcare is provided by women who are trying their best to serve the children in their care, with inadequate resources and inadequate pay. Paid caregivers may have to make the tough choice to compromise the quality of care they offer by having to take too many children into their homes or classrooms. My speculation is that caregivers' sensitivity is compromised, with adults becoming more frustrated, angry, and impatient as they try to meet the needs of the children in their care with inadequate resources and support (see Figure 11.1). The implications of such a model for intervention would suggest trying to reduce the stressfulness of the work environment for childcare providers, similar to interventions aimed at reducing the stressfulness of parenting in high-risk environments.

Applying McLoyd's model to childcare

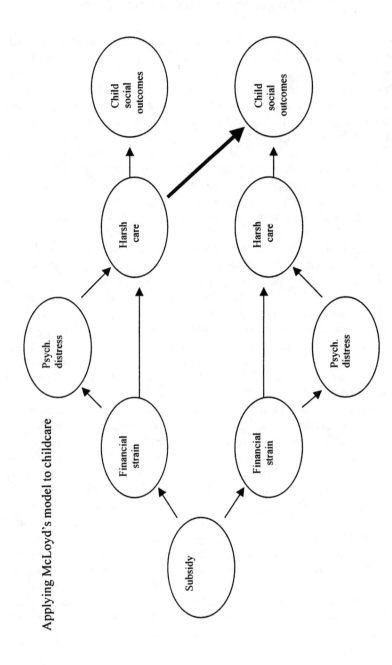

Figure 11.1. Model of financial strain and caregiving.

In short, parenting interventions have moved away from didactic models focused on teaching parents about developmental milestones to consider ways to aid low-income families to more effectively manage and reduce emotional stress. So too might providers be considered not for only what they know or do not know regarding child-centered beliefs, cognitive stimulation, etc., but for how they feel and whether they have adequate resources with which to carry out the highly demanding job of caring for other people's children. How are these models parallel? Is there any empirical evidence to support this perspective on childcare quality? To make a plausible case for the hypothesis that childcare workers' provision of lower-quality, more emotionally negative care may be at least in part dependent upon childcare workers' working conditions, I will briefly consider four points: childcare as an occupation; whether childcare work can be empirically characterized as stressful; whether the quality of care improves with the provision of supports that might reduce the stressfulness of the job; and implications of this model for public policy.

Childcare as an Occupation

First, consider Huston's suggestion that we examine childcare from the "supply" side. I would like to draw our attention to childcare as an occupation, with childcare work as a form of employment provided *by* low-income women. I draw here from my interests in women's employment in low-wage work in the context of welfare reform (Raver, 2002b). Research on women's participation in low-wage work underscores the reality that many low-income women were working before PROWRA was enacted, and that women's prospects for securing stable, high-paying, rewarding work (i.e., a "good" job) are relatively slim. Generally, few jobs "pay" in both psychological and economic terms, with the jobs held by ethnic minority, low-skilled women being most sensitive to recession, least likely to provide benefits, and most unstable (Bartik, 1997; Hoynes, 1999). As much work by Huston and others has shown in their analyses of welfare-to-work demonstration projects, work has not generally lifted women out of poverty, largely because of low pay.

Childcare is one job that is available to women leaving TANF. These women are substituting care within the home, where they receive TANF aid, for providing care to other people's children, either inside their home or outside of it, in other people's homes or in centers, for a wage. These women must in turn find care for their own children. In short, the labor supply for the care of low-income children face many of the same economic constraints and ecological stressors as the demand—it is low-income women with children who work as childcare workers, childcare aides, and family day care providers (Mocan & Tekin, 2000; Whitebrook, Howes & Phillips, 1998).

My own work on maternal employment and mental health and mothers' emotional expressiveness has tested the hypothesis that women carry the stress of work into the home. My research examines the impact of low-wage work from the perspective of whether these jobs are good or bad jobs, having a positive or negative impact on working mothers' mental health and their parenting of their own children. Following up on work by Menaghan and Parcel (1995), Ellwood (1988), Kalil et al. (1998), and Edin and Lein (1995), I ask whether low-wage work pays in psychological as well as financial terms, for mothers of young children. The opportunity to serve as discussant in this section alerted me to another question: how does the stressfulness of the job of childcare provider affect the children in the provider's care, *on the job*? I'll just briefly mention the findings of this study.

In my analyses, I tried to determine whether women's transitions into low- versus high-prestige jobs were associated with *changes* in their mental health and emotionally negative parenting, over time. My results suggest some evidence for the impact of the quality of mothers' jobs on parenting and maternal mental health. Specifically, lower prestige jobs were associated with increases in mothers' reports of depressive symptoms over a two-year period, even after taking their earlier levels of depressive symptoms into account. In addition, lower-prestige jobs were associated with an increase in mothers' use of more emotionally negative styles of parenting, over time, net of their use of negative parenting at baseline. These findings are congruent with extant research in the occupational stress literature that suggests that more stressful occupations are associated with workers' increased moodiness, anger, conflict, and physiological stress. In order to make a case for my speculation that childcare quality is compromised because of the stressful nature of childcare as an occupation, let us turn to a second point: does childcare work fit this characterization in terms of its stressfulness as an occupation?

Is Childcare Work a Good Job or a Bad Job?

The literature on occupational strain suggests that jobs that are highly demanding, that offer little control, and that provide workers with few resources, are said to be highly stressful (Curbow et al., 2000). It is clear that childcare workers in underfunded sites are likely to face low resources, high demand, and low control, a particularly deleterious combination. Curbow et al. (2000) designed a helpful inventory of worker stresses for childcare workers, and I will refer to these as a way of illustrating these three dimensions.

A Focus on Resources

Wages. Huston makes the astute observation that childcare workers essentially subsidize some of the cost of care by taking substandard wages (Huston, the volume, p.146). For former TANF recipients leaving the roll to work as childcare workers, wages per hour range from $5.26 (25 cents less an hour than the average wage by cashiers) to $7.33 for women hired as preKindergarten teachers (Bartik, 1997). Even when data are examined for center-based childcare workers more generally (where workers are more likely to be married, with higher family incomes), wages are still low and would not be sufficient to bring a family above federal poverty thresholds (Mocan & Tekin, 2000; Phillips et al., 2000).

Class size. Not just material capital, but human capital can be expended on children. Are teachers' patience, attention, and emotion spread too thin when they must care for large numbers of children? In Clarke-Stewart and colleagues' (2002) study of the regulable features of home-based care, caregivers cared for 5–14 children in their homes. Work by occupational psychologists on occupational stress among elementary school teachers suggests that teachers are constantly scanning their classrooms, trying to focus on "trouble-spots", trying to manage the multiple demands of teaching their academic subject, teaching behavior, maintaining children's attention, maintaining their physical safety, and giving emotional support simultaneously (Messing, Seifert, & Escalona, 1997).

Low Control, High Demand

Service work is generally relationally more demanding than manufacturing work, requiring "soft" or "people" skills—this is particularly true for childcare workers who must not only obtain compliance from preschool-age children but who must also negotiate work conditions, etc., with supervisors and adult purchasers of care. According to Huston, there are additional significant hassles of certification, and reimbursement for subsidy using TANF parents. Consider the stress that these hassles must cause for the childcare providers. Billing, certification, and reimbursement seem extremely taxing to navigate, and it seems questionable whether any other industry would put up with such low and troublesome reimbursement rates. The equation regarding demand, control, and resources would clearly be heavily negatively weighted by the lack of control in paying, and the lack of resources represented by the low subsidy.

Additional characteristics of the occupation that contribute to high levels of demand are the expectation reported by childcare providers and teachers that much preparatory work goes unpaid. Adults are often expected to prepare meals, design educationally oriented projects, order free tickets to the local museum, etc., on their own time.

Undoubtedly, some women find work as a childcare provider to be gratifying, important work (Blau & Mocan, 1999). Some teachers are clearly gifted at working with children in this employment context, and appear to derive considerable job satisfaction from their work. A number of ethnographic studies suggest the childcare providers believe that care for children is an important social contribution that has clear nonmonetary value, such as building loving relationships with the children in their care and supporting young children's growth and development. There are considerable non-salary financial benefits in moving care from the home into the paid sector, such as caregivers' eligibility for the Earned Income Tax Credit, a career and salary increase ladder, and emotional support from other adults in a workplace setting. Optimists in the welfare reform debate suggest that women will be able to earn more, over time, such that work does really "pay" (Kalil, Corcoran et al., 1998). In short, data from welfare reform demonstration programs suggest that many women making this transition are able to find and keep meaningful work (Moffitt, 2002). Childcare may be one good option that women elect to pursue as a job.

But in considering these benefits we must not overlook the stressors involved in the job of childcare: Specifically, workers clearly face inadequate material resources, face high demands on time, attention, and focus, and receive little instrumental or emotional support in the classroom. This has been conceptualized by the study of childcare workers' stress, where emotional responses to stressors at work for childcare providers may lead not only to turnover, but also may have negative consequences for the children in care (Curbow et al., 2000). Edin and Lein (1995) very effectively portray the strain of working in a succession of "dead-end" jobs where wages do not appreciably increase over time. Is childcare one of these types of jobs? Job stress not only has an effect on the women who are employed in the stressful occupation, but in this case would reasonably be expected to have an impact on the children in the workers' care.

Evidence to Support This Model?

Findings generated from experimental research would be ideal in providing more substantive evidence to support this model of quality of care. My third point is therefore to ask Huston whether there are effects of streamlining state childcare subsidy reimbursement for the *providers*. What were the effects of this intervention on the level of hassle experienced by *providers*? How much were their jobs and the quality of care provided to the children in their care improved by improving their work conditions? In other words, how malleable is quality, from this perspective, and how much do these factors make a difference in child outcomes? How can we maximize job satisfaction for those who provide such an important service and minimize job stress? What inputs would we recommend for improvement of the emotional climate of the classroom or family day care home?

Administrators quickly reach for less expensive solutions such as the purchase of staff training curricula, but it may be that reducing class size or providing emotional and instrumental support in the form of additional staffing, mental health consultation, etc., may make a greater difference. We would all probably agree that greater investment is needed, but how can we best improves the quality of the job for the provider as well as the quality of care for the child?

Conclusion

The fourth and last point to be considered in outlining this model of quality is to examine the implications of such a model for public policy. Huston notes that the public and policy makers are hesitant to take childcare "on" as a policy problem worth trying to fix. My thoughts are that childcare may be benefited by placing it in the arena of labor policy rather than only in the domain of early educational policy. This choice, of whether to view childcare as a work support rather than an early childhood intervention, calls to mind Gordon's history of the 1935 Social Security Act, *Pitied but not entitled* (Gordon, 1994). Because of white middle-class women's exemption from the need to work, and the payment of a family wage, women's labor has historically been obscured. For example, Gordon reports that from 1900–1930, over 90% of African American single mothers worked in domestic or farm work, yet both these occupations were exempted from unemployment insurance and labor protection policies (Gordon, 1994, pp. 22, 276). Gordon argues that labor policy has historically focused on men at work, while women have received attention through child and family policy administered through means-tested programs such as early educational intervention and welfare-style "relief". If we really mean to move women into the labor force, we have to also take a sanguine look at the ways in which the state must take responsibility for children, if the state no longer subsidizes women to take care of children in the unpaid context of the home.

Some data suggest that paying childcare workers more is associated with better care. In recent studies of an NICHD study sample of childcare homes (Burchinal et al., 2000), caregivers who were more emotionally positive and more responsive had children who were doing better later on in terms of school preparedness. Interestingly, informal forms of relative care, where relatives or friends agree to "watch" children while mothers work, have been found to be of lower quality than non-relative family day care by a provider who is motivated to pursue childcare as an occupation (Kontos et al., 1996). These data suggest that people who have good intentions to help out but who are not adequately rewarded do not always make the best providers of care over the long term. These findings are quite telling in light of Edin and Lein's (1995) portrayal of low-wage working parents' reliance on free care from relatives as one of the key ways to make ends meet. In Huston's analyses, families who benefited most from streamlined subsidy receipt were more likely to use center-based care. But some families will always prefer a family-based approach to their childcare needs, and we must find ways to test models of improvements in childcare quality through randomized design in these settings as well.

What Can We Do?

What are the solutions that follow from Huston (this volume) and my comments? The most obvious and regulable option is to cut down on the large number of children cared for by low-income providers in both home- and center-based contexts while also increasing reimbursement rates so that those providers can afford to care for fewer children. Group size has consistently been associated with quality of care (Elicker, Fortner-Wood, & Noppc, 1999; NICHD Early Child Care Research Network, 1996). When day care homes were in compliance with recommended age-weighted group size cutoffs, caregivers were able to provide more emotionally positive caregiving. It is likely that in these contexts, caregivers have greater resources (e.g., more of their own attention), fewer demands, and potentially more control than caregivers at the sites where group size is unwieldy.

How do we motivate a financially-strapped public to see the value of investing in high-quality childcare as a worthwhile public good? One way to do so is to highlight the costs. In my view, the costs are to three overlapping groups of people: overworked and exhausted childcare providers; stressed and unstably employed low-wage workers who cost companies much in absenteeism when their childcare breaks down; and most key to this discussion, children, to their schools and communities if they fail to be given the support they need to reach their full academic, social, and behavioral potential.

Acknowledgments

This work was completed with the support of the William T. Grant Foundation and the McCormick Tribune Foundation. The author gratefully acknowledges the research and editorial assistance of Breeze Luetke-Stahlman.

References

Arnold, D. H., McWilliams, L., & Arnold, E. H. (1998). Teacher discipline and child misbehavior in day care: Untangling causality with correlational data. *Developmental Psychology, 34*, 276–287.

Bartik, T. J. (1997). Short-term employment persistence for welfare recipients: The "effects" of wages, industry, occupation, and firm size. Unpublished manuscript.

Blau, D. M., & Mocan, H. N. (1999). The supply of quality in child care centers. *Review of Economics and Statistics, 84*, 483–496.

Burchinal, M. R., Roberts, J. E., Riggins, R., Zeisel, S. A., Neebe, E., & Bryant, D. (2000). Relating quality of center-based child care to early cognitive and language development longitudinally. *Child Development, 71*, 339–357.

Campbell, S. B., Shaw, D. S., & Gilliom, M. (2000). Early externalizing behavior problems: Toddlers and preschoolers at risk for later maladjustment. *Development and Psychopathology, 12,* 467–488.

Clarke-Stewart, K. A., Vandell, D. L., Burchinal, M., O'Brien, M., & McCartney, K. (2002). Do regulable features of child-care homes affect children's development? *Early Childhood Research Quarterly, 17,* 52–86.

Curbow, B., Spratt, K., Ungaretti, A., McDonnell, K., & Breckler, S. (2000). Development of the child care worker job stress inventory. *Early Childhood Research Quarterly, 15,* 515–536.

Edin, K., & Lein, L. (1995). *Making ends meet.* New York: Russell Sage Foundation.

Eisenberg, N., Cumberland, A., & Spinrad, T. L. (1998). Parental socialization of emotion. *Psychological Inquiry, 9,* 241–273.

Elicker, J., Fortner-Wood, C., & Noppc, I. C. (1999). The contexts of infant attachment in family child care. *Journal of Applied Developmental Psychology, 20,* 319–336.

Ellwood, D. (1988). *Poor support: Poverty in the American family.* New York: Basic Books.

Goldstein, N. E., Arnold, D. H., Rosenberg, J. L., Stowe, R. M., & Ortiz, C. (2001). Contagion of aggression in day care classrooms as a function of peer and teacher response. *Journal of Educational Psychology, 93,* 708–719.

Gordon, L. (1994). *Pitied but not entitled: Single mothers and the history of welfare, 1890–1935.* New York: Free Press.

Hoynes, H. (1999). The employment, earnings, and income of less skilled workers over the business cycle. In R. Blank & D. Card (Eds.), *Finding jobs: Work and welfare reform* (pp. 23–71). New York: Russell Sage Foundation.

Kalil, A., Corcoran, M. E., Danziger, S. K., Tolman, R., Seefeldt, K. S., Rosen, D., & Nam, Y. (1998). *Getting jobs, keeping jobs, and earning a living wage: Can welfare reform work?* (Discussion Paper No. 1170-98). Madison, WI: Institute for Research on Poverty, University of Wisconsin.

Kontos, S., Howes, C., & Galinsky, E. (1996). Does training make a difference to quality in family child care? *Early Childhood Research Quarterly, 11,* 427–445.

McLoyd, V. C., Jayaratne, T. E., Ceballo, R., & Borquez, J. (1994). Unemployment and work interruption among African American single mothers: Effects on parenting and adolescent socioemotional functioning. *Child Development, 65,* 562–589.

Menaghan, E. G., & Parcel, T. L. (1995). Social sources of change in children's home environments: The effects of parental occupational experiences and family conditions. *Journal of Marriage and the Family, 57,* 69–84.

Messing, K., Seifert, A. M., & Escalona, E. (1997). The 120-S Minute: Using analysis of work activity to prevent psychological distress among elementary school teachers. *Journal of Occupational Health Psychology, 2,* 45–62.

Moffitt, R. A. (2002). *From welfare to work: What the evidence shows* (Policy Brief No. 13). Washington, DC: Brookings Institution.

Mocan, H. N., & Tekin, E. (2000). *Nonprofit sector and part-time work: An analysis of employer-employee matched data of child care workers* (Working Paper No. 7977). Cambridge, MA: National Bureau of Economic Research

NICHD Early Child Care Research Network. (1996). Characteristics of infant child care: Factors contributing to positive caregiving. *Early Childhood Research Quarterly, 11,* 269–306.

Phillips, D., Mekos, D., Scarr, S., McCartney, K., & Abbott-Shim, M. (2000). Within and beyond the classroom door: Assessing quality in child care centers. *Early Childhood Research Quarterly, 15*, 475–496.

Pianta, R. C. (1999). *Enhancing relationships between children and teachers*. Washington, DC: American Psychological Association.

Raver, C. C. (2002a). Emotions matter: Making the case for the role of young children's emotional development for early school readiness. *Social Policy Report, 16*, 3–18.

Raver, C. C. (2002b). Does work pay, psychologically as well as economically? The effects of employment on depressive symptoms and parenting among low-income families. Unpublished manuscript.

Raver, C. C., & Knitzer, J. (2002). *Ready to enter: What research tells policymakers about strategies to promote social and emotional school readiness among three- and four-year-old children* (Policy Paper No. 3). New York: National Center for Children in Poverty, Columbia University.

Scarr, S., & Eisenburg, M. (1993). Child-care research: Issues, perspectives, and results. *Annual Review of Psychology, 44*, 613–644.

Webster-Stratton, C., Reid, M. J., & Hammond, M. (2001). Preventing conduct problems, promoting social competence: A parent and teacher partnership in Head Start. *Journal of Clinical Child Psychology, 30*, 283–302.

Whitebook, M., Howes, C., & Phillips, D. (1998). *Worthy work, unlivable wages: The National Child Care Staffing Study, 1988–1997*. Washington, DC: Center for the Child Care Workforce.

12

CHILDCARE FOR LOW-INCOME FAMILIES: PROBLEMS AND PROMISE

Martha Zaslow
Child Trends

Introduction

A recurrent theme in the chapter by Huston (this volume) is that of the *juxtaposition and integration* of differing approaches. The chapter underscores the progress that can be made when contrasting schools of thought or approaches are juxtaposed and successfully integrated, and the gaps and pitfalls that can occur with a lack of integration.

Huston juxtaposes and then integrates two research traditions to present a composite picture of the childcare experiences of low-income families: experimental evaluations of welfare reform programs, and longitudinal descriptive research focusing on childcare and its implications for children's development. There is real progress here, both within each of the separate bodies of research and then also from their juxtaposition and integration. The integration provides a more complete picture and also presents us with a new set of issues and questions.

Huston also juxtaposes two separate policy traditions in the United States: one focusing on childcare as a support to employment, and one focusing on childcare as fostering early childhood development. Here, however, Huston contends that lack of integration is a problem: there are separate policies, funding streams, and funding agencies for each policy tradition. She argues that a lack of integration across these policy streams is an obstacle to making progress in policy and programs for low-income families. I am going to differ from the perspective that the two policy streams are proceeding on entirely separate tracks. I will point to what I see as some encouraging signs of integration across these policy streams, and pose the question of whether these steps are cursory and perhaps fleeting, or rather reflect the beginning of a systematic integration.

Integration of Findings From Two Research Traditions

A central feature of the paper by Huston is its presentation and then integration of research findings from two separate bodies of work: (1) the experimental evaluations of welfare-to-work programs that incorporate a focused examination of impacts on children, and (2) descriptive longitudinal work that provides a fine-grained examination of children's early experiences in childcare and within the family, and the role that each of these contexts plays (separately and jointly) in children's development over time. (See Zaslow & Tout, forthcoming, for a further discussion of the different information these bodies of work can yield in considering the experiences of childcare by children in low-income families since welfare reform.)

In what I believe to be a breakthrough in understanding the impacts of childcare policies on low-income families and children, the Next Generation research group has analyzed the data from eight different welfare reform programs, dividing these programs into two groups according to whether or not the program provided enhanced childcare services to those in the program as opposed to the control group. That is, some of the welfare-to-work programs studied just provided more of the same childcare benefits to those participants who worked more and needed childcare more, but other programs studied provided qualitatively and/or quantitatively different, "enhanced" services to those in the program group. As Huston summarizes, the findings of the new analyses point to impacts on both the parental and child generation when there were enhanced childcare services in the program group. Children, especially young children, in families who received enhanced childcare services experienced greater increases in their participation in center-based childcare as opposed to home-based care. In the parental generation, mothers reported that childcare was not as great a barrier to employment, had increased use of subsidies, and reduced out-of-pocket expenses for childcare. The childcare subsidies contributed to more substantial gains in the overall economic resources of these families.

These findings provide evidence that the childcare-related elements of programs and policies, and the way these are implemented, *matter* both to employment and economic outcomes and to children's experiences. The fact that the data come from experimental studies, and that the patterns held when combining data from programs that differed on a range of features other than the childcare benefits, strengthens our confidence that the differences in experiences are attributable to the childcare treatment differences.

The results provoke a new set of questions. We know from this work that a package or set of differing childcare services and resources mattered for maternal and child outcomes. However, programs were assigned in the Next Generation categorization as providing enhanced childcare services if *any* of a set of policies or implementation practices were present. We do not know which was most important or which mattered to which outcomes. Was it the increase in the efficiency of subsidy payments, the provision of further information about childcare to families, the requirement to use regulated care when receiving a subsidy, or the encouragement to use formal childcare that was important to the outcomes for children and for mothers? The set of enhanced services includes elements that could be characterized as features of policy and also as approaches to implementation. For example, one might consider it a feature of policy that childcare subsidies could be used only for regulated care in certain programs, but an approach to implementation in other programs that childcare resource and referral personnel were co-located with the welfare office and more accessible to provide information on the subsidy application process and on locating childcare.

This distinction between policy and implementation practices is key in the research on childcare experiences of low-income families (Adams, Snyder, & Sandfort, 2002). From this first important step by the Next Generation research group, we cannot distinguish whether one or the other, or the combination, underlies the findings. New research following up on this set of findings will be critical, and should be forthcoming in a new set of experimental studies now in the planning phase to focus on childcare subsidy policy and practices in states. Hopefully the new work will enable us to understand whether the patterns observed occur only within the context of welfare-to-work programs, or also occur when enhanced childcare services are provided to working-poor families with no recent connection to the welfare system.

While the data analyzed by the Next Generation team has the particular strength of experimental design, the NICHD Study of Early Child Care has the different strength of extremely fine-grained examination of the quality and continuity of both early childcare experiences and of early experiences within the family, and consideration of both the childcare and family environments as predictors of children's development over time. From this different research tradition, as Huston summarizes it, we glean a critical new finding: while the quality of childcare in centers did not differ substantially for low-income as opposed to higher-income families in the sample, the home-based childcare settings experienced by these two groups did differ in quality, with the care received by low-income families of lesser quality. Further, from this and other studies (e.g., Tout et al., 2001), we learn that children in low-income families are more likely to participate in home-based childcare than are children in higher-income families. As a result, overall, the care received by children in low-income families in the early years is of lower quality.

One question raised by this work is whether and how it might be possible to improve the quality of home-based childcare experienced by children in low-income families. A recently released report by the U.S. General Accounting Office (September 2002) indicates that a substantial proportion (likely a majority)[1] of the funds that states are using to improve the quality of childcare is going to center care. The reasons for this are not clear. Is this occurring because center care is more accessible (in the sense that in this setting it is possible to work with more caregivers

---

[1]The GAO report notes that in 34 states that tracked the type of provider targeted by quality improvement initiatives, when six specific types of initiatives were considered, two thirds of the funds used to improve quality were going to center care. However colleagues at the Child Care Bureau (personal communication, 11/02) note that this figure needs to be qualified in that expenditures on resource and referral, enhanced inspections, and other activities to improve quality were not considered. Further, other states might have allocated their funding differently.

and in more spaces or classrooms at one location); are home-based childcare providers less interested or willing to participate in quality enhancement activities; or is it perceived to be more difficult to bring about improvements in the quality of home-based care? A special focus on enhancing the quality of home-based childcare (with both licensed and legally-unlicensed providers) is warranted given the quality differential noted in the NICHD study and the disproportionate reliance on such care by low-income families.

When the results of these two sets of studies, experimental and longitudinal/ descriptive, are juxtaposed and integrated, new insights and hypotheses emerge. Enhanced childcare assistance differentially increases young children's participation in center-based as opposed to home-based childcare, and the center-based care received by low-income families is not markedly different in quality from that received by higher-income families. Further, the NICHD study of early childcare suggests that participation in center-based care, above and beyond the influence of childcare quality, tends to foster young children's early cognitive development (though with less favorable social and emotional outcomes). Thus, the provision of enhanced childcare services may yield increased participation in a form of care with the potential to benefit the cognitive development and academic school readiness of children from low-income families. We need to follow up on this hypothesis, which is based on the integration of two research traditions, by explicitly examining a model testing whether enhanced childcare assistance contributes to improved early learning through increased exposure of children in low-income families to formal childcare (with a more elaborated model perhaps also considering the contribution of subsidies to the overall economic status of the family).

Policies Supporting Employment as Opposed to Early Development: Juxtaposition Alone or Emerging Integration?

Turning now to the issue of childcare policy traditions, Huston argues that two sets of policies are proceeding on parallel tracks with little integration. Indeed, Huston notes that there are points at which the two sets of policies have the potential for conflict. These policy "strands" (a) provide funding for childcare primarily as a support for maternal employment, and (b) support childcare and early education as a source of developmental enrichment.

National data on patterns of childcare use support the basic contention that families use early childhood care and education settings both as a support for employment and to foster their children's cognitive and social development. In a recent set of analyses with data from the National Survey of America's Families, colleagues and I found that while young children are indeed more likely to participate in nonparental care settings when their most involved parent is employed, nevertheless, between 44 and 57% of young children participate in nonparental care settings even when this parent is not employed (with the percent varying by family income). In accord with this pattern, we gave our paper the title, "Early Care and Education: Work Support for Families and Developmental Opportunity for Young Children" (Tout et al., 2001). It is noteworthy that use of nonparental care on a regular basis when the parent is not employed occurs less often among lower-than higher-income families, suggesting more limited use or perhaps access to early care environments for the purpose of enhancing children's development.

I also concur with Huston's contention that the two strands of policy can conflict. At the Head Start Research Conference held in June 2002, Rachel Cohen (Cohen, 2002) presented the results of a set of analyses which indicate that the overall pattern of favorable impacts of Early Head Start on children's development three years after enrollment did not hold for the subgroup of families receiving welfare. She hypothesized that the work requirements of welfare reform made it difficult for parents to participate actively in the family components of Early Head Start, and she pointed to data indicating that the program participation of families receiving welfare dropped off over time. Thus policies that support and require employment may indeed conflict with those that aim to foster early development, particularly those with family involvement components.

I acknowledge and agree with Huston's point about two policy traditions, and that the two sometimes conflict. Yet at the same time I also see more evidence of integration across the policy streams than she suggests.

Policies Focusing on Support for Employment

First, the existing policy stream that focuses on childcare as a support for employment has important components dealing with childcare quality, and thus the enhancement of children's development. The Child Care and Development Fund (CCDF) is the funding stream that focuses on provision of childcare as a support to employment, and state childcare administrators quite clearly view support for employment as their primary goal. Administrators express concern over the difficult choices they need to make in terms of establishing income eligibility thresholds for subsidies, co-payment levels, and subsidy payment levels, and how these influence the proportion of eligible families who will receive subsidies.

Yet this funding stream has an important component focusing on the enhancement of children's development. States are required to spend at least 4% of their CCDF funds on activities to improve the quality and availability of childcare (the "quality set aside"). Additional CCDF funds are "earmarked" for the improvement of access to and quality of infant and toddler care, for resource and referral services, and for school-age childcare, as well as for further quality-related activities (see overview in Tout & Zaslow, 2003).

How serious or enduring are the efforts to improve quality through the set-aside? According to the previously mentioned GAO report, many states are exceeding expenditures of 4% for quality-related activities. Of 42 states responding to a GAO survey, 23 reported spending beyond the required amounts, and states allocated up to 38% of CCDF funds toward quality activities. According to the Child Care Bureau, "in FY 2001, states spent $716 million in current and prior year CCDF funds (including state funds and funds transferred from TANF) to improve the quality of childcare services—this accounts for nine percent...of combined Federal and State expenditures."[2]

Research by Toni Porter and her colleagues on state use of the quality set-aside (Porter et al., 2002), as well as information collected by GAO point to a range of quality activities in the states, with funding going to initiatives that increase caregiver compensation and improve retention, on-site as well as off-site training for caregivers, the provision of incentives for facilities to move towards accreditation or other enhanced quality levels, improved enforcement of childcare regulations (e.g., through more frequent inspections of childcare facilities), funding to resource and referral agencies for a range of activities (such as helping families locate care for a child with disabilities), and safety and equipment improvements.

While state administrators are supportive of the quality set-aside, they are concerned about the difficulty of improving quality across the system with the current level of funding (Tout & Zaslow, 2003). Collins et al. (2000) report that many states distribute the funds to small, local projects or individual providers. Mezey et al. (2002) also highlight the promising but often small-scale efforts being undertaken in states. They recommend an increased percentage set-aside and also note the need for more evaluation of current efforts as well as technical assistance to states. In addition, the GAO report cautions that there has been, as yet, little systematic evaluation of the effectiveness of the quality initiatives. It points out that some evaluations are currently underway, such as the study of the provider wage initiative in Washington state, and the study of tiered reimbursement as a quality enhancement strategy in Minnesota (Tout & Zaslow, forthcoming). Porter and her colleagues are currently working on a project to provide tools and strategies for states to more systematically evaluate their quality initiatives. The experimental evaluations of subsidy policies will provide an important vehicle for examining specific quality enhancement strategies. But the point stands that at present we know little about the effectiveness of the strategies being undertaken. The states have engaged in a period of experimentation in terms of quality initiatives. It is time to harvest this experimentation through rigorous study.

There are further signs that the federal government views the funding stream that supports maternal employment through the provision of childcare subsidies as having the potential to enrich children's early development as well. The President's Good Start Grow Smart Initiative stresses the importance of early

---

[2]Personal communication (11/02) from colleagues at the Child Care Bureau (in alphabetical order): Brenda Coakley, Stephanie Curenton, Pia Divine, Ivelisse Martinez-Beck, and Karen Tvedt.

cognitive development for children's progress towards reading and success in school, and proposes to strengthen the range of early childhood settings to support early literacy. The initiative calls for a states "to develop quality criteria for early childhood education including voluntary guidelines on pre-reading and language skills activities that align with State K-12 standards" (p. 2).

In response to the Good Start Grow Smart Initiative, the Child Care Bureau is asking states to include in their state plans for the Child Care and Development Fund, to be submitted in July 2003, a discussion of the steps they are taking to develop early learning guidelines to apply across the range of early care and education settings, including childcare. Again, it will be important to ask how substantial a step this will be. These are voluntary guidelines, intended to provide a vision or set of goals in each state. Yet the inclusion of early learning guidelines in the state CCDF plans is again an indicator that funding streams are not seen at the federal level as focusing strictly on one goal or another: supporting employment or enhancing early development.

Policies Focusing on Fostering Early Development

I would argue that policies aimed primarily at fostering early development are also showing movement toward integration. One key example involves efforts to increase access to (and in some instances the supply of) childcare as part of policies and programs focusing specifically on enhancing early development. A noteworthy example pertains to Head Start. As indicated by Paulsell and colleagues (2002), "in 1997, the Head Start Bureau established collaboration offices in all states to facilitate linkages with state prekindergarten and childcare programs. In 1998, the Child Care and Head Start Bureaus launched a new training and technical assistance initiative— Quality in Linking Together: Early Education Partnerships (QUILT)—to help Head Start programs and child care providers develop partnerships" (p. 79). This collaborative work acknowledged that children participating in Head Start programs also often need to participate in childcare because these are usually part-day programs. These collaborations foster the coordination of programming, space, and funding arrangements to foster continuity for children and families across care environments. Thus, a program that aims to foster children's early development, Head Start, is acknowledging the need to provide care in connection with employment.

The collaborations that have been perhaps most carefully studied to date are those that involve Early Head Start-childcare partnerships (see Paulsell et al., 2002, for a discussion of such initiatives). When families participate in Early Head Start, if they need childcare beyond the hours that Early Head Start makes such care available, they must participate in settings that meet the Head Start performance standards. Yet in many communities there is a lack of appropriate care for infants and toddlers, let alone care that meets the performance standards. Accordingly, Early Head Start programs have developed partnerships with childcare providers to work jointly toward the development of new facilities that meet performance standards, or to move existing facilities toward improving quality so that they can meet the standards. Different funding strategies have been used to support these partnerships. These include having states pay for full-day infant/toddler care that meets Head Start performance standards, and having Early Head Start pay for the quality improvements, complementing funding through the subsidy system.

Observational studies of efforts to bring community-based infant/toddler childcare up to the Head Start performance standards confirm that the partnerships can lead to observable improvements in quality (Paulsell et al., 2001). What is important to point out in the present context is that the funding stream generally seen as fostering early development is here being used to increase childcare slots and support maternal employment.

Another example of this integrative strategy comes in the location of public prekindergarten programs in childcare settings. Georgia, which has a universal prekindergarten program, places these programs both in community childcare settings and in schools. At present, more than half of the programs are located in childcare facilities, strengthening the system of care to support maternal employment. Other states in which prekindergarten programs are being located in private as well as public settings include New York and Illinois.

State Programs that Combine the Two Policy Goals

Finally, in the past decade, we have seen the emergence of state-level initiatives that explicitly encompass the goals of supporting employment and fostering early development; that inherently integrate the two policy goals. I am thinking here of such state initiatives as Smart Start in North Carolina, First Steps in South Carolina, and First Five (funded by Proposition 10) in California. Interestingly, these initiatives are framed around the goals of supporting children's school readiness. Family's economic well-being and the quality of early care and education are both viewed as important contributors to children's school readiness. For example, the legislation for South Carolina's First Steps program calls explicitly for programs that strengthen families, including their economic well-being, as well as that enhance the quality of children's early care settings (Holmes, 2002). The First Steps initiative provides funding both to expand the number of families receiving childcare subsidies, and to improve the quality of childcare (Child Trends, 2003). In North Carolina, where approximately 70% of the Smart Start funding goes to improving childcare, Donna Bryant (personal communication, October 2002) estimates that about half of this goes to increasing capacity and the other half to improving quality, with the specific proportions varying somewhat across counties.

Here we need to ask whether there is evidence that such initiatives can simultaneously increase subsidies and childcare capacity, and improve the quality of early childhood settings. Evaluations of each of the state initiatives I have named are ongoing and will begin to yield some insights into these questions.

In conclusion, I do not see the strict segregation of policy streams that is noted in the paper by Huston. Rather, I think that we are seeing the emergence of (a) of policies intended to support employment that are providing funding and program components aimed at enhancing early development; (b) policies intended to support early development that are allocating funding and program components to increase the supply of childcare to support employment; and (c) state-initiated policies to support children's school readiness that involve integrations of the two sets of goals, supporting both early development and parental employment.

A key remaining question is whether these indicators of integrative efforts across the policy streams represent the starting point of meaningful change.

Acknowledgments

The author would like to thank the following colleagues (noted in alphabetical order) for their extremely helpful feedback on an earlier draft of this manuscript: Brenda Coakley, Stephanie Curenton, Pia Divine, Ivelisse Martinez-Beck, Kristin Moore, Kathryn Tout, and Karen Tvedt.

References

Adams, G., Snyder, K., & Sandfort, J. (2002). *Getting and retaining child care assistance: How policy and practice influence parents' experiences* (Assessing the New Federalism Occasional Paper No. 55). Washington, DC: Urban Institute.

Child Trends. (2002). *First Steps and further steps: Early outcomes and lessons learned from South Carolina's school readiness initiative.* Washington, DC: Author.

Cohen, R. (2002). Discussion at Roundtable on Welfare Reform and Head Start at the Head Start Research Meeting, Washington, DC.

Collins, A. M., Layzer, J. I., Kreader, J. L., Werner, A., & Glantz, F. B. (2000). *National Study of Child Care for Low-Income Families: State and community substudy interim report.* Cambridge, MA: Abt Associates.

Good Start, Grow Smart: The Bush Administration's Early Childhood Initiative. Retrieved from http://www.whitehouse.gov/infocus/earlychildhood/sect6.html

Holmes, B. (2002). *History of South Carolina's First Steps legislation* (Working paper). Columbia, SC: Office of First Steps.

Mezey, J., Schumacher, R., Greenberg, M., Lombardi, J., & Hutchins, J. (2002). Unfinished agenda: *Child care for low-income families since 1996—Implications for federal and state policy.* Washington, DC: Center for Law and Social Policy.

Paulsell, D., Kisker, E., Raikes, H., & Love, J. (2001, April). *Child care in Early Head Start: Challenges, successes, and strategies for supporting quality.* Paper presented at the Biennial Meeting of the Society for Research in Child Development, Minneapolis, MN.

Paulsell, D., Cohen, J., Stieglitz, Lurie-Hurvitz, E., Fenichel, E., & Kisker, E. (2002). *Partnerships for quality: Improving infant-toddler child care for low-income families.* Paper prepared for the Child Care Bureau, Administration for Children and Families, U.S. Department of Health and Human Services, by ZERO TO THREE and Mathematica Policy Research.

Porter, T., Habeeb, S., Mabon, S., Robertson, A., Kreader, L., & Collins, A. (2002). *Assessing Child Care and Development Fund (CCDF) investments in child care quality: A study of selected state initiatives.* New York: Bank Street College of Education.

Tout, K., & Zaslow, M. (2003). Public investments in child care quality: Needs, challenges, and opportunities. In R. M. Lerner, F. Jacobs, & D. Wertleib (eds), *Promoting positive child, adolescent, and family development: A handbook of program and policy innovations* (Vol. 1, pp. 339–366). Thousand Oaks, CA: Sage.

Tout, K., & Zaslow, M. (in press). *Tiered reimbursement in Minnesota child care settings. A report of the Minnesota Child Care Policy Research Partnership.* Washington, DC: Minnesota Department of Children, Families and Learning.

Tout, K., Zaslow, M., Papillo, A. R., & Vandivere, S. (2001). *Early care and education: Work support for families and developmental opportunity for young children* (Assessing the New Federalism Occasional Paper No. 51). Washington, DC: Urban Institute.

U.S. General Accounting Office. (2002). *Child care: States have undertaken a variety of quality improvement initiatives, but more evaluations of effectiveness are needed.* Washington, DC: Author.

Zaslow, M., & Tout, K. (in press). Welfare reform and children's experiences of child care. In *Welfare reform and children.* Washington, DC: U.S. Department of Health and Human Services, Office of the Assistant Secretary for Planning and Evaluation.

IV

How are the Challenges of Managing Work and Family Experienced by Low-Income Men and Women?

13

"MAKING A WAY OUT OF NO WAY": HOW MOTHERS MEET BASIC FAMILY NEEDS WHILE MOVING FROM WELFARE TO WORK

Susan Clampet-Lundquist
University of Pennsylvania
Kathryn Edin
Northwestern University
Andrew London
Syracuse University
Ellen Scott
University of Oregon
Vicki Hunter
Kent State University

Introduction

Monica is a 45-year-old white high school graduate from the high-crime, job-poor Kensington section of Philadelphia. She was receiving cash welfare, food stamps, and Medicaid when President Clinton signed the Personal Responsibility and Work Opportunity Reconciliation Act (PRWORA) in 1996. To meet her new work requirement, Monica started stuffing envelopes at a small firm within walking distance of her home, which provided full-time, minimum wage employment from April through November each year. Her low-wages ensured continued eligibility for a small amount of cash welfare and food stamps plus a medical card. However, the annual layoff hit hard, as it took the welfare department two to three months to adjust her benefits, so for two to three months each year she had little to no income. To resolve her dilemma, she tried to find year-round employment but she was unable to do so. In the interim, she resorted to selling prescription drugs illegally to local drug addicts.

When she started her job stuffing envelopes, both of Monica's children, ages 7 and 12, were still young enough to qualify for subsidized childcare. Even though Monica knew welfare was supposed to provide these subsidies, her fight to secure them took nearly two years. Her repeated requests for assistance churned through multiple caseworkers who claimed, one after another, that the forms had been "messed up" by the previous caseworker. During this time, her common-law husband watched her children during the summer and before and after school, refraining from searching for work himself. This meant he could contribute no resources to her strained family budget. After she received the childcare subsidy, she paid the children's grandmother to watch the youngest before and after school, and the eldest, now 13 years old, was on his own.

Throughout the transition from welfare to work, the family's health needs were covered by Medicaid. One month, though, her pay check included some overtime hours and her caseworker told her that her earnings that month ($1,000 before taxes) pushed her over the income limit.[1] She went without coverage that month, a potentially serious situation for Monica, as she was soon after diagnosed with cervical cancer.

Moving from welfare to work is about more than trading a welfare check for a paycheck. For Monica, family and fiscal management before welfare reform were never easy, but the welfare benefits were at least stable, and she did not have work-related expenses such as childcare. She was the one who supervised the children since she remained at home. And though her small cash welfare allotment never covered all her bills, she could count on its steady stream of income each month, plus the food stamps and medical card. She filled the gap between her welfare benefits and her expenses by relying on the contributions of family, and a trip or two to the food pantry each year.

Monica responded to the new mandates of welfare reform by going to work. Once she made the transition, she faced months with hardly any legitimate source of income ($10–15 from the welfare grant) because of the seasonal nature of her work and the delayed response of the welfare department. Her friends and family,

---

[1] According to the State Policy Documentation Project, the eligibility level for Medicaid recipients in Pennsylvania is $1,088/month for a family of three. If Monica did not count her husband in her family composition, she would have been just on the cusp of eligibility for Medicaid. More importantly, she was still eligible for Transitional Medicaid, which extends to 185% of poverty, and her income that month was well within this range.

already stretched thin, could not fill this large income gap, but turning to crime to pay her bills left her both ashamed and fearful. Good mothers, she believed, did not break the law.

Like many low-wage workers, Monica desperately needed the work supports that were, in theory, available to parents who left welfare for employment. But obtaining those benefits meant complying with a plethora of new requirements, including the need to submit a set of forms and her pay stubs in a timely manner each month. Her fight to obtain her childcare subsidy involved repeated trips and phone calls to the welfare office, and her "mistake" of working overtime left her without health coverage for a month, due to a caseworker error.

Nine months out of the year, her earnings exceeded what she'd received from welfare, but her minimum wage job did not generate enough surplus funds to cover the months when little legitimate source of income was coming in. Since Monica, like most parents in our sample, viewed raising her children as her most important job, her struggle to ensure their well-being in the face of this annual fiscal crisis left her feeling uncertain about whether the children were benefiting from her efforts to play by the rules (see also Scott, Edin, London, & Mazelis, 2001).

The authors of PRWORA were not oblivious to the fact that for the typical welfare recipient employment alone might well fall short of providing enough disposable income to meet basic family needs. Accordingly, the federal law mandates that all new state TANF programs ensure transitional childcare, food stamps, and Medicaid to those leaving welfare for low-wage work. But it is one thing to have these provisions on the books and another to successfully deliver them to the families who so desperately need them. In the new world of welfare, securing such benefits requires detailed knowledge of the benefits the welfare office is supposed to provide, the cooperation of a competent, well-trained caseworker, a family situation that allows the family to "take up" these benefits in the form the welfare department provides them, and just plain luck.

In the years following welfare reform, researchers have found that the take-up rates for childcare, food stamps, and Medicaid are lower than should be expected. Nationally, only 10–15% of eligible children receive a childcare subsidy from the Childcare and Development Fund—the main source of federal funding (Giannarelli & Barsimantov, 2000). These eligible children include those whose parents have never been on welfare, parents who have left welfare, and parents who are still on the welfare rolls. Although the national-level data do not allow us to distinguish the welfare from the non-welfare recipients of childcare subsidy recipients, some state welfare-leaver studies show that the percentage of welfare-leavers who receive childcare subsidies is higher than that of the larger eligible population. However, in many of these states, less than one third of the welfare-leavers reported any childcare subsidy use (Schumacher & Greenberg, 1999).

Even before welfare reform was implemented in the states, a steady decline in participation in the Food Stamp Program (FSP) among the pool of eligible families was evident, and this trend has grown over time. Between 1994 and 1999, there was a 40% drop in food stamp usage nationwide. Using household-level data from the Current Population Survey, Wilde et al. (2000) concluded that although 28% of the decline in the mid- to late-1990s could be attributed a drop in the number of families who were income-eligible, over one half of the decline was due to a decrease in the proportion of income-eligible people who participate. Most relevant to this analysis, however, is the astonishing drop in FSP participation for those families who move off of cash welfare, the majority of whom continue to be eligible. Using data from the 1999 wave of the NSAF, Zedlewski (2001) found that two thirds of families who left welfare between 1997 and 1999 also left the Food Stamp Program, even though most of these families were still income-eligible.

Welfare-leavers can have a difficult time retaining their Medicaid benefits too. In an analysis of the 1997 NSAF, Garrett and Holahan (2000) found that despite the special Medicaid provisions for welfare-leavers, a large proportion of welfare-leavers reported no Medicaid benefits for themselves and their children. At the time of the NSAF interview, 4 of 10 welfare-leavers received Medicaid or another form of state public health insurance, and about 2 of 10 were covered by private or employer-sponsored health plans. However, 41% remained uninsured.[2] Most of these uninsured leavers remained income-eligible for Medicaid. In fact, almost 60% had incomes below the federal poverty guidelines. Yet even in this very low-income group of recent leavers, only 44% had Medicaid.[3] Although some of these uninsured welfare-leavers may have used up their time limit for Transitional Medicaid, fully one third of the women who left welfare within the last six months were uninsured—a time period clearly within the range of Transitional Medicaid.

As we will show, a sizeable portion of our respondents, particularly those in Philadelphia, lost their childcare, food stamps, or Medicaid benefits at some point during our study. When they talked about losing their food stamps or Medicaid benefits, many of our respondents in both Cleveland and Philadelphia used the language of "sanctioning." However, official sanctioning does not occur when recipients miss appointments or when paperwork is filled out incorrectly or lost. Rather, when these events occur, cases can be closed. Although the effect on the client is essentially the same—the loss of benefits—these two actions differ in terms of how quickly people can reinstate their benefits. When cases are closed, recipients can usually get their benefits reinstated as soon as they turn in the proper documents or keep an appointment with their caseworker. Sanctioning practices

---

[2] These percentages do not add to 100% because some respondents reported multiple sources of coverage.

[3] The children of welfare-leavers fared better than their parents, as half of them received Medicaid or another public health insurance and only 25% were uninsured. This was probably due to newly implemented health insurance programs for children (SCHIP), available in all states, which provide benefits to children whose parents earn less than 200% of the poverty threshold regardless of their parent's past or current relationship to the welfare department.

vary by state and they remain in effect for a proscribed period of time. Furthermore, the welfare department counts sanctions and case closures differently. When states report on their sanctioning rate, these figures do not include cases that have been closed either because of procedural issues or caseworker error. In their analysis of over 1,000 families who were currently or recently receiving welfare, Cherlin et al. (2002) found that when families lost benefits, it was usually due to missed appointments or problems with paperwork, rather than violations of work or child support requirements. In the Cherlin study, 17% of these families reported a partial or full loss of benefits in the past two years "because the welfare office said they were not following the rules" (p. 395).[4] The primary rule violations turned out to be missing appointments or having problems with paperwork, and these violations do not result in official sanctioning, but rather case closure, often at the caseworker's discretion. These families came from three cities—Boston, Chicago, and San Antonio—and the rate of benefits lost varied across the cities, reflecting differences in welfare reform implementation and caseworker practices. Twenty-six percent of the families in Chicago reported losing their benefits, compared to 15% in San Antonio and 10% in Boston. Similar to other studies, Cherlin et al. found that families who lost their benefits were more likely to have worse health, lower education, and more children than those who did not lose their benefits, indicating that families with factors linked to poorer employment outcomes are also vulnerable to losing their benefits.

Thus far, we have only cited statistics on take-up rates of publicly subsidized benefits. Another possible source of support for women moving from welfare to work is their individual private safety nets. Researchers have found that, indeed, some low-income people are able to rely on kin and friends for babysitting, food, or financial support (Edin & Lein, 1997; Stack 1974). However, the celebrated tight network of support that Carol Stack found in The Flats not only has the potential to strain one's individual resources, but the level of resources exchanged also pales in comparison to that exchanged through more affluent networks (Riley & Eckenrode, 1986). Those who have few resources individually tend not to have connections with people much different than themselves (Hogan, Eggebeen, & Clogg, 1993; Roschelle, 1997). In this chapter, we will also examine the types of private safety net supports that the respondents in our sample draw from to cover their childcare, food, and medical expenses.

We use data from a longitudinal, in-depth, qualitative study of families in Cleveland and Philadelphia to tell the story—from the viewpoint of families—of how they struggled to meet basic needs when they transitioned from welfare to employment. In this analysis, we examine how families in two quite different policy regimes managed the challenges of meeting their food, childcare, and medical care needs. For each expense domain, we look at the role of the public and private safety nets. We first analyze the transitional benefits each state is supposed to

---

[4] They excluded the families who had lost their eligibility to these benefits from this measure.

provide, and the constraints within the service delivery that may affect take-up rates. Second, we look at what non-public sources of support families turn to in addition to or in lieu of these state benefits and find that personal networks and private charities play an important role for some people. However, we find that families still can end up falling through the public and private safety nets and suffer material hardship.

Methods

In this paper, we analyzed a longitudinal ethnographic sample of 74 welfare recipients from Cleveland (N=40) and Philadelphia (N=34). The ethnographic study was a part of the larger Manpower Demonstration Research Corporation's Project on Devolution and Urban Change, a study of four urban counties (see Quint et al. [1999] for more details about the larger Urban Change study).[5] This larger study incorporated research on the implementation of welfare reform, and the impact of welfare reform on neighborhood institutions, as well as other components measuring the effect of welfare reform at the county level. A survey was conducted in all four counties in two separate waves in order to gain a broader look at the effect of welfare reform on families. We use data from this survey throughout our findings as a backdrop for findings from our smaller sample. In the ethnographic phase of the study, researchers in each of the four counties chose three to four moderate to high-poverty neighborhoods from which to draw a sample of 10–15 families. In Philadelphia and Cleveland, we chose two African American neighborhoods, and one white neighborhood. One of the African American neighborhoods in each city had a poverty rate of 40% or above, and the other two neighborhoods, one African American and one white, had poverty rates just over 30%. In each neighborhood, interviewers contacted respondents through local neighborhood institutions, through fliers, by going door-to-door in the selected neighborhoods, and through referrals from other participants. All respondents received cash welfare at recruitment, all were at least 18 years old, and all had at least one child under 18. We followed each family for three to four years, beginning soon after the implementation of welfare reform in each city. There was very little attrition among our respondents since we maintained contact with them in between annual interviews. In Philadelphia, we conducted baseline interviews in fall 1997, and in Cleveland, from winter 1997 to summer 1998.

---

[5] Because welfare practices are decided on state and county levels, Urban Change focused on counties rather than cities. Philadelphia is unique in that its city and county boundaries are the same. Cleveland is part of Cuyahoga County, but all of our ethnographic respondents reside in the city of Cleveland. The other two counties are Miami-Dade and Los Angeles, where the ethnographic study focused on immigrant populations. Cleveland and Philadelphia were the most similar in terms of industrial history and current racial composition.

Data were collected primarily through a series of in-depth in-home interviews we held with respondents once each year. In these interviews, we asked participants about experiences with caseworkers; knowledge of the specifics of welfare reform; attempts at finding jobs; work, training, and educational histories; relationships with their children and boyfriends/spouses; health; neighborhoods; material hardships; and network supports, among other topics. We also asked for a detailed accounting of each family's income and expenditures over the last year. Each year, the interviews lasted between three and nine hours, and often occurred over several meetings. In between the annual interviews, interviewers kept in regular contact with respondents, either by phone or by dropping by for a brief chat or interview, and either recorded their observations in fieldnotes or taped the interviews and phone conversations. We taped these interviews, transcribed them, and coded both transcripts and fieldnotes in machine-readable form.

Since we are focusing on the transition from welfare to work in this analysis, for most of this chapter, we only use data from the respondents who worked at some point during the course of the study (Philadelphia: $N=28$; Cleveland: $N=31$). These workers include those who moved off of TANF cash benefits entirely, or those who combined (formal) work and cash welfare. Therefore, when percentages are given about how many respondents received childcare subsidies, etc., we use only respondents who worked as a denominator. However, when we discuss accessing network and institutional resources to cover food expenses, or when we analyze food and medical hardships, we include the entire sample.

Much of this chapter analyzes how transitional benefits are or are not used by the respondents as they move from welfare to work. This story of implementation is one-sided, as we use data only from current and former welfare recipients rather than from their caseworkers. Understandably, this limited perspective raises a methodological question about whether we are getting an accurate picture. Fortunately, in the implementation component of the Urban Change study, Quint and Widom (2001) studied the same welfare offices that our respondents used. They interviewed and observed caseworkers about their provision of food stamps and Medicaid benefits. Their findings coincide with ours, namely, that although caseworkers claimed to the interviewers that they told recipients about the availability of benefits in their one-on-one meetings with them, they were less likely to do so in practice.

Findings

By the end of the study, respondents in both Philadelphia and Cleveland who worked reported significant gains on average over what they were taking in at baseline, and had more income (net work-related expenses) than those respondents who were not working.[6] Workers in both cities said that by the end of the study, they were able to provide their children with more of the material goods than they had before. Analyzing 1997–1999 panel data from the Women's Employment Survey, Danziger et al. (2002) had similar findings. Women who worked and were no longer receiving cash assistance were better off financially than those who were on welfare and not working. However, nearly one half of the welfare-leavers were still living below the poverty line.

These income gains in our sample were not, however, purely due to their labor market effort (Scott, Edin, London, & Kissane, 2001). In fact, they reflect the rather large growth in the work-based safety net over the last few years. In the pre-welfare reform environment, Edin and Lein (1997) found that single women who worked low-wage jobs averaged $180 more each month than their welfare counterparts, but that gain was more than swamped by the additional costs of going to work. Since then, most states have used the new flexibility that PROWRA allowed to dramatically enhance earnings disregards. That, together with the expansion of the Earned Income Tax Credit (EITC), the increased availability of childcare subsidies, and the extension of Medicaid benefits to some low-wage working parents and their families, was a crucial part of the package that made moving to formal work a more attainable goal for the families in our study.

However, these averages mask a great deal of variance within the sample; for example, some women had to pay childcare out of pocket, while others were able to use a childcare subsidy or to place their children in the free or low-cost care of a relative. This variability of "income" sources and support occurred for two reasons. First, the method the states used to deliver transitional benefits was not always consistent and this may have reduced take-up. Second, the private safety nets these parents and children had to fall back on were far stronger for some than for others. The inequality of the public and private resources meant that we observed a broad array of outcomes for families and children. For those lucky enough to access the array of transitional benefits the welfare office was supposed to supply, the cost of going to work was radically reduced, and parents and children saw meaningful material gains, especially given the EITC. For those with strong private safety nets, a similar story can be told. However, what is not told by these numbers is how onerous the process of gleaning support from the state is, a process that, in itself, can frustrate parents' efforts to remain employed and adequately fulfill the responsibilities of parenting. Nor do these numbers tell the story of the often costly process of securing private support, or of its questionable quality in some cases.

---

[6] Scott et al. (2001) calculated income change for the full samples in Philadelphia and Cleveland up through the second round of interviewing. Their analysis differs from this disposable income calculation in that they did not figure work-related expenses into the analysis, and they compared the respondents to themselves (at baseline and Round 2), rather than comparing workers with non-workers. Similar to this analysis, they found that, in general, those who worked and did not receive cash assistance by Round 2 were the most likely group to have an increase in their income. Those who combined work and welfare or cycled between the two were less likely to have increased income than the work-only group, but more likely to have increased income than the welfare-only group.

In sum, beyond the demands of managing the new job and the commute, families also face the challenge of securing enough outside resources to cover their family's basic needs. This challenge is both incredibly arduous and ongoing, and presents another layer of difficulty and frustration to fiscal and family management. One of our Philadelphia respondents, Marcia, claimed that mothers who survived on welfare would be able to meet this financial challenge of low-wage work. She said, "If anyone can survive off of welfare, they can survive off of anything. Those are some true survivors, that survive off of a welfare check. Because that's no money. They straight making way outta no way."

Childcare

Public-sector childcare resources. When we talked with our 74 families the first time, just as the states were implementing their new TANF programs, they generally expressed enthusiasm for work (London et al., 2001). However, they also feared that a move from welfare to work would create unmanageable fiscal and logistical problems. Not surprisingly, they worried a great deal about how they would mange to cover the costs of childcare. They also worried that the sheer logistical problems of arranging for childcare, especially for evening, night, or weekend shifts, would defeat their efforts to both hold down a job and ensure adequate supervision for their children (Scott, et al., 2001).[7]

Both Pennsylvania's and Ohio's TANF programs guarantee childcare assistance for families with children up to 13 years of age, both while the mother seeks work (through a job search or independent job search program), or is involved in a state-approved "work activity" (short-term training or unpaid work experience) and while she combines welfare and work. Those moving off cash welfare entirely are also eligible for a childcare subsidy, which is assessed on a sliding scale for income. In Cleveland, this benefit is available as long as a family's income remains under 185% of the poverty threshold; and in Philadelphia, a family is eligible until their income reaches 235% of poverty (State Policy Documentation Project, 2000). An important difference between the two sites was that Philadelphians could use their voucher to reimburse unlicensed caregivers, such as relatives and friends, for childcare, but in Cleveland, only licensed providers could be reimbursed. Technically, people in Cleveland can go through the process of getting their relatives licensed, but none of our respondents did so. One respondent described the process as too onerous, so she gave up.

In both cities, TANF recipients receive their subsidies through the welfare office. But in Philadelphia, parents who have worked their way off cash welfare entirely must submit their requests for childcare assistance to a different state

---

[7] Researchers analyzing the 1997 National Survey of American Families (NSAF) have shown these mothers' fears were not misplaced: low-income families (below 200% of the poverty line) pay about $217 a month on average for childcare, comprising 16% of their earnings, while the rate for more affluent families is only 6% (Giannarelli & Barsimantov, 2000).

bureaucracy, called Childcare Resources, which is responsible for issuing the voucher and monitoring ongoing eligibility. At Childcare Resources, recipients are only required to submit their pay stubs every six months unless there is any change in their income in the interim. In Cleveland, once a family leaves cash welfare another division of the welfare office, Cuyahoga Health and Nutrition, handles the subsidy. At Cuyahoga Health and Nutrition, re-certification of income eligibility is required annually.

In both cities, the rules governing childcare subsidy receipt were quite straightforward. Yet a surprisingly high number of our respondents—mainly in Philadelphia—claimed their caseworker withheld information about the availability of childcare subsidies, provided false or misleading information, or even denied their existence to recipients who asked about them.[8] While it is entirely possible that client error was involved, the stories were so similar across our different neighborhoods we believe caseworkers were also part of the problem, and observations of caseworker-client interaction in local welfare offices from the implementation component of the Urban Change study (in the same welfare offices our respondents used) bears this out in terms of the caseworkers forgetting to mention benefits such as food stamps and Medicaid (Quint & Widom, 2001).

When we first interviewed our families, both states' childcare subsidy programs were in place, but families knew little or nothing about them. One year later, some families knew a little more, but even so, less than one third of those families who reported some work activity said they had received any kind of subsidy.[9] By the end of the study, roughly four years after implementation began, the proportion of respondents who'd worked and used a subsidy in the previous year had increased somewhat, to 33% in Cleveland and 36% in Philadelphia. This is despite the fact that at the start of the study, just over half had children under the age of 6, and nearly all had children under the age of 13.[10]

We looked at our data to see why more respondents had not taken up the childcare subsidy. First, we tried to assess whether the working respondents in our study were eligible for the subsidy. We found that one year into our study, the median monthly income for nearly all of our working families was well below the income eligibility cut off (Scott et al., 2001). Thus, excess income cannot be the reason the majority of families did not take up the benefit. The data offer two

---

[8] Their stories are similar to the findings of Adams, Snyder, and Sandfort (2002) in their focus group research with parents who were current or recent TANF recipients. As they tried to get their childcare subsidies, they encountered missing paperwork, unhelpful caseworkers, and inflexible welfare office practices across the twelve states in the study.

[9] This estimate includes those who did not receive any cash assistance, and those who combined welfare and work.

[10] Nationally, 10–15% of income-eligible children receive the childcare subsidy, so our rates of 33% and 36% seem high in comparison. However, these figures are not comparable. The 10–15% estimate measures subsidy utilization at one point in time, where our figure covers subsidy use for any child in the family at any point of time over a one year span. In addition, the denominator for the 10–15% estimate is income-eligible children, and the unit of analysis for our denominator is sample families who were on welfare recently or currently. Most states favor welfare recipients and welfare-leavers when they allocate childcare subsidies (see Huston, this volume).

other possible explanations for the low take-up rate: poor implementation of the program or a mismatch between the form of the subsidy provided and the preferences and needs of families.

The first year of our study coincided with the first year of welfare reform implementation in each of our sites. Thus, we were able to observe the unfolding story about how changes in welfare influenced families' day-to-day lives. The dominant theme of the baseline interviews was one of confusion and chaos. Respondents reported that their caseworkers seemed poorly trained and overwhelmed, that the cast of characters they interacted with at the welfare office was expanding, and that there was a high rate of staff turnover. In both sites, caseworkers had the job of contacting recipients and calling them in to describe the new rules and benefits. The chief piece of information they were charged with imparting was that welfare was ending and that recipients must work. Thus, information about transitional supports for work, if mentioned at all, received short shrift (Quint & Widom, 2001).

As we outlined above, in Cleveland the transitional childcare subsidy could only be used for licensed care (a childcare center or a licensed in-home provider). In Philadelphia, low-income families with childcare subsidies could use unlicensed providers such as family and friends. Several respondents in both sites voiced a strong preference for relative care, mostly because they feared their children would be abused at the hands of strangers, but also because the licensed providers were often located some distance away and were typically less flexible than their work schedules required. This bias against formal care, taken together with the different site rules governing the type of providers who could be paid with a subsidy, may have affected the take-up rate for respondents in Cleveland.

However, Philadelphia respondents faced far more hassle in actually securing and maintaining a subsidy than their Cleveland counterparts. Data from the 2001 wave of the Urban Change survey reveal that 18% of Philadelphia respondents who worked in the last year and 27% of Cleveland respondents with age-eligible children had received childcare help from a government agency. The following stories from Philadelphia reflect this struggle. Mary's story is quite typical. Between rounds 1 and 2[11], Mary participated in job club, independent job search, and short-term job training. During this period, she said her caseworker repeatedly told her she was not eligible for a childcare subsidy for any of her three young children. When she heard from other recipients that she should have received one, Mary was furious and charged her caseworker with "…act[ing] like the childcare money is coming out of her paycheck." At round 2 she was combining work and welfare and still not receiving the subsidy. This time, she said she thought she knew the rules, but her understanding was far from accurate. She told us, "Once you give them [the welfare office] a notice saying that you want to apply for the transitional

---

[11] The annual interviews are referred to as "rounds".

childcare, you can't get [any] cash [welfare] for a year." Since her job was only part-time, she thought applying for a subsidy would be too risky, as she believed her cash welfare benefits would be terminated. The last time we interviewed Mary, she had recently turned in her childcare paperwork and was expecting her reimbursement to begin soon.

Even when the respondents had a fairly accurate understanding of the rules, many said their caseworkers still blocked them from obtaining a subsidy. Danielle, a white Philadelphian, had already applied for a subsidy when we first interviewed her. She'd survived a bout with cancer and was recovering from chemotherapy while working part-time. Though proud of her ability to sustain employment, she felt betrayed by the welfare office's early promises of support, and felt her caseworker was "working against" rather than for her. She said, "[The welfare office] tell you — you get a job, we'll provide childcare, we'll provide the bus fare. No they don't. I pay for the bus fare, I pay for the childcare, and I only come home with sixty-five, seventy-five dollars a week." When she told her caseworker she had to quit her job during the summer months if she didn't receive a subsidy, her caseworker reportedly replied, "That's your problem." At round 2, Danielle, now unemployed, was trying to get a subsidy so she could participate in job search. She felt pressed because her caseworker told her she could only get the subsidy if she was willing to forgo the clothing allowance that job search recipients were entitled to, and Danielle felt she needed both. In reality, both benefits should have been readily available to a job search participant. By the end of our study, Danielle had still never received a childcare subsidy.

Once a parent obtained a subsidy, maintaining it was often an ongoing struggle. Eileen, a white mother of six from Philadelphia, managed to land a childcare subsidy after months of effort, but several months later, the welfare department informed her that she was no longer eligible. Eileen claimed that the welfare office gave her no reason for the cut off, but suspected malice on the part of her caseworker, who had accused her of having "attitude" when she'd complained about a prior sanction. She felt that her ongoing dealings with her caseworker to try to maintain her transitional benefits were unlikely to yield a long-term positive result. Since she was already struggling to maintain both full-time and part-time jobs, she felt she didn't have the time or energy to deal with the "hassle".

> Uh, I'm, I'm to the point where, I mean, I'm tired of [welfare]. I'm tired of fighting them.... I'm tired of putting appeals in —it [takes] so much time. And then like, by me being in there all the time, I'm always coming in to work] late. I'm like on the border line of getting fired. And I, I... [Interviewer: So, have you tried to get it in the past and they've given you the run around?] Yeah, they, they do that to me all the time. But now it's to the point where my...job's

on the line .... My jobs are more important right now, because
that's the only ... money I have [coming in right now]. I
mean [I've got to be worrying about] supporting my family.

Another challenge to keeping a subsidy was the welfare department's
paperwork requirements from the provider, along with a frequent delay in
processing the subsidy payment. Some mothers elected to forgo the subsidy in
order to keep a trusted provider who'd become disgruntled with these paperwork
and payment problems. By round 2, Marcia, an African American mother from
Philadelphia, was working full-time and paying her babysitter $80 per week out of
her pocket. In return, her babysitter, an elderly neighbor, provided supervision for
her two children after school. Marcia told us, "I pay for it myself ... that's because
I don't feel like going through all that hassle." In addition, Marcia said, she didn't
want her babysitter "bitching" about where her money was any longer.

Certainly some of the respondents, particularly those in Cleveland, received
the subsidy in a smooth, virtually hassle-free manner. Debbie, an African American
Cleveland resident, worked full-time during the last two years we knew her, and in
the final year, left cash welfare behind. The children's father worked part time,
and could monitor the two older children before and after school. However, her
toddler—who required all-day supervision the father couldn't provide—had a
subsidized slot in a licensed in-home daycare facility. Her subsidy also covered
all three children's all-day summer care. Tina, an African American respondent
from Philadelphia, had two children under the age of 5 in full-time care. Her
childcare subsidy covered all but $40 of the $700 in monthly fees. She repeatedly
claimed she would be unable to stay employed without the subsidy, since she had
no one in her network who could watch the children all day for free.

Non-public childcare resources. The above examples make it clear that the
implementation of the childcare subsidy benefit was not without significant
problems. Paperwork and misinformation barriers in Philadelphia sometimes made
it difficult, if not impossible, for some families who could have clearly benefited
from a subsidy to get or maintain one. But it is also true that for a number of
women in Cleveland, the structure of the subsidy led to rejection of a subsidy
offer. As we alluded to earlier, in Cleveland, respondents were much more likely
to know they were eligible for a subsidy, reported far fewer cases of caseworkers
who gave misleading or false information, and faced less administrative hassle
when they applied for the subsidy. However, the Cleveland subsidy program was
far from perfect in respondents' eyes, because unlicensed providers, such as
relatives, could not be used unless the relative was willing to go through a complex
process of becoming licensed; yet, as we said before, respondents in both sites
voiced strong preferences for relative care. None of our Cleveland respondents'
relatives went through this licensing process. Those Cleveland families with infants
or toddlers requiring all-day care usually felt they had little choice but to send

them to licensed providers. Though they could often persuade a relative or friend to provide a few hours of light supervision for an older child after school, few knew anyone willing to provide full-time care to a demanding infant or toddler for little or no money.

Probably partly because of the differing structure of the subsidies in the two sites, more Philadelphia workers used relatives (including husbands and boyfriends) to care for their children than did Cleveland respondents. Nearly 80% (N=22) of Philadelphia workers used this type of care at some point while they were working; whereas only 58% (N=18) in Cleveland did so.[12] However, in practice, the subsidies were so hard to secure and maintain that only 6 of the 22 workers in Philadelphia who used relative care were actually able to secure a subsidy to pay those caregivers. Taking away these 6 respondents would leave the proportions using this type of care the same in the two cities.

In cases where the respondent's personal network was strong, mothers were able to exercise their preferences with relatively little strain on their budgets. Hallie, a white mother in Cleveland, rejected a subsidy offer for center-based care because her mother, who lived close by, was willing to watch her kindergartener after school. She saw the informal care option as a healthier and safer option. She explained, "Yeah, they asked me if I wanted it. Like I told them, with the kids [in daycare] getting meningitis and things like that, my son better stay at home with my Mom. There's not too many people I'd trust with my son anyway."

Many of the respondents echoed Hallie's sense that relative care was of higher quality than more formal options. But this was not always the case. Danielle, whose fruitless struggle to obtain a subsidy from the state we detailed above, reported leaving her youngest child, age 4, with her mother. But for Danielle, this option was clearly second-best. She said, "I don't know...she's weird... she screamed like, my landlord told me the other day, she was screaming and cursing at them. I was like, "Oh my God." That was so embarrassing... She disgusts me...." Four years after we met her, Danielle still had no reliable source of childcare even though she worked most of the time during those years. Her children were now in school, but they still needed care after school and in the summer. Her mother filled in, but when the interviewer asked Danielle how she felt about this arrangement, she replied that she was "horrified." Also in Philadelphia, Kitina also used her mother to watch her 3-year-old daughter because despite repeated attempts, she could not get the subsidy she should have qualified for. She confessed to the interviewer that she wasn't pleased with the care her mother provided; the house was always dirty and Kitina believed she did not discipline or adequately supervise her granddaughter. Thankfully, she said, her daughter would start school the next year and be free of her mother's environment.

---

[12] According to the 2001 Urban Change survey, 38.5% of Cleveland respondents and 41.8% of Philadelphia respondents who worked in the previous year used a grandparent or father/boyfriend as their primary source of childcare.

Almost 40% of Cleveland respondents and 29% of Philadelphia female respondents who worked used their husband or a boyfriend, usually the child's father, to provide childcare at some point during the study. But sometimes this type of care did not add up to a safe and reliable environment. For example, Linda, a white Cleveland respondent, was married but on welfare because her husband was disabled. His severe mental illness was going untreated because Medicaid wouldn't pay for the drugs his psychiatrist prescribed. At the end of our study, she was working full-time, leaving their daughters in his care after school and in the summers.[13] When we first met Alice, a white Cleveland mother of three, she told us about a recent incident. She had been leaving her infant with the baby's father while she worked 60 hours a week at a pizza shop. After a few months of this arrangement, she realized that her daughter was not developing properly. She found that the baby's father had left his child with a "friend" while "running the streets." The father and his friend had neglected the baby to the point where, at 8 months old, she was not sitting up and was only drinking a couple of bottles a day:

> She lacked malnourishment [sic]. She lacked attention. She lacked someone to talk to, play with. You get her up and soon as I stopped working, within a month the girl was sitting up and starting to crawl. So, she improved. She never ate food, bottles. You know what I'm saying? That scared me a lot. And probably scared me away from working for a little while, until I can't make it no more. You just kind of get to that point where you just can't take it no more. But that was very scary ... And this was being done by her own father. You know what I'm saying? If he wasn't understanding of what was going on...So, if your own father would let this happen, I don't trust nobody!

Eileen used several different family members for childcare during the course of our study. Her oldest son provided babysitting for his youngest siblings, ranging in age from 6–10 at baseline. He was in his early 20s and did not live at home, and provided the care grudgingly, even though he was paid a reasonable fee through her childcare subsidy. Since Eileen's younger children were all school-aged, he was only responsible for them after school and in the summer. When she lost her childcare subsidy, he refused to watch them for free, partly because he then had to find another job to pay his bills. Because of this, Eileen was forced to make do with other arrangements, such as leaving the children with her severely retarded adult daughter who still lived at home and did not demand pay, or leaving the children home by themselves. When she resorted to these latter two options, she

---

[13] Linda, however, believes the quality of the children's father's care is excellent.

made sure that she turned the gas off in the house so they could not turn the stove on. When we last interviewed Eileen, she was still trying to piece together better childcare arrangements, this time involving her cousin who was frequently undependable due to her drug addiction. One day, when her cousin did not show up, Eileen enlisted the help of the children's father, whom she had left because of serious domestic abuse.[14] While he was in charge, her 9-year-old ended up falling down the stairs on her bicycle and he brought the child to Eileen's workplace with her face swollen and covered with blood. The father had refused to help clean her up, saying, "that's a mother's job."

The climax of Eileen's story came just after the end of our study. Eileen returned home from her third-shift job one day and found the children's father high, sitting on the steps of a house across the street. He pointed to the smoke coming from her windows and told her that there was a fire in the kitchen. He remained on the stoop and watched while she and the neighbors rushed in to get her sleeping children and their belongings out of the house.

In the last year of the study, nearly one in four of the Cleveland mothers and one in three of the Philadelphia mothers who did not use a voucher but had an age-eligible child regularly left children at home without adult supervision before or after school and in the summer.[15] Fortunately, in every case but three, there was also an adolescent child at home. However, the pressure on the adolescent caregivers was sometimes detrimental to their own development (see Gennetian et al., 2002). Throughout the course of the study, Tina, a Philadelphia mother with five children still at home, relied heavily on her adolescent children to take care of their younger siblings. This added responsibility affected her daughter's ability to get to school on time and complete homework. Because Tina had to leave the house at 5:30 every morning in order to be at work on time (a 90-minute commute by public transportation), Tamara, a ninth-grader, had to wait with the younger children for the Head Start van. However, the driver was often quite late, so Tamara was frequently 20–30 minutes late for school. Tina worried about what the tardiness would mean when her daughter applied for the magnet high school she dreamed of attending. When we interviewed her for the last time, Tamara was taking the children to Head Start on the way to her school, but still had problems with lateness:

> 'Cause she's late every day for her school, every day. And
> what the school says to me is they're gonna, they gotta do
> what they, what's their policy. She's gotta stay after school,

---

[14] Two other papers give a comprehensive picture of the intersection of domestic violence and welfare reform (Scott, London & Myers, 2002a; Scott, London, & Myers, 2002b).

[15] Other mothers who did use vouchers also left their children home alone. In the 2001 Urban Change survey, 10% of working Cleveland respondents and 12% of working Philadelphia respondents used an older sibling as their primary source of childcare.

do her detention, um things like that because she didn't, or she'll lose her credit out of her, out of that morning class cause she didn't get there on time. So she feels sad and I, I feel bad because I gotta be at work at 7.

Renee, an African American respondent from Philadelphia, put her oldest child, 10-year-old Marcus, in charge of his two younger siblings, ages 6 and 1. When she started back to work after a brief stint on welfare, Marcus usually watched both full-time, six to seven days a week, as it was summer and his mother worked two jobs. One hot summer afternoon, one of our interviewers dropped by the house and found the 6- and 1-year-old outside on the sidewalk, unattended. They were locked out of the house and didn't know where Marcus was. The street did not have heavy traffic, but had a high level of visible drug activity. The interviewer went to the corner store to get the children something to eat, and when she came back, Marcus was climbing through a window to get inside and unlock the front door. At the end of the study, Renee's children were 12, 8, and 3, and the older two were still left alone for periods of time while she was working. She paid a local day care center for the full-time care her 3-year-old required, because two jobs left her with no time for the hassle that obtaining a subsidy would entail. At the end of our study, Renee reflected on the situation that she had put her children in, and attributed Marcus' current severe behavioral problems to the responsibilities she had laid on his shoulders.

Sometimes mothers put older children in charge of younger siblings who have serious behavioral and health issues. Wendy, a white Cleveland respondent, had a 14- and 12-year-old at round 2. Her youngest child had been diagnosed as having ADHD, bipolar disorder, and schizophrenia, and frequently set things on fire and expressed thoughts of homicide. It was difficult to find someone who was willing to care for such a disturbed child, although the children's father (who was abusive to them and to Wendy) watched him frequently. She sometimes enlisted his 14-year-old sister to provide the care during Wendy's shifts at a video store.

[I: How did you handle childcare, while you were working there?] I had to pray a lot. Because they were here by themselves...unless, I was doing the day shift...She [her daughter] is so responsible it spins my head at times...[I: Can she care for Bobby, you know, like a lot of the times?] She used to be able to until he got into the teenage thoughts and, it's hard for her to control him...[I have to] go to work and pray that all hell doesn't break loose here at the house when I'm working.

Food

Public-sector food resources—The Food Stamp Program. Per federal guidelines, nearly all welfare recipients are automatically eligible for food stamps, as are non-welfare families whose gross household income does not exceed 130% of the federal poverty level.[16] Just as is true with childcare subsidies, there is a key difference in how welfare officials in Cleveland and Philadelphia implement the Food Stamp Program (Quint & Widom, 2001). Workers who remain eligible for food stamps in Philadelphia must provide verification of their ongoing eligibility on a monthly basis, and benefit adjustments are made on the basis of each monthly report (this is also true for Philadelphia's cash welfare program). Ohio's program, in contrast, required recipients to submit this paperwork quarterly rather than monthly.

Our ethnographic data revealed that the seemingly small variation in program requirements in Ohio and Pennsylvania had a dramatic effect on the daily lives of poor families. While putting a completed form and a copy of a pay stub (and occasionally, additional documentation such as verification from employers when employees were laid off or fired) in the mail each month may not seem like an undue burden, the overwhelming majority of Philadelphia respondents who worked reported routine problems with the monthly reporting routine. Some of these problems stemmed from their own inability to keep up with the paperwork or fill out the forms correctly, for the forms were fairly complicated. More often, at least according to our respondents, it was caseworker error. We were startled by the number of respondents, for example, who reported that their caseworkers "lost" or misfiled paperwork they claimed they sent in on time. The problem was so epidemic that in all three neighborhoods we observed in Philadelphia, some respondents who wanted to remain on the program adopted the strategy of bringing their monthly paperwork in to the welfare department in person, and demanding verification of receipt. Thus, the monthly task of collecting the documentation and filling out the forms was compounded by a bus, train, or car trip to the welfare office before or after work, a logistical nightmare for many since most offices were only open from 8 a.m. to 4 p.m.

Not surprisingly, our Cleveland families had far fewer problems keeping their food stamp benefits than the Philadelphia group, though some did have to deal with mistakes made by their caseworkers. In the last year of the study alone (when most of our respondents were working), nearly 30% of the Philadelphia respondents who worked reported problems with food stamp paperwork. More importantly, a few of the Philadelphia families who remained eligible found the paperwork burden and the hassle too great to bear, and opted out of the program altogether, whereas this was far less common in Cleveland.

---

[16] This limit is extended slightly for families in Ohio and Pennsylvania – food stamps are guaranteed to TANF leavers up to 133% of the poverty level (Brock, Nelson, &Reiter, 2002).

When we first spoke to families in our study, welfare reform had just been implemented in our sites, and only a few respondents had experienced reductions or cutoffs of food stamps as a result. This typically happened when women were working, but got cut off for missing the face-to-face meetings with their caseworkers all recipients were required to attend. For their part, respondents often claimed they hadn't been notified by their caseworkers of the appointment, or that the appointment interfered with their work hours and their caseworker was unwilling to change the time. However, with less than 15% of the sample working, problems with the Food Stamp Program were rare.

When we interviewed families a second time, many—especially in Philadelphia—were eager to relate stories of hassles with the Food Stamp Program. Some had had their food stamps incorrectly (from their viewpoint) reduced, while others had been cut completely off. When Lynn, in Philadelphia, started working part-time in a welfare-to-work program, she claimed her caseworker vowed her food stamps would not be cut at all. But the following month, her food stamp debit card contained only $80 rather than the $245 she usually received. She went to the caseworker, and then to his supervisor with her complaint, and her benefit was increased to $140 per month, still over $100 shy of what she'd been getting previously. The revised amount was likely correct, but Lynn resented the time and energy it had taken to get the additional $60. She blamed her problems on poor caseworker training and high turnover: "I'm like, what are they doing? And then they keep changing your caseworkers so much, this one don't know…the difference [when they've made a mistake]."

Celena, a white Philadelphian respondent, had similar problems. Though she'd enrolled in job search at round 2, she had not begun working.

> I went to go grocery shopping—this is [so] embarrassing— went in the store, had all my groceries, I had nothing [on the EBT card]. Nothing. And the lady just looked at me— Thank god my mom was with me and she used her cash. I came home and called the um, caseworkers, they had cut my food stamps. I asked, "Why they did cut my food stamps?" And she said "well…, you're working, right?." And I'm like, "No. I'm on that [job search] program." She was like, "I don't know [what I can do for you]." Well, here I just found out that they fired that lady [the caseworker]. She no longer works for the state or nothing.

In the beginning of our study, Brenda, in Cleveland, told us of a recent job experience. When she told her caseworker she'd landed a part-time job, he "took" half of her food stamps away the following month, and at the same time allegedly informed her that she only had thirty days of eligibility for food stamps and Medicaid left. This was clearly not the case, as the job Brenda had taken paid only minimum wage and offered only 20 hours per week. Fearing the loss of these benefits, Brenda told her caseworker she would probably quit work to keep the benefits. But the caseworker reportedly told her that if she quit voluntarily he'd sanction her benefits for three months. Brenda resolved the situation in an innovative way: "I purposely got myself fired so I could keep my benefits, because they were [worth] more than my job. And at the same time, I went and I found a job that paid cash under the table."

Quint and Widom (2001) interviewed and observed welfare caseworkers in Cleveland, Philadelphia, and two other cities in order to assess how welfare departments actually implement the various transitional benefit programs like food stamps. In our cities, these interviews were conducted in the same welfare offices our respondents used. Though in staff surveys and focus groups caseworkers claimed they'd informed their clients of ongoing eligibility for all transitional benefits, including food stamps, observations of caseworker-client interactions revealed that in actuality these conversations rarely took place. While our respondents told us their caseworkers spent much time in the face-to-face interviews talking about work requirements and the time limit they had to find a job, and our Cleveland respondents seemed to have an accurate knowledge about childcare subsidies, information regarding ongoing food stamp eligibility was hit or miss, and they perceived that caseworker information was sometimes incorrect.[17]

Our families reported that they were cut off from food stamps because their caseworker claimed that they (the respondents) had failed to complete the necessary paperwork correctly or on time. In Philadelphia, one in five workers lost their food stamp benefits during the study, and all but one lost them because of paperwork problems.[18] Though more families in Philadelphia lost their food stamps more often than in Cleveland, it is notable that one in eight workers in Cleveland lost their food stamps during the course of the study. As the reader might recall, in Philadelphia, respondents often felt a trip to the welfare office was necessary to get the paperwork in, but for Tina, the routine burden this imposed sometimes proved too much. This mother of six was left scrambling to find money for food after her case was closed for not handing her paperwork in on time one month in the middle of our study:

> Since I work from 8:00, 'til 4:30, I really don't have time to get this report [down to the welfare office] … I'm trying to keep my position at work, so I don't want to be late. I leave out of here about 5:30 [a.m.]. I have to [be on the bus] at

---

[17] In addition, Quint and Widom (2001) found that caseworkers frequently cut off food stamps when their clients exceeded the earnings limit for cash welfare. As the eligibility threshold is much higher for the former than the latter, these caseworkers were in error. However, this practice is probably the cause of some of the benefit cutoffs our clients experienced but could not explain.

[18] Celena was sanctioned after she missed a mandatory day of her welfare training program. She couldn't go in to school that day because she had been beaten up the day before by her children's father.

> 6:00 to get to my job on time. But my report, I don't know
> ... It comes in so [often] that it seems like you just miss it
> [sometimes]. You [have to go down and] give them the same
> information that they just asked you for, you know, all over
> again.

These difficulties were ongoing for Tina and others like her. At round 3, Tina estimated that she either didn't get her paperwork in on time or the caseworker lost her paperwork roughly every other month over the prior year. Her paperwork burden was especially high because she worked through several different temporary agencies, and had to get documentation from the employer each time she moved from one assignment to the next.

> Well, I just received a letter stating that I probably have an
> incorrect [monthly report] and that my benefits, if I don't
> send them, fax them three companies that I worked for; they
> need verification that I don't work with them anymore, that
> I left the company or whatever. So I need to get that in to
> them as soon as possible. [The caseworker wants it] [t]o
> verify the last transaction, I guess, that we had together
> because that's how they determine what and where you're
> working at. So, with me, I always work at these different
> companies. So I'm never at one place, and I'm never at one
> place very long, so it's kinda stressful on me when I have to
> go there and say, "Oh, um, could you please fax over this
> information for my caseworker?" Because, you know, and
> it's embarrassing. I don't like doing this.

Melissa, a white mother of four in Philadelphia, lost her food stamps for several months while she was out of work during the last year of our study. She told us that her case closure was a result of the paperwork hassle combined with bad blood between her and her caseworker:

> Well, she kept telling me [I lost my food stamps because]
> she wasn't getting my pay stubs. And I would send them
> and send them. And I would send her two copies a month,
> because she kept sending me forms telling me she ain't got
> them ... [I: Okay, and so then how did you get back on?]
> Well, I called her supervisor and told her supervisor that
> she was always copping [an attitude with] me on the phone
> ... [This time,] she told me she *had* the pay stubs and, she
> just cut the food stamps because she felt like it. So I went

down there, gave her all the things she needed, and she
finally put me back on. She gave me everything.

Like Tina, Melissa claimed that while she was working, the welfare office
lost her paystubs, which she continued to mail in "at least every other month."
When this happened she would have to copy the paystubs again and get them to
her caseworker as soon as possible. She found this constant running around
"frustrating" enough to let her benefits lapse.

Our working respondents in Philadelphia had to submit paperwork twelve
times during the year to continue their food stamp benefits; in Cleveland, our
sample respondents only had to submit paperwork four times a year. Even with
this less frequent verification process, some respondents in Cleveland experienced
trouble in maintaining their food stamp benefits. In the round 3 interview, Alice
told us how her food stamps were cut off. She did not submit all of the required
documentation for her three-month eligibility verification and her entire family's
case was closed for two months. "So um, I had a three month evaluation thing and
I didn't have everything she wanted and it took me some time to get [it], and I was,
she cut me off. [This was] two months ago. Till this month … [They took away]
everything. It was really hard."

These examples amply illustrate how the seemingly small task of verifying
income, even if only quarterly, can have a large impact on families as they try to
negotiate the more complex daily routines that regular employment requires (see
also Cherlin et al., 2002). By round 3, most respondents worked full time, either at
one job or by combining two part-time jobs. Commutes to and from work could
take an additional hour or two of their day. Meanwhile, these working respondents
were also raising children, dealing with childcare arrangements and children's
schools, and working to maintain those network bonds that proved so useful in
times of crisis. As respondents faced reductions or their food stamps were
sanctioned, they had to find new ways of coping.

Non-public sources of food resources. When in need, many families turned to
members of their own personal networks and private charities. By the end of the
study, over one half of all the Philadelphia respondents and one third of Cleveland
respondents said they'd received help in the food domain from the family and
friends in the preceding year. For those who did not, some said they didn't need it.
But for others, their networks were simply too thin to provide much help, or the
social costs these exchanges exacted proved too great for parents already juggling
family and work.

In 2000, Brenda, a white Cleveland respondent, was off cash welfare, food
stamps, and Medicaid while she moved to another state working a handful of jobs.
When she moved back to Cleveland, she got a job but did not have time to take off
of work to come in for an appointment to apply for benefits, so she remained
without benefits. At one point during this year, she took a temporary job but had to
wait two weeks for the first paycheck. In the interim, she ran short of food. Luckily,

a generous neighbor watched her daughter after school and provided her with dinner. Philadelphia respondent Sarah's food stamps were reduced when she left cash welfare for a job, but since rent, utilities, and transportation to work consumed nearly all of her paycheck, she still ran short of food. Her sister, who was slightly better off, bridged the gap. Kitina, also from Philadelphia, was able to buy food "on credit" at a small neighborhood grocery store owned by family friends, and they knew she always paid them back. Toni, an African American mother from Philadelphia, was cut off because her earnings were just above the food stamp income limit. When she ran short on food, as she often did, she called on her aunt and her mother. Her aunt swapped her food stamps for transportation for her weekly round of errands, which Toni was able to provide because she had a car. Her mother, an additional resource, held a job at a local nonprofit and had ready access to their food pantry, so her kitchen cupboards were always well stocked.

> Like when I run low on canned goods and stuff, I just go to her house and just stock up... a couple times a month. [It would cost] about a hundred dollars [if I were to buy it]. Because I go there, and I get whatever I need even down to the toilet paper and stuff like that, you know? She has everything. Anything you need... Like if I run out of cereal, she has all kinds of stuff. I'll go get a couple of boxes of cereal, juice- you know what I mean. Anything that I might need. So that's a big help that saves me a lot of money.

This "back up" for food was a valuable resource for those who were lucky enough to have it. Janice, from Cleveland, said,

> Well, I know that if I run out of anything, you know a couple friends of mine that I've known almost thirty years – if I need something, I can call them, you know, and they usually get it for me somehow. So, as far as worrying about running out, I worry about it, but I know if I really need it, I can get it.

Although many respondents relied heavily on the food contributions of family and friends, they also talked about the wide array of factors that limited their ability to draw on network support. For example, Marcia, from Philadelphia, outlined her strategy as follows: "My girlfriends will help me out with some food, I don't really go to my family for stuff like that. I don't like them to know when I am in need, I don't know why—it is kind of the pride."

Sometimes families and friends simply did not have the resources to help. In Philadelphia, Tina's father shared what he had with her and her five children when she asked. However, Tina expressed a reluctance to go to him for help because he was disabled. Thus, she worried he would run short and might not be able to quickly replenish his food supply, especially during the winter. By round 3, Maria, a white Cleveland respondent, had been working for three years, but was cut from food stamps (perhaps in error) when she started working full-time and left cash welfare. Each week after that, Maria and her four children ate several meals at her mother's house, but her mother's resources were stretched thin by a sister and children in even worse circumstances. In order to help feed her children and grandchildren, Maria's mother began taking the cash set aside for her mortgage and used money to pay for groceries.

Kathy, in Cleveland, expressed similar difficulties when it came to asking already hard-pressed relatives for food:

> They can't exactly just hand us cash money 'cause everybody's having financial problems of their own. No, we don't. We don't get to actually ask our relatives if they can just hand us cash. But, like, we, we need help with something we can borrow it or pay 'em back some other time, some other way. Like I said, if we were really, really hungry and we didn't have any food, my relatives would take care of it.

It was also true that sometimes network members who were not financially strained simply chose not to help out. Monica, the respondent who suffered the annual layoffs from the envelope-stuffing job, claimed that her mother was unresponsive to her situation when she was laid off:

> I mean, you know, like even when I got laid off and, you know, she [mom] knew that things weren't good here, okay? But she never even offered the kids nothing, you know. I can fend for myself, and go down to the mission or something, you know, but she didn't even say to the kids, 'Well are you hungry? Do you want something to eat?' Nothing.

Around one third of our full sample in each city had to use food pantries to supplement their stock of food.[19] Some of the respondents saved by not shopping for items they knew they could get at the food pantry. Lisa, an African American mother of six from Philadelphia, began volunteering part-time at a neighborhood church food pantry and she was "paid" with a weekly stock of groceries.

---

[19] According to the 2001 Urban Change survey, 9% of Cleveland working respondents and 4% of Philadelphia working respondents went to a food bank in the month previous to the survey.

> Usually, I make it through because the food I get from the church, the way I do it, I get most of my vegetables from the church. And when I go shopping, I go to the meat market, and I buy meat. I usually don't have to buy them. Like I get bags of rice from the church, and so usually it's mostly meats [I have to buy with my food stamps]. And like cereal and milk....

Food pantries and soup kitchens, whether they are located at churches or community centers, only offer food at certain times, offer a very limited amount of food (generally a one- to two-day supply), and sharply curtail how often families can receive assistance. Even the most generous among them do not generally allow use more than once a month. Thus, families who used pantries often had to expend a good deal of time for a rather meager benefit. Gayle, a white Cleveland resident, told us, "And I don't even know if I can get to the church [for food] because you're only allowed to go to those churches every other month. I don't understand that. You run out of food all the time, not every other month. The food stamps don't last that long."

In round 3, when most respondents were working, one third of workers reported some form of food hardship.[20] As we showed previously, mothers could sometimes appeal to friends and family, or by visiting a food pantry. However, many respondents told us that they could find no such remedy, and avoided food hardship by adopting more extreme strategies. One Philadelphia respondent with five children, currently a prep cook at a local diner, had resorted to stealing meat from a grocery store in order to feed his five children during a time when he was unemployed. Right before our study began, Linda, from Cleveland, lost her food stamps when she missed an appointment with her welfare caseworker, so she sold plasma to get the money to buy food. In the last year of our study, Brenda prevented her young daughter from going hungry by circumventing the rules of several local food pantries; she used a different name and address each time she went and alternated days, hoping in this way to avoid confronting the same volunteer she'd had earlier. Like Linda, Brenda also sold blood for food money during several difficult months, sometimes twice per week (she gleaned about $17 each time).

Almost universally, parents were quick to tell us that even though they might have to go without food, they made sure their children did not. In the last year of our study, our respondents from both cities told us about this struggle. Wendy, from Cleveland, said holiday times put a special strain on her food budget: "And then toward the end of th[ose] month[s], you know, I'll go maybe three days at a

---

[20] This ranged from not having enough money to buy food to actually skipping meals or not eating for a day. This estimate is slightly lower than that found by Polit, London, and Martinez (2000) in an earlier analysis of food insecurity with Urban Change Respondent Survey data. They defined "food insecurity" by respondents' answers to the Household Food Security Scale, and found that over 40% of respondents in the four Urban Change cities who worked experienced some form of food insecurity. This measure is different than that used in the current chapter, since we used qualitative data from the interviews to explore whether food hardships were experienced.

time without eating just so the kids can have their three meals a day." Joe, from Philadelphia, claimed he went hungry about three times a week so that his children would not. Renee, also from Philadelphia, lost food stamps when she took not one, but two, jobs. Nonetheless, she'd gone hungry several times since she'd been working. She too, made sure her children had food while she went without. "Sometimes [I've] gone hungry because we had no food...I send my kids over there to my sister. That's the only one I would ask—other than that, I won't ask nobody because see I know she always—she's got four kids, she stays with [welfare] and she gets food stamps—I know she's got food."

Health

Public-sector health care resources. Medicaid was part of the standard "package" that welfare-reliant families received in the years prior to PWRORA, and families who left welfare for work were supposed to be assured continued eligibility for six months, regardless of income. If their income stayed below 185% of the poverty line, they remained eligible for a year. PRWORA modified these rules by unlinking Medicaid eligibility from TANF eligibility, allowing families who are income eligible but who may never have been on welfare to receive a medical card (Garrett & Holahan, 2000). However, special provisions remained for those leaving welfare for employment. While those who were not recent welfare leavers were only eligible if their income fell below 135% of poverty, those leaving welfare for work but with higher incomes, up to 185% of the poverty threshold in our sites, could keep their Medicaid for a year.

Most individuals who leave welfare for work find employment in a low-wage job with no health insurance (Families USA, 1999; Loprest, 1999; Polit, London, & Martinez 2001). Therefore, unless they marry someone who has access to family health insurance, Medicaid is their only health insurance option. Yet, as we cited in the introduction, a large proportion of welfare-leavers who are income-eligible for Medicaid still are not receiving it (Garrett & Holahan, 2000). Why would welfare-leavers who remain income-eligible and within the time limit not have Medicaid?[21] The Urban Change implementation study, conducted in Cleveland and Philadelphia and two other cities, found that caseworkers did not always inform their clients that they might be eligible for Medicaid if they stopped their TANF cash assistance (Quint & Widom, 2001). Our data from the client's side offered us insight into their perceptions of eligibility, as well as other barriers to Medicaid receipt. We found that as with the Food Stamp Program, caseworker error, sanctions or case closures, and confusion over eligibility sometimes put our respondents' medical coverage in jeopardy. Nonetheless, most of our respondents were able to retain their Medicaid coverage for the bulk of our study.

---

[21] Garrett and Holahan (2000) suggest that administrative hassles, caseworker misinformation, and stigma may be potential causes for the drop in Medicaid receipt, although their data cannot address these issues directly.

At round 1, few mothers felt any confidence that they could land a job that would insure them, much less their families (see also Polit, London, & Martinez, 2001). They frequently expressed concern that complying with the new welfare rules and finding work would leave them and their children uninsured, particularly since so many of the adults and children had chronic health conditions. When we interviewed Tasha, an African American mother in Cleveland, at baseline, her daughter had severe disabilities brought on by regular seizures that stemmed from a negative reaction to a DPT immunization as an infant. Tasha did not worry about losing cash assistance since she was confident she could out-earn her welfare benefit. However, the prospect of losing medical insurance was downright frightening for her, as her daughter regularly required doctor's visits, medication, and a home health aide. She said, "... if we ever lose Medicaid, I'm in trouble." Fortunately, none of the children with severe health problems in the study lost health coverage, but several asthmatic mothers did.

Unlike childcare subsidies and, to a lesser extent, food stamps, many respondents were aware they were eligible for transitional Medicaid benefits once they started work. A fair number, though, were clearly misinformed about the nature of the benefit. When we first interviewed Wendy, a mother of two from Cleveland, she'd come away from a recent meeting with her caseworker believing that once she found work, only she, and not her children, would continue to be eligible for Medicaid. As her 11-year-old son was disabled and on SSI, she saw this as a serious problem. Beyond the frequent doctor visits he required were his medications, including Ritalin and blood pressure pills, and their cost was far beyond her means. Misinformation such as this, whatever its source, can act as a deterrent to work. Tasha's and Wendy's confusion at baseline reflects the depth of misinformation for some of the respondents, since both of their children who required so much medication would continue to be covered by Medicaid through their SSI status. Most of the families in our study maintained their Medicaid between round 1 and 2—a period of about 18 months—even though many went to work. But by round 3, several had lost Medicaid for themselves, and some had lost benefits for their children as well. According to the 2001 Urban Change survey, 31.8% of Cleveland respondents and 23.1% of Philadelphia respondents who had worked in the previous year were without health coverage at some point in that year.

In our ethnographic sample, 30% of working respondents in Cleveland were without any kind of health coverage at some point during the study, while 40% of workers in Philadelphia were without coverage.[22] By talking in depth with respondents who'd lost benefits, we were able to divide the probable reasons for

---

[22] In their analysis of the first wave (1997–1998) of the Urban Change Survey, Polit, London, and Martinez (2001) found that former welfare recipients who were working and not receiving any cash assistance were more likely than those still on welfare to be uninsured at some point in the previous year (42% compared to 13–14%). Similarly, in their analysis of the Women's Employment Survey, Danziger et al. (2002) found that welfare-leavers were significantly more likely not to have health coverage and to forego medical and dental care than those who remained on welfare.

the cutoffs into those resulting from sanctions or case closures, from caseworker errors, and those triggered by the program's time limit or income eligibility threshold.

According to the federal law, states cannot sanction children's Medicaid. Additionally, in Pennsylvania and Ohio, adults cannot have their Medicaid sanctioned for failure to fulfill work requirements, though they can be sanctioned for other reasons (State Policy Documentation Project, 2000).[23] However, our respondents' stories indicate that these protections may be poorly enforced since in a few of our cases, children lost their Medicaid benefits because of sanctions or case closures. Of those who worked, four respondents in Cleveland and four respondents in Philadelphia reported losing their Medicaid benefits because of paperwork problems or caseworker error in the last year of the study, or nearly 15% of the working families in the entire sample.

Eileen, in Philadelphia, lost her Medicaid for problems related to the paperwork required for ongoing eligibility. For much of the time we knew her, Eileen worked two jobs; a full-time job at a laundromat and a part-time job at Dunkin Donuts. When the management at the Dunkin Donuts changed, the outgoing owners did not pay her for the final month she'd worked. Thus, she did not have a paycheck to submit to her caseworker that month. She told us her caseworker did not believe her employer had cheated her in this way and demanded the nonexistent paycheck. When she could not produce it, he cut off her food stamps and Medicaid. Eileen thought her caseworker had it in for her anyway, because just before this incident she lost her childcare subsidy because the caseworker claimed her caregiver, an adult son, had filled out the provider forms incorrectly. (When she appealed the loss of the childcare subsidy to her caseworker, the caseworker laughed and told her that her son was "stupid." Enraged, Eileen appealed to the supervisor, who reversed the caseworker's decision.) Eileen reasoned that the most recent cut-off had been levied by her caseworker as revenge for the prior complaint. About a year later, Eileen lost a monthly paystub and could not get a copy from her employer. Her caseworker responded by taking away her daughters' Medicaid (she had already lost her Medicaid for a reason she couldn't name).

> I had an incident where, I had lost one of my pay stubs. Because I couldn't produce that pay stub, that's when they sanctioned me ... And, they took away my medical and, uh, the food stamps for 30 days, just to teach me a lesson that I don't lose pay stubs. [I: So, they took off the whole family or just your case?] No, see, I'm not on it. Only my three little ones are on there ... That was to teach the mother don't lose your pay stub. [I: That's what they told you when they cut you?] Yeah.

---

[23] In Ohio, a non-pregnant adult can lose their Medicaid if they are facing their third sanction.

Another respondent in Philadelphia described a similar type of conflict with a caseworker. At round 2, Andrea had been laid off of work and one of her children, Crystal, had just been diagnosed with diabetes and a debilitating joint condition. Andrea decided to put off looking for another job until her daughter's health situation was stabilized. When she applied for SSI benefits for her daughter, her caseworker demanded that Andrea write a letter explaining why she was not working, and describing her daughter's health, which she had already detailed for the SSI application. Her caseworker told her that he would cut Crystal off of Medicaid if she did not comply.

> [My caseworker said] if you don't cooperate, she's gonna be taken off the medical, knowing she needs her insulin, you know, and the things that goes with it. The sugar testing, the, you know, they don't care. You know, what good is the [food] stamps if she can't have medical? She won't be around to use them, to eat off of.

In the first year of our study, Kitina, a white mother of one in Philadelphia, lost her Medicaid for several months because she elected to attend medical assistant training full-time rather than fulfill her job search or work requirement (In Pennsylvania, welfare recipients had to work 25 hours a week in addition to school [State Policy Documentation Project, 2002]). However, it was through this training that she was able to secure a relatively good job later on, which, incidentally, provided private heath insurance.

Four Cleveland workers had lost their Medicaid benefits through sanctions or case closures in the last year of our study. In three cases, the whole family lost their benefits, not just the mother. Each of the four worked enough hours to fulfill the work requirements their state imposed, but in each case the caseworker claimed the client had made an error in the ongoing paperwork required or had failed to make a recertification appointment with their caseworker in a timely enough manner. As work requirements put more and more of our families in the time bind that full-time employment, solo parenting, and long commutes impose, they had more difficulty meeting these requirements. Since they felt their top priority ought to be keeping their jobs, many felt they had to choose between showing up at work on time and making the morning meeting with the caseworker. In those cases where the job won, the mother and her children risked benefit loss, including the all-important benefit of Medicaid (see also Quint & Widom, 2001).

Tamara's caseworker cut her and her son off all benefits, including Medicaid, just before the round 2 interview. The caseworker claimed Tamara had worked at a country club in Southern Ohio and had failed to report her income.

... they tried to tell me I worked at a place called Chillicothe Country Club that I've never heard of. I ain't never been to Chillicothe and I don't plan on going. I [tell her] I'm not trying [to fight her anymore]...I'm going to work. I don't have time for this. So they terminated my case. [I: Do you think they got you mixed up with someone else?] Yeah. I know they did.

When transitional Medicaid ended, another public-sector benefit—health clinics—sometimes allowed families to meet their healthcare needs. Cuyahoga County, which encompasses Cleveland and its inner suburbs, has two of these clinics, while Philadelphia County, which is contiguous with the city limits of Philadelphia, has a network of ten neighborhood-based clinics where clients pay based on their income. In Philadelphia, prescriptions can be filled for free at these clinics as well. Although some of our respondents reported using these clinics, the hours of operation made it difficult for those who worked (they were open from 8 a.m.–4:30 p.m. on weekdays only), particularly since they believed that they would have to wait several hours to be seen. Renee lost her Medicaid benefits for herself and her family because she'd exhausted her transitional Medicaid benefits. She paid out of pocket for her children to been seen by their regular doctor rather than go to the local health clinic, claiming she had no time to wait half a day for them to be seen. She told us, "I don't have to pay at the free clinic but it's too much stuff you got to go through and you have to do all this paperwork for them. You get there at 8:00 in the morning when they open the door, and you still leaving out at 1:00 ... Me and the free clinic don't click at all."

Over the course of our study, a new program was making its way in the knowledge base of each of the communities we studied: the State Children's Health Insurance Program [SCHIP], called Healthy Start in Cleveland and CHIP in Philadelphia. In Cleveland, Linda's transitional Medicaid ended six months before our last interview, and she was able to move to her employer's insurance plan to cover her own health needs. However, the cost of the family plan was too expensive. Luckily, her children were able to transition into Healthy Start after their Medicaid eligibility ended. Like Linda, two other workers in Cleveland got coverage for themselves from their employers and benefits for their children through Healthy Start. Another had no insurance for herself, but was able to obtain Healthy Start for her kids. Several other mothers still on transitional Medicaid expressed detailed knowledge of Healthy Start, and said they felt confident that they could cover their children through the program when their transitional Medicaid benefits expired. However, in Philadelphia, CHIP was far less utilized, perhaps because few families there had worked long enough or steadily enough for their transitional Medicaid to have expired, or possibly because the program was less well known. In fact, only one Philadelphian, Renee, successfully placed two of her three children on CHIP by the end of our study (her eldest retained Medicaid through his SSI), but only after the children had gone without any insurance for a year.

During the three to four years we studied these families, most were protected from Medicaid loss because they combined welfare with work and thus maintained eligibility, or because of the one-year extension of benefits for those leaving cash welfare entirely. Tina, from Philadelphia, was an exception. Just before our round 3 interview, her caseworker cut her off food stamps and Medicaid, claiming that she made too much money to render her family eligible for any of the programs. As Tina's income fell below the poverty line for a family of five, the food stamp cutoff was clearly in error. She also remained income-eligible for Medicaid, yet she'd used up her 12 months of transitional benefits. Since her caseworker did not tell her that her children were still eligible for Medicaid or CHIP, her children went uninsured.

Also in Philadelphia, Lisa had been without Medicaid for several months when the state removed her six children from her care because of her drug addiction. She successfully completed a drug treatment program, found a job as a nurse's assistant, and by the end of the study had regained custody of her children. However, because she'd been off cash welfare for 11 months, her caseworker told her she was only one month from the time limit. Lisa worried about how she would deal with the loss in the face of some rather serious health problems.

> I still get medical benefits but they trying to tell me they going to cut me off at the next month because I've been working [full-time] for [12 months], but I'm trying to fight it because I'm a diabetic and I'm Type II, which is uncontrolled. So I don't think that they should be able to cut me off. So I'm going to have to fight that.

Non-public sources of health care resources. By the end of the study, 26% of the Cleveland respondents who'd worked in the past year had insurance through their jobs, and three of these policies also covered the children. In Philadelphia, 24% of those who had worked in the past year had been covered by their employer's health insurance, and had employer-sponsored coverage for their children. Five other workers across the two sites, including Lisa, had been offered private coverage, but had not taken it because the co-payment was too costly.[24] For the one third of our sample who were without health insurance coverage at some point during the study, half of the time their children were without coverage as well as the adults.

---

[243] Danielle, a white mother of two in Philadelphia, said it would take more than half of her paycheck for the family to take advantage of her health insurance program. Brenda, a white woman in Cleveland, was a receptionist at a manufacturing firm when we last talked to her. She was offered insurance as well, but would have had to pay $289 a month for family benefits, a hefty amount despite her relatively high wage of $10 per hour.

For those who'd lost Medicaid, relatives or friends in the medical profession occasionally helped out. Maria, a white mother of four children in Cleveland, worked several jobs over the four years we knew her but consistently failed to find jobs that provided health insurance. Fortunately, her mother worked at a pharmacy and was able to get the medicine that she needed for a discount. Others "borrowed" the unused portions of common prescription drugs from family and friends. In the last year of our study, Melissa, from Cleveland, and her three children were uninsured for three months while she waited for her employer's health insurance and Healthy Start to cover them. Her elementary-school aged son had ADHD, but Melissa could not afford to buy his Ritalin. An acquaintance from her son's school stepped in to help out:

> That was something though, those three months, cause we ran out of pills, his Ritalin. And one of the ladies at school had some leftover from her kid and she gave them to me...She gave me a prescription of five, was it five? No it was tens and twenty's. [I: Milligrams?] Yeah, cause he takes ten. 'Cause she had a bottle, a full prescription of twenty's, which meant I could split the pills and take that full prescription and last the two, three months...I cut him back, cause he's supposed to take 'em three times a day. I cut him back just to two times in school during that time.

Another strategy the uninsured sometimes employed was to go to the emergency room, where many believed they could not be turned away for lack of coverage, and to convince a doctor to provide them with a large supply of free samples. Maya, an African American Philadelphian with one daughter, had recently started working as a full-time teacher when we interviewed her a second time. She'd just graduated from college with a teacher's degree and quickly found two part-time teaching jobs, which provided just enough salary to put her over the Medicaid guidelines. She went without insurance, and got her daughter covered under her father's policy. Once she was hired full time, she waited for coverage for another 90 days. During that time, she suffered two serious health problems related to her chronic asthma. Fearing the large medical bill she would incur, Maya did not seek treatment the first time. The second time, her sister convinced her to go to the emergency room. She was successful in convincing the doctor to provide her with enough free samples to keep her asthma and allergies under control until her insurance kicked in, but she now carries the debt on the unpaid emergency room bill.

After problems with paperwork and conflict with her caseworker, Eileen lost her Medicaid benefits and did not get them back for the remainder of the study. She had serious health problems, including asthma, and occasionally received free samples from a local doctor who provides care on a sliding scale.

Well, if he has samples and stuff like that, like he'll give
them to me. Initially, if he don't, then I have to pay for the
prescriptions. My one prescription for my breathing pills is
$200.00 [every two months]. My inhalers, I use four of them
a month, they're $28.00 apiece. Then my Prednisone is
$31.00 a month.

Conclusion

This analysis draws on three to four years of longitudinal ethnographic data on 74
families who experienced first-hand the most significant changes in the federal
safety net for poor families with children in recent history. Our focus is on how
those who transition to employment meet their family's basic needs for childcare,
food, and health care by accessing both the public and their own private safety
nets.

Our interest in this question was motivated in two ways. First, policy makers
identified these domains when fashioning the package of transitional benefits to
aid families in making the move to employment. Second, though most respondents
we followed were actively seeking employment, they expressed doubts about their
ability to effectively meet their family's needs in these domains, and worried that
their children would suffer because working would mean the eventual loss of food
stamps and Medicaid, and would force them to entrust the supervision of their
children to others.

In another analysis of these data (Scott et al., 2001) we've shown that most of
these families, all receiving cash welfare when we met them in 1997 and 1998,
had bought the rhetoric surrounding welfare reform, supported its goals, and had
adopted the premise that only by working could they be adequate role models for
their children. Good mothers, they reasoned, had to model the value of work
themselves in order to motivate their children to do those things that would lead to
their own labor market success, such as doing one's homework and staying in
school. They also believed that trading a welfare check for a paycheck would
mean their children would experience significant material gains. Buoyed by the
experiences of family and friends in the wake of an astonishingly strong economy,
they believed they would not only find jobs, but good jobs. Thus, they were quite
confident the costs of going to work, i.e., the loss of food stamps, Medicaid (if no
employer-sponsored insurance was provided), and the ability to supervise their
children themselves, would eventually be more than outweighed.

These views were in sharp contrast to what a similar group of AFDC recipients
told Edin and Lein (1997) in the early 1990s, several years prior to welfare reform.
The 215 welfare recipients Edin and Lein spoke to almost universally wanted to
work, but felt that unless they were able to land an usually good job, the costs of
working would swamp any gain in earnings they might enjoy. They also believed

that full-time year-round work would compromise their ability to parent their children effectively. For most, the solution was to use the time on welfare to invest significantly in their own human capital, or to simply wait until the "costs" of working were lower (i.e., their need for childcare was reduced). This contrast suggests that the strong economy, with the carrot of work supports and the stick of work requirements, may have changed the calculation of the costs and benefits for the average welfare recipient.

Thus, if our families are any guide, at the dawn of welfare reform recipients were fully on board with the goals of welfare reform and had embraced them as their own. Over the ensuing three years, the vast majority of families proved they meant what they'd said at baseline, and struggled valiantly to get and maintain employment. In theory, a whole host of transitional benefits should have been available to aid them in meeting their family's basic needs along the way, but as often as not, the welfare department's rhetoric didn't match the real experiences of families. Most families making the move to a job desperately needed these benefits, and when they were forthcoming, a family's transition was considerably eased. However, the ability of respondents to secure transitional childcare, food, and health care resources depended a great deal on the quality of program implementation in their city or state. When they could not secure these benefits, the vast majority could not replace these resources through the market, since they could not afford to do so.

Our sample across the two cities is small, but the lessons we have taken from this analysis highlight ways that the operation of the public safety net can be improved so that families' transition from welfare to work can occur without significant hassle or hardship. For a policy change as dramatic as welfare reform, it is important to study it from many vantage points so as to not be only describing one part of the elephant. This paper highlights the experiences of welfare recipients, but the broader Urban Change study includes the experiences of caseworkers and neighborhood institutions.[25] It is beyond the scope of this study to identify where the breakdown in service delivery occurred across these various programs, but anyone who spends a day in a local welfare office can easily see how the administrative nightmares so many of our families experienced could have been caused by any number of factors. For example, if welfare administrators do not adequately brief frontline workers on the array of transitional benefits offered, the caseworkers cannot effectively communicate this information to clients. Even caseworkers who understand the new landscape of benefits for welfare-leavers must be trained and monitored to ensure the information gets to the client, and must have a motivation to do so. And though state systems monitor and identify those who are getting benefits in excess of what is allowed, we know of no system to flag cases in which a client has been denied a benefit they are eligible for but not receiving, or have been sanctioned in error.

---

[25] These reports are available at http://www.mdrc.org.

Certainly, the nature of the low-wage labor market, where jobs are often short-lived and variable in hours, makes the average caseworker's job of assessing ongoing eligibility and benefit levels difficult. The vast majority of the women in our sample cycled among a number of jobs with varying hours and pay, so their caseworkers' jobs were especially taxing. Their caseloads may not have been adjusted for the increased burden of each case they were responsible for. Yet in order to make the transition to work manageable for welfare-reliant families, state bureaucracies need to work with these changes in a way that doesn't create logistical nightmares for poor single parents who are trying to play by the rules. Those who know quite well what they're eligible for from the welfare department sometimes simply do not have the time or energy to deal with the administrative hassle involved. Even the small differences in the reporting requirements between Cleveland and Philadelphia (i.e., monthly versus quarterly) seemed to make a great deal of difference in the experiences of families.

Parents who are juggling work and family on a limited income do not have the time or the resources to do the research on the benefits they should be receiving, so many do not have the expertise or courage to challenge their caseworkers, even if they suspect the caseworker is in error. Additionally, most respondents realize that they do not hold the power in this relationship, and the stakes for them are high if they challenge the system. Thus, state welfare systems must ensure that recipients are adequately and accurately informed about all aspects of the state TANF program, including the carrots (transitional benefits) and the sticks (time limits and sanctions). The high rate of turnover among caseworkers makes this an enormous problem. But our analysis shows that securing access to the work-based safety net is crucial for ensuring the needs of families with children are being met.

In lieu of public-sector supports for childcare, food, and healthcare, families often turn to non-public resources, including their personal networks, private charities, and, in the case of Medicaid, their employers. Many assume that those with private resources do not need access to the work-based safety net, or even that the quality of non-public resources exceeds those provided by the public sector. While this assumption is occasionally correct, it is often in grave error. In the childcare domain, though some children without subsidies were able to spend time with a caring and competent grandmother, others were left in the care of adults who were, in their mother's view, verbally abusive, unreliable, struggling with drug addictions or mental illness, or even downright neglectful. In a few situations, children were left caring for children, sometimes to the detriment of both the recipient and giver of the care. Some of these mothers would much rather have used licensed care, but couldn't get access to the subsidy. In the food domain, parents could often get a meal from a family member or friend, but several knew they were putting pressure on a set of network resources that were already spread thin. Food pantries provided some relief, but the stringent limitations they put on the receipt of food and the stigma they imposed increased the transaction costs of employing this strategy. In the healthcare domain, the main non-public resource was the employer, who seldom provided healthcare benefits and when so, often charged a higher co-payment than the family could afford to pay.

Equally important, neither the quality nor the availability of non-public childcare, food, or healthcare resources are evenly distributed among the poor. Edin and Lein (1997) showed that those families with the most ready and valuable offers of support from kin, friends, and institutional sources, were those same families who were already advantaged in other ways; namely, whites, those living in better neighborhoods, and those who'd been on the rolls a shorter amount of time. Other analyses of social network support have also shown higher rates of receipt among the more advantaged (Hogan, Eggebeen, & Clogg, 1993; Roschelle, 1997). Thus, an over-reliance on the private safety net may exacerbate, rather than ameliorate, inequality.

We conclude by offering a warning to the reader. The story we tell here might be unduly rosy. When we left our families in 2000 and 2001, the economy was still strong and most had not yet exhausted the broad array of supports the welfare department offered those who began working. Those who benefited from the ability to combine welfare and part-time work and keep most of their earnings will soon reach the five-year life time limit for cash welfare benefits. Those who've left cash welfare behind may have also now lost Medicaid benefits because they've hit the time limits. Others will have earned their way just above the eligibility thresholds for these programs, which may cause a sudden spike in their work-related expenditures. Some will find their earnings are insufficient to make up the difference. As the economy sags, federal and state officials may feel tempted to cut back on the already-weakened public safety net at a time when it is most needed. The message we have learned from the families in our sample, however, is that this safety net is crucial to their well-being. In addition, those who care about the well-being of families with children must think seriously making sure that these benefits are delivered to needy low-wage workers and their families in a smooth, hassle-free manner.

Finally, we want to note that throughout the course of our study, state officials in both Ohio and Pennsylvania did make modifications to their systems to try to increase their support of families moving from welfare to work. In Ohio, officials amended their computer eligibility verification system so that caseworkers could close the cash assistance benefits for a recipient but not terminate Medicaid benefits. Furthermore, Cuyahoga County launched an advertising campaign to increase awareness of the State Children's Health Insurance Program. In the beginning of 1999, Childcare Works went into effect in Philadelphia. This program increased and expanded childcare funding for working poor families who no longer received cash assistance. Implementation of policies as major as welfare reform can be a continuously changing process. The point of our story about barriers to accessing benefits is not to criticize implementation in specific locales, but rather to point out pitfalls that can occur in any county's delivery of services to families moving from welfare to work.

Acknowledgments

This research is a joint production of the Project on Devolution and Urban Change and the Next Generation project. Both of these research projects are funded through the Manpower Demonstration Research Corporation. The Project on Devolution and Urban Change is funded by the Ford Foundation, Charles Stewart Mott Foundation, Pew Charitable Trusts, W.K. Kellogg Foundation, Robert Wood Johnson Foundation, U.S. Department of Health and Human Services (including interagency funds from the U.S. Department of Agriculture), Annie E. Casey Foundation, John S. and James L. Knight Foundation, Joyce Foundation, Cleveland Foundation, George Gund Foundation, William Penn Foundation, James Irvine Foundation, California Wellness Foundation, and Edna McConnell Clark Foundation. The Next Generation project is funded by the David and Lucile Packard, William T. Grant, and John D. and Catherine T. MacArthur Foundations. The authors would like to thank Averil Clarke, Lorna Dilley, Ralonda Ellis-Hill, Karen Fierer, Tasheika Hinson, Rebecca Joyce Kissane, Mirella Landriscina, Joan Mazelis, Leondra Mitchell, Samieka Mitchell, Keesha Moore, Kagendo Mutua, Laura Nichols, Enid Schatz, and Sarah Spain, who worked with us to recruit the samples, interview the families, and code and analyze the data. We are especially grateful to the families in Cleveland and Philadelphia who shared their experiences with us over the last few years.

References

Adams, G., Snyder, K., & Sandfort, J. R. (2002). *Getting and retaining childcare assistance: How policies and practices influence families' experiences* (Assessing the New Federalism Occasional Paper No. 55). Washington, DC: Urban Institute.

Brock, T., Nelson, L. C., & Reiter, M. (2002). *Readying welfare recipients for work: Lessons from four big cities as they implement welfare reform.* New York: Manpower Demonstration Research Corporation.

Cherlin, A. J., Bogen, K., Quane, J. M., & Burton, L. (2002). Operating within the rules: Welfare recipients' experiences with sanctions and case closings. *Social Service Review, 76*, 387–404.

Danziger, S., Heflin, C. M., Corcoran, M. E., Oltmans, E., & Wang, H. (2002). Does it pay to move from welfare to work? *Journal of Policy Analysis and Management, 21*(4), 671–693.

Edin, K., & Lein, L. (1997). *Making ends meet: How single mothers survive welfare and low-wage work.* New York: Russell Sage Foundation.

Families USA. (1999). *One step forward, one step back: Children's health coverage after CHIP and welfare reform* (Families USA Publication No. 99-106). Washington, DC: Author.

Garrett, B., & Holahan, J. (2000). *Welfare leavers, medical coverage, and private health insurance.* Washington, DC: Urban Institute.

Gennetian, L., Duncan, G., Knox, V., Vargas, W., Clark-Kauffman, E., & London, A. (2002). *How welfare and work policies for parents affect adolescents: A synthesis of research.* New York: Manpower Demonstration Research Corporation.

Giannarelli, L., & Barsimantov, J. (2000). *Childcare expenses of America's families* (Assessing the New Federalism Occasional Paper No. 40). Washington, DC: Urban Institute.

Hogan, D. P., Eggebeen, D. J., & Clogg, C. (1993). The structure of intergenerational exchanges in American families. *American Journal of Sociology, 98*(6), 1428–1458.

London, A. S., Scott, E. K., Edin, K., & Hunter, V. (2001). *Juggling low-wage work and family life: What mothers say about their children's well-being in the context of welfare reform* (The Next Generation, Working Paper). New York: Manpower Demonstration Research Corporation.

Loprest, P. (1999). *Families who left welfare: Who are they and how are they doing?* (Assessing the New Federalism Discussion Paper 99-02). Washington, DC: Urban Institute.

Polit, D. F., London, A. S., & Martinez, J. M. (2000). *Food security and hunger in poor, mother-headed families in four U.S. cities* (The Project on Devolution and Urban Change, Working Paper). New York: Manpower Demonstration Research Corporation.

Polit, D. F., London, A. S., & Martinez, J. M. (2001). *The health of poor urban women: Findings from the Project on Devolution and Urban Change.* New York: Manpower Demonstration Research Corporation.

Quint, J. C., Edin, K., Buck, M. L., Fink, B., Padilla, Y. C., Simmons-Hewlitt, O., & Valmont, M. E. (1999). *Big cities and welfare reform: Early implementation and ethnographic findings from the Project on Devolution and Urban Change.* New York: Manpower Demonstration Research Corporation.

Quint, J., & Widom, R. (2001). *Post-TANF Food Stamps and Medicaid benefits: Factors that aid or impede their receipt.* New York: Manpower Demonstration Research Corporation.

Riley, D., & Eckenrode, J. (1986). Social ties: Subgroup differences in costs and benefits. *Journal of Personality and Social Psychology, 51*(4), 770–778.

Roschelle, A. (1997). *No more kin: Exploring race, class, and gender in family networks.* Thousand Oaks, CA: Sage.

Schumacher, R., & Greenberg, M. (1999). *Childcare after leaving welfare: Early evidence from state studies.* Washington, DC: Center for Law and Social Policy.

Scott, E. K., Edin, K., London, A. S., & Kissane, R. (2001). *Unstable work, unstable income: Implications for family well-being in the era of time-limited welfare* (The Next Generation Project, Working Paper No. 5). New York: Manpower Demonstration Research Corporation.

Scott, E. K., Edin, K., London, A. S., & Mazelis, J. (2001). My children come first: Welfare-reliant women's post-TANF views of work-family tradeoffs. In G. Duncan & P. Chase-Lansdale (Eds.), *For better and for worse: Welfare reform and the well-being of children and families.* New York: Russell Sage Foundation.

Scott, E. K., London, A. S., & Myers, N. A. (2002a). Living with violence: Women's reliance on abusive men in their transitions from welfare to work. In N. Gerstel, D. Clawson, & R. Zussman (Eds.), *Families at work: Expanding the bounds* (pp. 302–316). Nashville: Vanderbilt University Press.

Scott, E. K., London, A. S., & Myers, N. A. (2002b). Dangerous dependencies: The intersection of welfare reform and domestic violence. *Gender & Society, 16*(6), 878–897.

Stack, C. (1974). *All our kin.* New York: Basic Books.

State Policy Documentation Project (2002). *Joint project of Center for Law and Social Policy and Center on Budget and Policy Priorities.* Retrieved from http://www.spdp.org

Wilde, P., Cook, P., Gunderson, C., Nord, M., & Tiehen, L. (2000). *The decline of Food Stamps participation in the 1990s* (Food Assistance and Nutrition Research Report No. 7). Washington, DC: United States Department of Agriculture.

Zedlewski, S. R. (2001). *Former welfare families continue to leave the Food Stamp Program.* (Assessing the New Federalism Discussion Paper 01-05). Washington, DC: Urban Institute.

14

SHOULD PROMOTING MARRIAGE BE THE NEXT STAGE OF WELFARE REFORM?

Benjamin R. Karney
Shauna H. Springer
University of Florida

Clampet-Lundquist et al. (this volume) paint a moving portrait of the challenges that mothers face when transitioning from welfare to work. Their stories reveal that policies designed to help low-income families can be insensitive to the obstacles those families actually face. The result, as the authors effectively point out, is that some people fall through the cracks, obstructed in their efforts to manage their lives by the very services charged with helping them. In their struggles to obtain adequate food, healthcare, and childcare, the women interviewed for this study display remarkable courage and tenacity, making their successes all the more inspiring and their failures all the more poignant. A compassionate reader learning of their experiences can only ask: how might the needs of these families be better served?

The authors offer no easy answers, but their data do suggest a few promising directions. They describe links between success at maintaining employment and the availability of childcare subsidies. It makes sense that women who do not have to choose between their jobs and the well-being of their children will be able to pursue those jobs more effectively. Thus, one way to facilitate the transition from welfare to work would be to make childcare subsidies more widely available. They describe how case workers, overtaxed by the federally mandated changes in their own roles, create unnecessary obstacles for many women, failing to provide information and sometimes providing incorrect information about the benefits available. These stories suggest that welfare reforms will be more effective when accompanied by a commitment to the effective and fair implementation of those reforms. Finally, the authors note that the women who were most in need were the ones least likely to possess access to nonpublic resources. These cases suggest that if the most needy women and their children are to be protected, public resources must be maintained and enhanced.

Welfare Reform and Marital Stability

Despite these implications, however, current proposals for new legislation to help low-income families address none of these directions. Instead, during the years since the 1996 legislation was enacted, further welfare reform has been explicitly linked to promoting marital stability. In spring 2002, for example, the Bush administration urged Congress to allocate $300 million of welfare money to programs encouraging marriage, explicitly as a means through which women may exit poverty. The proposal follows on the heels of a wave of similar measures that have been passed or are currently being discussed at the level of state government. Florida, for example, was the first state in the nation to mandate relationship education. As of 1998, Florida's ninth- and tenth-grade students are required to take classes on relationship values and skills, engaged couples in Florida are offered a discount of $32.50 on their marriage licenses if they provide evidence of receiving premarital education, and couples contemplating divorce are required, if they have a minor child, to undergo up to three months of counseling. Louisiana, Arizona, and Arkansas have each passed legislation allowing couples to enter into a covenant marriage, distinguished from a regular marriage in that couples must prove that they have received premarital education, and are required to receive counseling before divorcing. More than 20 other states are currently considering bills instituting their own versions of covenant marriage. Arizona, in addition, has appropriated funds allocated for the Temporary Assistance to Needy Families (TANF) program to pay for marriage education classes. Oklahoma Governor Frank Keating has devoted $10 million of welfare money to fund similar classes. West Virginia, as of July 2000, awards a monthly $100 bonus to couples on welfare who are married and remain married. These examples by no means exhaust the list of state and federal government programs promoting marriage in the United States, but they suffice to make a point. In most cases, efforts to encourage marriage have been an element of broader efforts directed towards reducing dependence on government subsidies.

The logic behind linking welfare reform and marriage promotion seems to be as follows. Data from several national surveys, most recently the National Survey of Family Growth (Bramlett & Mosher, 2002), indicate that rates of marriage are significantly lower and rates of divorce are significantly higher in neighborhoods with higher rates of poverty and lower household incomes. Longitudinal data reveal associations between marital disruption and declines in income for women (Morgan, 1991), and have demonstrated long-term negative outcomes for children of dissolved marriages (e.g., McLanahan & Bumpass, 1988). Although these findings have all been correlational, it has nonetheless been thought that they indicate the presence of causal relationships from marriage to poverty. Thus, promoting stable marital unions has been held up as a means of simultaneously preventing the declines that lead families to rely on welfare and allowing low-income couples and their children to raise themselves up out of poverty. Because some studies have shown that relationship education and improved communication skills predict more stable marriages (e.g., Halford, Sanders, & Behrens, 2001), federal funds have been devoted specifically toward relationship education and communication development programs, all in the name of diminishing reliance on government welfare.

Among policy makers invested in welfare reform, this sort of logic has been explicit. For example, the Florida Marriage Preparation and Preservation Act of 1998 begins with the statements that "Relationship skills can be learned" and "When effective coping exists, domestic violence, child abuse, and divorce and its effect on children, such as absenteeism, medical costs, and learning and social deficiencies, are diminished." From these premises, the legislature of Florida reached the conclusion that government money devoted to teaching coping skills to couples may be a more effective social policy than giving those finds directly to individuals in the form of welfare.

Problems with Marriage Promotion as Welfare Reform

Are the conclusions reached by an increasing number of policymakers at the state and federal levels justified? Are programs designed to promote marital stability likely to improve the lives of low-income families? Data from Clampet-Lundquist et al. offer cause for concern about the answers to these questions. One is the fact that research on the beneficial effects of relationship education and communication skills training has yet to be conducted on samples that contain low-income couples and families. On the contrary, research on the causes and consequences of marital stability has been conducted almost exclusively on samples consisting primarily of white, middle-class, relatively well-educated couples, and nowhere is this more true than in research on marital communication (Karney & Bradbury, 1995). To the extent that marriages among low-income families differ in important ways from marriages among middle-class couples, results from prior research are unlikely to generalize. For example, couples who live well above the poverty line can take for granted that they will have flexible time in which to communicate with each other. Low-income families may not have that flexibility. After taking multiple jobs, caring for children, and completing the complex requirements for obtaining their benefits, the families described by Clampet-Lundquist et al. seem unlikely to have a spare moment to communicate with each other at all, much less practice the communication skills taught by marital education programs. The idea that a good marriage takes work seems especially apt here. Just as Clampet-Lundquist et al. described those forced to chase down their own benefits and find suitable childcare as those who were also most limited in their ability to maintain employment, lack of time to communicate and enjoy each other may also limit the ability of low-income couples to maintain their relationships. Thus, lack of time for communication may be the source of difficulty in the marriages of low-income families, rather than a lack of skill in communicating. Until marital education is shown to be effective in couples who face significant challenges external to their relationships, redirecting welfare money towards marital education programs may be premature.

A second concern with current proposals is that they may rest on a confusion between different kinds of marital outcomes (Karney, Bradbury, & Johnson, 1999). The premise of these proposals is that the state of being married carries tangible benefits for couples and children. It may be more accurate to say that the state of being happily married carries those benefits. Being in an unhappy marriage, to the contrary, has significant negative consequences for physical and mental health (Veroff, Kulka, & Douvan, 1981), and long-term negative consequences for children (Booth & Amato, 2001). Promoting marriage, especially to the extent that couples who no longer wish to be married are prevented from divorcing, may therefore have the unintended consequence of prolonging the suffering of couples and their children.

Stress and Marital Satisfaction

Among low-income families, marital distress may be a particular concern because these couples face the sorts of chronic and acute stressors that make marital distress more likely. Our own recent longitudinal work has explored the processes through which challenges external to a relationship may affect the development of the marriage. Although this work has not examined low-income couples directly, it has revealed processes that may generalize to these couples.

For example, one study (Karney, Story, & Bradbury, in press) confirms that it is harder for even initially satisfied couples to maintain their relationships when facing chronic stress. Newlywed couples were asked to discuss in detail and then rate the quality of their finances, their jobs, their health, and their relationships with friends and family, every six months for the first four years of their marriages. We expected that, in general, couples who faced higher levels of chronic stress (e.g., ongoing health problems, job instability, lack of financial security) would report lower levels of marital satisfaction, even as newlyweds. This prediction was confirmed. Furthermore, we predicted that, even controlling for differences in their general levels of satisfaction, couples facing more severe chronic stress would also experience greater declines in their marital satisfaction over the first years of marriage. This prediction was also confirmed, suggesting that chronic stress interferes with efforts at preserving a happy relationship, presumably by draining resources and energy that spouses might otherwise spend on each other.

In the same study, we also examined the effects of acute stress, those specific events (e.g., car accidents, acute illnesses, natural disasters) that arise over the course of a marriage and require communication to resolve. If chronic stress affects a marriage by draining a couple's coping resources, then high levels of chronic stress should make coping with acute stressors especially difficult for couples. Indeed, marital satisfaction tended, on average, to be lower after periods during which couples faced many acute stressors, and higher after periods that were relatively low in acute stressors. For couples facing high levels of chronic stress, however, these effects were significantly stronger. In other words, the marital satisfaction of couples facing serious chronic stress was more reactive to the experience of acute stressors, whereas couples facing little chronic stress were able to deal with their acute stress in ways that left their marriages unaffected.

How do stressors external and presumably unrelated to a relationship affect spouses' evaluations of the marriage? Our most current work (Neff & Karney, under review) develops a model proposing two routes through which external stress may affect marital satisfaction. The first, and most direct, route is through the effects of external stress on the content of the relationship. As noted earlier, couples facing severe challenges outside of the relationship are likely to have less time to interact with each other, and less time to discuss problems that might arise in the marriage. Couples facing external stress may therefore experience fewer opportunities for affection and more unresolved conflicts. To evaluate this idea, we examined a second sample of newlywed couples, assessing their marital satisfaction, levels of acute stress, and experience of specific marital problems every six months for the first four years of the marriage. Consistent with our predictions, fluctuations in acute stress covaried with fluctuations in perceptions of specific problems, and those perceptions mediated the effects of acute stress on marital satisfaction. Thus, when couples experienced higher than normal levels of stress, they tended also to experience more marital problems. This accounted for their lower marital satisfaction during these periods.

A second route through which external stress may affect evaluations of a marriage is more indirect. Stress may affect not only the nature of each spouse's experiences in the marriage, but also the way each spouse understands and processes those experiences. It has been well-established, for example, that satisfied spouses make allowances for their partners' occasional negative behaviors (Bradbury & Fincham, 1990). By making an external attribution for a partner's lapses, a spouse may recognize the behavior without linking that behavior to a broader judgment about the marriage (McNulty & Karney, 2001). Such processes require effort, however, and it seems reasonable to suggest that under conditions of stress a spouse's ability to engage in these processes would be diminished. To evaluate this possibility, the same study described above examined whether fluctuations in acute stress covary with the kinds of attributions spouses make for negative events in their marriages, controlling for their perceptions of marital problems (Neff & Karney, under review). Consistent with our predictions, the nature of each spouse's attributions for their partner's behaviors also and independently mediated the association between acute stress and marital satisfaction. Thus, stress external to a relationship seems to affect evaluations of a marriage in two ways: first, by giving rise to negative experiences and minimizing opportunities for positive ones, and second, by limiting the ability of each spouse to process those experiences in a relationship enhancing manner.

Are similar effects likely to describe relationships within low-income families? The range of chronic and acute stress reported by couples in both of the studies described above was quite narrow. Yet even within that range, variability in stress was associated with variability in marital processes and marital outcomes. How much more substantial may these effects be among couples who are experiencing the severe stressors described by Clampet-Lundquist et al.? To the extent that couples experiencing relatively mild chronic stress experience report lower marital satisfaction, couples struggling daily to provide adequate food and healthcare for their children may be exceptionally prone to marital distress. To the extent that couples experiencing mild elevations in acute stress seem less able to forgive their partners for minor negative behaviors, couples who face life-threatening challenges may find their perceptions of the relationship highly fragile. From this perspective, current proposals to reduce reliance on welfare by preserving marriages seem particularly misguided. This line of research suggests that without a context in which basic needs for food, childcare and healthcare are met, marriages are not likely to be worth preserving. The direction of causality, in other words, may run from poverty to poor marital outcomes, rather than the other way around.

Conclusion

The detailed ethnographic data of Clampet-Lundquist et al. reveal the difficulties and injustices that may arise when families are forced to transition off welfare without readily available supports for making that transition. In doing so, they offer a model with which to understand the potential problems that may arise from the current wave of welfare reform legislation targeting marriage. Laws that require marital skills training for couples who must struggle to feed and clothe their children may not only be wasting resources on a population that could benefit from more direct interventions, but may in fact impede families who are already overburdened with the requirements of obtaining their welfare benefits. Laws that make marriages more difficult to end without providing resources that make marriages easier to maintain may ultimately prolong suffering rather than reduce it.

The lesson may be that the difficulties inherent in meeting basic needs are inseparable from the difficulties inherent in maintaining a relationship. Poverty rates and divorce rates may not be associated problems; they may be symptoms of a single underlying problem. Clampet-Lundquist et al. demonstrate that those who do best over the transition from welfare to work are those who are already advantaged. The same seems to be true in marriage: couples who have the advantage of resources to devote to the relationship are likely to have better relationships than those who lack such resources. Reducing divorce rates, therefore, may require less education and more attempts to extend the relevant advantages to low-income families. Rather than promoting marriage as a way of reducing poverty, serious welfare reform might consider directly attacking poverty itself. From a rich soil in which basic needs for food, healthcare, and childcare are met, healthy families may grow by themselves.

Acknowledgments

Preparation of this article was supported by grant no. MH59712 from the National Institute of Mental Health awarded to the first author. This research was also supported in part by a grant from the Fetzer Institute awarded to the first author.

The authors wish to thank Lisa Neff and Catherine Cohan for their valuable insights and assistance with the preparation of these comments.

References

Booth, A., & Amato, P. R. (2001). Parental predivorce relationships and offspring postdivorce well-being. *Journal of Marriage and the Family, 63*, 197–212.

Bradbury, T. N., & Fincham, F. D. (1990). Attributions in marriage: Review and critique. *Psychological Bulletin, 107*, 3–33.

Bramlett, M. D., & Mosher, W. D. (2002). *Cohabitation, marriage, divorce, and remarriage in the United States* (Vital and Health Statistics Series 23, No. 22). Hyattsville, MD: National Center for Health Statistics.

Halford, W. K., Sanders, M. R., & Behrens, B. C. (2001). Can skills training prevent relationship problems in at-risk couples? Four-year effects of a behavioral relationship education program. *Journal of Family Psychology, 15*, 750–768.

Karney, B. R., & Bradbury, T. N. (1995). The longitudinal course of marital quality and stability: A review of theory, method, and research. *Psychological Bulletin, 118*, 3–34.

Karney, B. R., Bradbury, T. N., & Johnson, M. D. (1999). Deconstructing marital stability: Distinguishing between marital dissolution and the trajectory of marital satisfaction. In J. M. Adams & W. H. Jones (Eds.), *Handbook of interpersonal commitment and relationship stability* (pp. 481–499). New York: Plenum.

Karney, B. R., Story, L. B., & Bradbury, T. N. (in press). Marriages in context: Interactions between chronic and acute stress among newlyweds. In T. A. Revenson, K. Kayser, & G. Bodenmann (Eds.), *The developmental course of couples coping with stress*. Washington, DC: American Psychological Association.

McLanahan, S., & Bumpass, L. (1988). Intergenerational consequences of family disruption. *American Journal of Sociology, 94*, 130–152.

McNulty, J. K., & Karney, B. R. (2001). Attributions in marriage: Integrating specific and global evaluations of a relationship. *Personality and Social Psychology Bulletin, 27,* 943–955.

Morgan, L. A. (1991). *After marriage ends: Economic consequences for midlife women.* Newbury Park, CA: Sage.

Neff, L. A., & Karney, B. R. (under review). Influences of negative external stressors on cognitive processes within relationships. Manuscript submitted for publication.

Veroff, J., Kulka, R. A., & Douvan, E. (1981). *Mental health in America: Patterns of helpseeking from 1957 to 1976.* New York: Basic Books.

15

MAKING OUR WAY TOGETHER: COLLABORATION IN THE MOVE FROM WELFARE TO WORK

Lynne A. Bond
Amy M. Carmola Hauf
University of Vermont

As states throughout the U.S. struggle with welfare reform, policy makers, media, and the public look for data to demonstrate a decrease in numbers of recipients of welfare, food stamps, and Medicaid, and an increase in individuals who are employed. This fervent search for *evidence of success* presses on. But too rarely do we pause to consider what might truly indicate "success" in the welfare-to-work transition, which are the highest priority goals, and what constitutes supporting "evidence" for their achievement.

Clampet-Lundquist et al. (this volume) provide an intriguing account of mothers' rocky road in "making a way out of no way" as they attempt to "meet basic family needs while moving from welfare to work." This chapter clearly illustrates the sorts of gaps and unmet needs that too often arise in the course of policy and program development and implementation. In fact, it is not only the mothers' words, but also what is missing from their accounts that suggest more effective strategies needed for undertaking the journey from welfare to work, and the importance of acknowledging that we must take this journey *together*.

In this chapter, we use Clampet-Lundquist et al.'s account as a springboard for considering: (a) the pressing need for conducting systems analyses to frame program development, (b) the necessity of incorporating ongoing program monitoring and evaluation that build on this systems approach, (c) the critical roles of safety nets that harness the strengths of diverse components of these systems, and (d) the resources that emerge when we name, acknowledge, and build upon individuals' achievements in coping within challenging systems. We argue that significant gains in each of these directions will result from pursuing a more *collaborative partnership* that engages diverse stakeholders in a joint venture through planning, implementing, monitoring, and revising welfare reform.

The Importance of a Systems Analysis

Mothers' tales of their journeys from welfare to work (Clampet-Lundquist et al., this volume) attune us to the many different layers of individuals, groups, and

251

systems that both influence and are influenced *by* the trajectory and tenor of welfare-to-work transitions. The roles played by these individuals, groups, and systems are ever changing and complex, developing and unfolding over time. To date, the story of welfare-to-work is too often told from the perspective of state and federal system employment and welfare statistics. Yet, it is obviously far more complex as it touches the lives of so many different stakeholders. For example, we learn of the ways in which mothers' own attitudes, relationships, resourcefulness, and skills shape (and are shaped by) the journey; moreover, we also begin to discover the roles assumed by other stakeholders: the mothers' children, partners, other family members; friends, neighbors, and childcare providers; their caseworkers and caseworkers' supervisors; the mothers' new coworkers, employers, and work settings; and the state and federal bureaucracies, regulatory systems, and policy makers. We can project characters.even beyond this list, including, for example, the broader not-for-profit and for-profit business sectors, healthcare and social service providers, politicians, taxpayers, and more. Clampet-Lundquist et al. have amplified the voices of welfare mothers as authors. In so doing, they help us to recognize the need for an even broader collaborative team of storytellers nested within different systems that are involved in the process. In fact, it is easy (and exciting!) to imagine a volume of "The Collected Stories of Welfare to Work" that incorporates not only the chapter by Clampet-Lundquist et al. but also a series of chapters authored by each of the different groups of constituents just mentioned—each with the opportunity to recount their experiences in the welfare-to-work transition.

The Need for and Value of Ongoing Monitoring and Evaluation

It is difficult to learn of mothers' struggles in the welfare-to-work transition without feeling shock and frustration regarding the apparent hurdles, service gaps, and misinformation introduced by various players and systems. Glitches arise in any new program during the transition from design to implementation; this is neither inexcusable nor unexpected. However, *every* program, regardless of how broad or narrow its scope, must include a system for ongoing monitoring and program evaluation as well as responsive program modification. In fact, ongoing monitoring and evaluation are among the most prominent characteristics shared by highly successful prevention and promotion programs (Bond & Carmola Hauf, in press) because this evaluation permits ongoing refinement of program design and implementation to more effectively achieve intended effects and respond to unintended effects (e.g., see Dalton, Elias, & Wandersman [2001] for a description of Comprehensive Quality Programming).

These comments are not intended to suggest that state welfare reform programs have remained completely isolated or unresponsive. As Clampet-Lundquist et al.

note, most states have increased the "work-based safety net" over the recent past in the form of new earned income disregards and tax credits, childcare subsidies, and extension of Medicaid benefits. In fact, the authors (this volume, p. xx) conclude that these changes have "in conjunction with the actual employment ... made the difference in leaving welfare." However, without ongoing monitoring of the mothers' own experiences, we would not have been able to identify the need for and contributions of such work supports. Such monitoring—and the flexibility and commitment to respond to it—must be an integral part of welfare reform programs. Moreover, the insight we glean through listening to mothers recount their experiences offers a glimmer of what we might learn from monitoring the experiences of other stakeholders and systems as well. Considering the multiple nested systems involved in welfare reform, it becomes clear that ongoing monitoring at multi-systems levels is essential for constructive outcomes.

The very process of engaging diverse stakeholders in monitoring and evaluation also focuses us in important strategic directions. We are led to ask, what are the different components and processes of the program that contribute to its success and deserve review? What are the many and varied sources of information (e.g., multiple stakeholders in diverse contexts) that can provide data relevant to these program components and outcomes? What are the shared and divergent goals of the stakeholders and how might they complement as well as conflict with each other? Accordingly, what are the various ways in which we might define as well as measure program success, with this array of goals in mind? Although each of these considerations is central to successful program design and implementation from the start, these questions are too often ignored in the absence of careful evaluation (e.g., see Carmola Hauf & Bond, 2002). We are fortunate to have useful models such as (Linney & Wandersman's 1996) *Prevention Plus III* approach for "identifying program goals and outcomes, evaluating program process, and evaluating attainment of desired program outcomes and wider impacts" (Dalton et al., 2001, p. 405). An increasing emphasis upon empowerment evaluation (e.g., Fetterman, Kaftarian, & Wandersman, 1996) supports a move to establish fuller collaboration among evaluation specialists, program planners, and developers so that the latter, including program participants themselves, are empowered to name and assess progress toward their goals and outcomes.

The Need for Safety Nets in Multiple Systems

Building upon the importance of a systems perspective and ongoing program monitoring, we come to recognize the need for and value of safety nets in multiple systems, so vividly illustrated in Clampet-Lundquist's account. Because different strengths and vulnerabilities are associated with each of these nets and systems, it is vital to have access to a variety of safety nets linked to diverse networks.

On the one hand, these safety nets include formal, institutionalized systems of support such as the federal and state work supports (e.g., childcare subsidies, food stamps, earned income tax credits, etc.). These formal supports are often presumed to be equally accessible to individuals in need, yet mothers' stories convince us that this is not the case within, and especially across, state borders. By witnessing the ways in which certain people fall through the holes in formal safety nets (e.g., when caseworkers levy sanctions, or when paperwork becomes overwhelming for mothers, childcare providers, or welfare staff), we discover not only the harm that these gaps create but also some of the ties that can hold the nets together (e.g., flexible responsive caseworkers, transitional work supports). The prominent role of formal, institutionalized safety nets is accentuated by the finding that "seemingly small variation in program requirements in [the two states examined] had a dramatic effect on the daily lives of poor families" (Clampet-Lundquist et al., this volume, p. 239). While this is disheartening from the perspective that the viability of a general policy is so vulnerable to state implementation, it is nevertheless encouraging to know that state systems *truly can* facilitate progress toward federally mandated goals. So many people have been ready to give up on the potential for our unwieldy state and federal bureaucratic systems to affect progress and change at all.

On the other hand, mothers' accounts of their welfare-to-work transitions also highlight the importance of safety nets comprised of informal microsystems that engage, for example, family members, friends, and neighbors who provide or barter services and share resources (e.g., childcare, food, and medicines, as Clampet-Lundquist et al. illustrate). Ironically, as is the case with formal institutional supports, there may be an implicit assumption that all individuals who are in need have access to informal safety nets. However, Clampet-Lundquist et al. provide striking testimony of existing disparities in both the existence of informal safety nets (e.g., family and friends with needed competencies and resources) as well as in mothers' abilities to access such networks (e.g., related to the women's self esteem, self-confidence, and resources available for barter).

To the degree to which we can facilitate the development of constructive safety nets that build upon already existing, stable systems and institutions (whether formal or informal) in the mothers' lives, the women and their families will benefit from more stable and sustainable supports. Thus, neighborhood gatekeepers (e.g., store clerks, neighborhood leaders and organizations, post office staff, school personnel, bank cashiers, transportation workers, childcare providers, and the like) may serve particularly important roles.

Acknowledging and Building upon Creative Coping and Resilience

In addition to the power of formal and informal safety nets to support welfare-to-work transitions, Clampet-Lundquist et al. illustrate many mothers' own capacities for creative coping and resilience in the face of pressing financial, family, and social stressors. We hear of one mother who sold her blood plasma to obtain money for food, another who used different names to access different food shelves in order to feed her family, the practice of securing childcare by swapping food (obtained through food stamps), accessing the hospital emergency room for service and free medicine samples, and more. Each of these examples reflects creative problem solving and coping strategies that help mothers make "a way out of no way."

It is remarkable how rarely we name and acknowledge such creative coping, especially among those who are relatively marginalized from mainstream socioeconomic success. It becomes difficult to hear a full range of voices and observe diverse forms of adaptation given the structures that frame our techniques for information gathering (e.g., our research sampling, telecommunications tools, community decision-making practices, and systems for political advancement and policy development). However, when we make the effort to capture, name, and acknowledge the strategies for coping that, for example, poor marginalized women have devised with remarkably little support (e.g., see Banyard, 1995; Belenky, Bond, & Weinstock, 1997; Romich & Weisner, 2001; Saegert, 1989), we develop not only a rich appreciation of the initiative, skills, resourcefulness, and sometimes complex strategizing involved, but also insights into processes (in this instance, created by the mothers) that we might be able to expand upon to everyone's advantage. For example, in a study of mothers who participated in the New Hope project (a community-initiated antipoverty program in Wisconsin) and qualified for the Earned Income Tax Credit (EITC), Romich and Weisner (2001, p. 212) note that one mother "purposely opened a bank account far away so she wouldn't take her money out so often." Consider the potential for amassing resourceful strategies such as this to fuel visions for program improvements. For that matter, imagine what creative coping strategies other stakeholders (e.g., the children, partners, neighbors, caseworkers, health care providers, etc.) may contribute as well, based upon their experiences maneuvering the welfare-to-work transition; these can all contribute to constructive program revision.

Reframing Welfare Reform as a Collaborative Venture

Much of our thinking about the implications of Clampet-Lundquist et al.'s paper has been influenced by our own work involving successful prevention and intervention programs (Bond & Carmola Hauf, in press) and, in particular, *collaborative partnerships* for designing, implementing, evaluating, and modifying such programs (Carmola Hauf & Bond, 2002). In fact, each of the four major issues we have examined in this chapter—the importance of a systems analysis, ongoing evaluation and monitoring in these diverse niches, promoting accessibility of diverse safety nets, and identifying and building upon creative coping strategies of the mothers and other stakeholders—can and perhaps *must* be addressed, in part, through the adoption of a more collaborative partnership in welfare reform.

Collaboration builds upon the contributions of a range of relevant stakeholders—those individuals and groups who both influence and are influenced by the issues being addressed. Collaborative programs are flexible and context-dependent; the structure of any given collaboration and the relative quality and quantity of stakeholder responsibilities depend upon the nature of the particular issue being addressed and the availability of resources. At the same time, an underlying premise of any collaborative effort is that "resources, power, and authority are shared and people are brought together to achieve a common goal that could not be accomplished by a single entity, individual, or organization independently" (Colby & Murrell, 1998, p. 191). Reframing welfare reform as a more collaborative venture appears essential if we are to resolve and prevent many of the problems revealed by Clampet-Lundquist et al.

While many features of collaborative partnerships are relevant to this discussion, we will emphasize three that are closely linked with the issues we've raised above: (1) acknowledging multiple and diverse stakeholders, (2) identifying clearly defined goals that incorporate the needs and perspectives of key stakeholders, and (3) building upon the varied and often unique resources that different stakeholders contribute to achieving jointly defined goals.

Acknowledging Multiple and Diverse Stakeholders

Collaborative efforts acknowledge and engage a potentially wide range of stakeholders that influence and are influenced by the issues or goals being addressed. The inclusion of multiple stakeholders stems from—and is best achieved by—the consideration of influential factors within many different systems. By bringing together a range of stakeholders affiliated with diverse but relevant systems, collaborative ventures not only profit from the varied perspectives that each offers but also promote the commitment of each group through acknowledging their ties to the issue, empowering each to influence the future course of action, and promoting ownership of both the process and the outcomes. Collaborative partnerships not only bolster each stakeholder's ties to the issue, but also their links to one another. Collaboration promotes recognition that they are all in this together, with shared responsibility for outcomes.

As Clampet-Lundquist et al. powerfully illustrate, mothers are not simply recipients or targets of the welfare-to-work program. Rather, as key stakeholders, they are active participants in shaping their own experiences as well as influencing the experiences of their families, friends, employers, caseworkers, and the state system as a whole. These mothers contribute to and are affected by the program's successes and challenges as they fight to access transitional benefits (e.g., traveling repeatedly to the welfare office, completing complicated and tedious paperwork), access—and construct—a range of personal safety nets when public-sector supports are not available (e.g., finding family and friends to provide childcare, relying on food pantries, bartering for food stamps), and resort to sometimes risky measures for filling the gaps (e.g., selling prescription drugs, going without medical care). Within a more collaborative model, mothers and their families, neighbors, caseworkers, policy makers, the business sectors, and others would work together in an ongoing fashion towards achieving welfare reform—with each explicitly acknowledging, engaging, and building upon the contributions of the others.

Of course, the adoption of a more collaborative approach would not be without challenges. Clampet-Lundquist et al. point out several obstacles that may stand in the way of each group's willingness to recognize the other as a fellow stakeholder and to work collaboratively: for example, caseworkers and mothers may have antagonistic relationships due to lack of trust and prior bad history; they may feel defensive about sharing information or power; and coming from different "cultures" may make communication difficult. Perhaps the greatest obstacle is that caseworkers and mothers may have and/or *perceive* themselves as having different goals. In fact, the process of collaboration can help immensely to clarify these differences and support the development of jointly accepted goals (and thereby address other obstacles such as distrust and miscommunication).

Identifying Goals that Incorporate the Needs and Perspectives of Key Stakeholders

Effective programs are characterized by having clearly defined and agreed-upon goals. By bringing stakeholders together, collaborative partnerships establish opportunities to explore commonalities and discrepancies among their goals. Each partner has the opportunity to voice its perspective, reflect on one another's views, and negotiate the future, thereby promoting everyone's ownership of and commitment to the program as ultimately construed.

The mothers interviewed by Clampet-Lundquist et al. generally endorse and devote effort to achieving the state and federally defined welfare-to-work program goals; they seek out training and employment opportunities and identify and access transitional work supports. However, these mothers are also driven by other, sometimes conflicting goals (e.g., securing and sustaining safe and reliable childcare, providing for the basic health and nutritional needs of their families, balancing their personal needs with those of their children and other family members, many of whom may be lacking resources). Each of these goals is reasonable and at least equal in importance to the goal of full-time employment. We find that mothers often turn to personal networks, such as relatives and friends, in their efforts to achieve the dual goals of working and caring for their families. Yet, as with all stakeholders the relatives and friends have life goals of their own (involving their personal needs and those of their families, friends, employers, communities, and others) that alternatively complement and compete with those of the mothers they are being asked to support. Their goals can and must also be considered within a more collaborative approach to welfare reform planning, implementation, and evaluation.

Without a collaborative approach, it is difficult to avoid the misunderstanding, disappointment, and frustration that characterize the relationships Clampet-Lundquist et al. portray between the caseworkers and their clients. According to those authors, although the stated goal of the state welfare departments was to provide transitional support to those moving from welfare to work, the "welfare department's rhetoric didn't match the real experience of families" (this volume, p. xx). Mothers described instances in which their caseworkers misplaced or deliberately failed to file paperwork, provided limited, inaccurate, or misleading information about benefits, imposed sanctions by withdrawing benefits that should have been guaranteed, and generally were "out to get" the women they were supposed to be helping. And yet we, like the mothers, have little sense of what actually underlies caseworkers' actions in these scenarios. Is it inadequate information and training related to high rates of turnover and insufficient support and supervision, low motivation, frustration and commitment to a punitive disciplinary approach toward their clients, as Clampet-Lundquist et al. suggest? Does the program create added work for the caseworkers? What is their understanding of the department, state, and federal goals, and their own roles vis-à-vis their clients, supervisors, and others? A better understanding of caseworkers' experiences, assumptions, and goals would help us understand what leads to service gaps and how they can be avoided in the future. Meanwhile, the simple fact that mothers perceive caseworkers as undermining their success illustrates the necessity for stakeholders to share perspectives and construct mutual priorities and strategies for achieving them.

Building upon the Resources of Different Stakeholders

Effective human development programs are generally characterized by a multi-system, multi-level perspective that acknowledges multiple influences on and pathways of development. Their success arises, to a significant degree, from influencing *relationships between systems* and *trajectories* of development rather than isolated behaviors and events (Bond & Carmola Hauf, in press). Collaborative partnerships in program design, implementation, and monitoring allow us to build upon the varied expertise and flexibility introduced by diverse stakeholders. Different stakeholders are affiliated and experienced with different systems that are relevant to program goals. Collaborative efforts pool stakeholders' skills, experience, and points of access for dealing with various contexts, systems, and trajectories of development.

This means that collaborative partnerships help to increase coordination and avoid gaps (as well as redundancies) of services, such as those (e.g., in childcare, healthcare, and food benefits) that Clampet-Lundquist et al. reveal are so prevalent in the journey from welfare to work. Similarly, collaboration permits multiple systems and parts of systems to be part of the solution rather than simply part of the problem, unlike the current situation in which, for example, mothers and their caseworkers often see one another as presenting obstacles to maneuver around, given the other's lack of understanding and appreciation of the bigger picture.

Different stakeholders have access to different types of resources that may be needed to make any particular program effective, such as money, personnel, credibility, political connections, and legitimacy. By engaging diverse stakeholders as collaborative partners, there is greater opportunity to develop understanding and respect for the perspectives, history, and resources each may offer. Clampet-Lundquist et al. provide moving examples of mothers', as well as their family's and friends', capacities for coping and resilience in the face of financial, personal, and family stress. These are stakeholder resources that contribute to program success. At the same time, caseworkers and other state employees have resources to contribute, such as knowledge of policies and available benefits, access or input (although perhaps too limited) to welfare program planners and administrators, and connections with other human service agencies. Through effective collaboration, each group's resources are made apparent and available to other stakeholders, promoting mutual respect and commitment to the partnership, and mutual benefit. More broadly, collaboration and resource sharing provides opportunities for building trust, sustained communication, and shared responsibilities and expectations.

Children as Stakeholders in the Welfare-to-Work Transition

In closing, we wish to consider a group of stakeholders (and potential collaborators) from whom we hear too rarely in the process of program development, implementation, monitoring, and revision—the children of families receiving welfare. In an earlier analysis of the same data described in this volume, Scott, Edin, London, and Mazelis (2001) demonstrate that mothers are quite focused upon the possible positive and negative effects of the transition from welfare to work on their families. Clampet-Lundquist et al.'s current analysis of the ways in which mothers meet basic family needs en route from welfare to work suggests an urgent need to examine those effects. Earlier literature warned of potential hazards of welfare reform and related policy changes for parenting and child development (e.g., Brady-Smith, Brooks-Gunn, Waldfogel & Fauth, 2001; Wilson, Ellwood, & Brooks-Gunn, 1995), but reports of relevant outcome research are only beginning to emerge.

Summarizing the earlier (Scott et al., 2001) analysis of their data, Clampet-Lundquist et al. (this volume, p. 211) note that most families they interviewed:

... bought the rhetoric surrounding welfare reform, supported its goals, and had adopted the premise that only by working could they be adequate role models for their children. Good mothers, they reasoned, had to model the value of work themselves in order to motivate their children to do those things that would lead to their own labor market success....

Some research evidence suggests that there may be reason to be optimistic about childrearing and child development outcomes of welfare-to-work transitions. Brooks-Gunn, Klebanov, Smith, and Lee (2001) report that on cognitive and behavioral assessments, the children of mothers who combine public assistance and employment score similarly to children of mothers who work and receive no public assistance, while children of mothers who only receive public assistance show more negative cognitive and behavioral outcomes (and the mothers provide less stimulating home learning environments). Stable employment among single, low-income mothers who are transitioning from welfare has been associated with higher child performance on math assessments (Gyamfi, 2002). An analysis of the Minnesota Family Investment Program, a welfare program that began prior to the 1996 federal welfare reform legislation, revealed that participants experienced increased employment and decreased poverty, and these mothers perceived their children as less likely to show problem behaviors and more likely to have greater engagement and better performance in school (Gennetian & Miller, 2002).

Examining Clampet-Lundquist et al.'s account of welfare-to-work transitions, we find related reasons to anticipate the potential for beneficial child outcomes. The authors report overall increases in net income (which includes work-related benefits such as childcare and healthcare support). We imagine that in some situations there may be advantages to having fathers and other family members more engaged in childcare—to the extent to which they are able, effective, and feel positive about it (which was *not* always the case); mothers might accrue additional support networks through their co-workers; and the acquisition of new work-related skills, sustained employment, and decreased dependency on public assistance may boost mothers' sense of self-esteem, confidence, pride, and effectiveness as a parent and role model.

At the same time, there are a number of reasons to worry about potentially adverse effects of welfare-to-work transitions on children. As Parcel and Menaghan (1997) warn, women's working conditions can influence the ways in which they parent as well as the ways in which they structure the home environment. If welfare recipients are able to secure only low-paying, stressful jobs, then employment may, in fact, be costly for the well-being of the family and the child. Similarly, Heymann and Earle (1999) examine parents who voluntarily left welfare for work during the early 1990s and find that "thirty-six percent of mothers who returned to work from welfare lacked sick leave the entire time they worked, in comparison with 20% of mothers [who had never received welfare]" (p. 503) and that mothers returning to work are also less likely to receive other paid leave or flexibility. Those authors conclude that welfare recipients required to return to work under the 1996 legislation may "face working conditions that make it difficult or impossible to succeed in the workplace while caring well for their children's health and development needs" (Heymann & Earle, 1999, p. 504).

Clampet-Lundquist et al.'s account of mothers' experiences in trying to meet basic family needs en route from welfare to work allows us to identify a variety of possible threats to effective childrearing and child outcomes. We learn of various circumstances that lead to dangerous childcare situations, ranging from leaving young children unattended to relying on the children's fathers, siblings, or grandparents, or other acquaintances who lack the skills, maturity, emotional stability, and/or social-cognitive resources to attend to the children's health, safety, and social and cognitive growth. In some instances, young siblings are called upon to care for brothers or sisters with extraordinary health and behavioral needs (prevalent among this population), threatening the well-being of both the care-giving and care-receiving siblings. We also find that the paperwork burden experienced by many childcare providers contributes to their stress and irritability, leading some to refuse to provide continuing service, and causing some mothers to forego use of their childcare subsidy in order to retain a provider (thus taking on additional financial strain). Each of these circumstances undoubtedly influences the child's environment in adverse ways (e.g., increasing instability of childcare, creating caregiver and maternal strain, and decreasing family resources).

In terms of healthcare, we learn of situations in which income with overtime pay surpasses the Medicaid ceiling, leaving the family without healthcare insurance for the month. We hear of circumstances in which mothers reduce the dosage of their children's prescribed medications and/or use friends' "left-over" medications when their own supplies dwindle. And Clampet-Lundquist et al. inform us (citing Garrett & Holahan, 2000) that a significant proportion of women who leave welfare report no Medicaid benefits for themselves or their families despite their continued eligibility, most likely due to the administrative hassles that are involved, potential stigma, and caseworkers' misinformation as well as use of sanctions. These scenarios pose serious threats to child healthcare.

Even in the best of times, when supports (e.g., food stamps, Medicaid, and childcare subsidies) are available, the time demands of process and paperwork appear overwhelming to some mothers, undoubtedly affecting their sense of availability and energy for their children. That being said, we can only imagine the tenor of the household when there are gaps in work supports. Not only are the needed resources (food, child supervision, healthcare) insufficient, but associated tension, stress, and perhaps maternal guilt will likely disturb childrearing and family interactions. Yoshikawa (1999) reports a relationship between support services (such as childcare) and maternal earnings and child math, reading, and vocabulary scores, suggesting the value of "welfare reform approaches that emphasize long-term human capital development" (p. 779). Clampet-Lundquist et al. conclude their analysis by emphasizing that the *need* for transitional benefits is not short-term, contrary to the program's assumptions. A more collaborative approach to welfare reform would introduce stakeholders and resources that could help to support a longer-term provision of benefits, thus securing more long-term success and sustainability in the transition from welfare to work. At the same time, it is clear that we need to conduct research that goes beyond analyses of simple relationships between welfare-to-work transitions and child outcomes. We must examine mediators of these relationships, such as the sorts of family and parenting dynamics that may link maternal stress, employment, and skill development to outcomes.

Conclusion

As we venture forward on this journey through welfare reform, it is clear that we can only be effective if we do this together, that is, if the many and diverse stakeholders are engaged in a collaborative effort to inform and improve program design, implementation, monitoring/
evaluation, and revision. By drawing diverse stakeholders into this problem-solving process, we benefit from the knowledge, skills, and resources each brings to the effort; we prosper from the stakeholder coordination, network, and shared commitment that is created; and, at the same time, we build the strengths and capacities of each partner individually, as well as together. Our own work with extremely poor, isolated, rural mothers of young children reveals that contexts which foster the development and acknowledgment of voice and mind are powerful settings for nurturing women's abilities to support their own development as well as the development of others (Belenky et al., 1997; Bond, Belenky, & Weinstock, 2000). Thus, the very process of engaging in highly mutual, respectful collaboration itself should go a long way in helping to achieve a number of the goals of welfare reform and to promote mothers' abilities to support themselves, their families, and their communities.

Early in this chapter, we suggested the creation of a volume of "Collected Stories of Welfare to Work" that would augment Clampet-Lundquist et al.'s account of mothers' experiences with additional chapters by each of a variety of stakeholders: children, grandparents, partners, and other family members, caseworkers, state and federal administrators and policy makers, local employers, and co-workers, among others. These chapters would provide us with a starting point for reviewing and refining welfare reform programs to be more effective in addressing stakeholders' diverse needs, goals, and joint responsibilities. Of course, rather than limit the volume to a collection of separately authored chapters, we hope that ultimately such a book could conclude with a chapter co-authored by all of these constituents. That chapter would recount a *collective journey* that reflects the collaboration of stakeholders in program planning, implementation, review, and modification. Unlike earlier chapters, the concluding piece would blur many of the previous distinctions between stakeholders' perspectives because shared understanding and responsibilities will have merged these to some degree. Collaborative partnerships are not simple, but we have increasing guidelines for ways in which to forge them with greater ease (e.g., see Carmola Hauf & Bond, 2002). Without such collaboration it seems inevitable that the road from welfare to work will be overburdened with the frustrations and harm to a variety of stakeholders that Clampet-Lundquist et al. have brought to light.

References

Banyard, V. L. (1995). "Taking another route": Daily survival narratives from mothers who are homeless. *American Journal of Community Psychology, 23,* 871–891.

Belenky, M. F., Bond, L. A., & Weinstock, J. S. (1997). *A tradition that has no name: Nurturing the development of people, families and communities.* New York: Basic Books.

Bond, L. A., Belenky, M. F., & Weinstock, J. S. (2000). The Listening Partners Program: An initiative toward feminist community psychology in action. *American Journal of Community Psychology, 28,* 697–730.

Bond, L. A., & Carmola Hauf, A. (in press). Taking stock and putting stock in primary prevention: Characteristics of effective programs. *Journal of Primary Prevention.*

Brady-Smith, C., Brooks-Gunn, J., Waldfogel, J., & Fauth, R. (2001). Work or welfare? Assessing the impacts of recent employment and policy changes on very young children. *Evaluation and Program Planning, 24*(4), 409–425.

Brooks-Gunn, J., Klebanov, P., Smith, J. R., & Lee, K. (2001). Effects of combining public assistance and employment on mothers and their young children. *Women & Health, 32,* 179–210.

Carmola Hauf, A. M., & Bond, L. A. (2002). Community-based collaboration in prevention and mental health promotion:. Benefiting from and building the resources of partnership. *The International Journal of Mental Health Promotion, 4,* 41–54.

Colby, S. M., & Murrell, W. (1998) Child welfare and substance abuse services: From barriers to collaboration. In R. L. Hampton, V. Senatore, & T. P. Gullotta (Eds.), *Substance abuse, family violence, and child welfare: Bridging perspectives* (pp. 188–219). Thousand Oaks, CA: Sage.

Dalton, J. H., Elias, M. J., & Wandersman, A. (2001). *Community psychology: Linking individuals and communities.* Stamford, CT: Thomson Learning.

Fetterman, D. M., Kaftarian, S., & Wandersman, A. (Eds.). (1996). *Empowerment Evaluation: Knowledge and tools for self-assessment and accountability.* Thousand Oaks, CA: Sage.

Garrett, B., & Holahan, J. (2000). *Welfare leavers, medical coverage, and private health insurance.* Washington, DC: Urban Institute.

Gennetian, L. A., & Miller, C. (2002). Children and welfare reform: A view from an experimental welfare program in Minnesota. *Child Development, 73,* 601–620.

Gyamfi, P. (2002). When welfare-dependent mothers become employed: Implications for single black mothers and their children. *Dissertation Abstracts International, 62*(10). 4817B (UMI No. 3028526).

Heymann, S. J., & Earle, A. (1999). The impact of welfare reform on parents' ability to care for their children's health. *American Journal of Public Health, 89,* 502–505.

Linney, J. A., & Wandersman, A. (1996). Empowering community groups with evaluation skills: The Prevention Plus III Model. In D. Fetterman, S. Kaftarian, & A. Wandersman (Eds.), *Empowerment evaluation: Knowledge and tools for self-assessment and accountability* (pp. 259–276). Thousand Oaks, CA: Sage.

Parcel, T. L., & Menaghan, E. G. (1997). Effects of low-wage employment on family well-being. *Future of Children, 7*(1), 116–121.

Romich, J. L., & Weisner, T. S. (2001). How families view and use lump-sum payments from the earned income tax credit. In G. J. Duncan & P. L. Chase-Lansdale (Eds.), *For better and for worse: Welfare reform and the well-being of children and families* (pp. 201–221). New York: Russell Sage Foundation.

Saegert, S. (1989). Unlikely leaders, extreme circumstances: Older black women building community households. *American Journal of Community Psychology, 17,* 295–316.

Scott, E. K., Edin, K., London, A. S., & Mazelis, J. M. (2001). My children come first: Welfare-reliant women's post-TANF views of work-family trade-offs and marriage. In G. J. Duncan & P. L. Chase-Lansdale (Eds.), *For better and for worse: Welfare reform and the well-being of children and families* (pp. 132–153). New York: Russell Sage Foundation.

Wilson, J. B., Ellwood, D. T., & Brooks-Gunn, J. (1995). Welfare-to-work through the eyes of children. In P. L. Chase-Lansdale & J. Brooks-Gunn (Eds.), *Escape from poverty: What makes a difference for children?* (pp. 63–86). Cambridge: Cambridge University Press.

Yoshikawa, H. (1999). Welfare dynamics, support services, mothers' earnings, and child cognitive development: Implications for contemporary welfare reform. *Child Development, 70,* 779–801.

16

THE GROWING COMPLIANCE BURDEN FOR RECIPIENTS OF PUBLIC ASSISTANCE

Andrew J. Cherlin
Johns Hopkins University

Whether women who move from welfare to work increase their net income has been much debated. In the early 1990s, it appeared that gains in earnings were largely erased by losses in benefits and work-related expenses (Edin & Lein, 1997). But during the 1990s, the Earned Income Tax Credit (EITC) rose sharply, the minimum wage was increased, and the economy grew ever stronger. By the end of the decade, it appeared that moving from welfare to work did pay. Daniziger et al. (2002) report that in a sample of welfare recipients in Michigan followed for two years, work did lead to a net gain in income, on average. But this average incorporates substantial variation in individual outcomes. The chapter by Clampet-Lunquist et al. (this volume) suggests that whether a woman ends up on the positive or negative side of the average depends, in part, on whether she is successful in obtaining a post-TANF package of benefits. The findings from their ethnographic study suggest how difficult it is for mothers who have recently left welfare to comply with the procedures for obtaining and maintaining all the benefits they need.

In this chapter I will present some evidence that bears upon these points from a survey of low-income families in Boston, Chicago, and San Antonio. I will argue that the compliance burden is rooted in administrative practices and procedures that place a higher priority on avoiding the provision of benefits to the unqualified than to providing benefits broadly to all who may be eligible. Federal and state agencies require recipients to file documentation repeatedly and attend meetings frequently in order to remain eligible for benefits. I will discuss the origins of the current compliance burden and suggest some reasons why obtaining a reliable stream of benefits may now be more difficult than ever.

The Origins of the Compliance Burden

The need for recipients to fill out many forms, provide considerable information, and attend regular meetings did not originate with PRWORA. The rise of the compliance burden can be traced to two developments in the 1960s and 1970s. First, the AFDC caseload doubled between 1965 and 1975, creating public concern about the cost of the program. Second, there was a general realization that the composition of the AFDC caseload had shifted since the origins of the program in the 1930s. At first most of the recipients were widows, and they were largely white. But by the 1960s, the majority of recipients were divorced, separated, or never-married; moreover, they were disproportionately black and Hispanic. Whether rightly or wrongly, the general public was much less sympathetic to providing cash assistance to the latter group, especially as AFDC expenditures increased. Anecdotal reports of individuals who were abusing welfare abounded, although few were substantiated. As a result, federal officials pressured state welfare agencies to reduce error rates and to eliminate "waste" and "fraud" or face financial penalties. State officials, in turn, encouraged caseworkers to enforce strict rules that required frequent filings of information on employment, income, household composition, and the like, and attendance at meetings at regular intervals and upon request of the caseworker (Handler, 1995).

Officials argued that agencies have the right to the information needed to determine eligibility and that no eligible family need be punished. But as Lipsky (1984) observed in his essay on bureaucratic disentitlement, "From the bottom up, however, the developments looked like increases in harassment and the addition of degrading difficulties in maintaining eligibility" (pp. 8–9). To judge from the Clampet-Lundquist et al. chapter, they still do. These complex requirements pose a considerable challenge for parents with little education, language barriers, health problems, or tumultuous daily lives. Yet these are some of the very families who are now, for the first time, being pushed into the labor force in large numbers as work requirements reach down to the less educated.

Moreover, this system—designed at a time when fewer welfare mothers and middle-class mothers worked—paradoxically assumes that mothers who need assistance are not working outside the home. Therefore, the system assumes that parents have the time to visit a social service agency whenever a caseworker thinks it necessary and to fill out forms regularly. But now, because of work requirements and time limits, more and more low-income mothers are working. Consequently, they have serious time constraints and often cannot take the time to make the multiple visits to agencies that are required to obtain the benefits they need and are entitled to get.

Sanctions for Noncompliance

Findings on sanctions and administrative case closings from a study of low-income families complement the examples presented by Clampet-Lundquist et al. on the difficulties that families have in complying with the rules required to obtain and keep program benefits. The study is being carried out in Boston, Chicago, and San Antonio. It includes a longitudinal survey of over 2,000 families with children 0–4 years of age and 10–14 years of age in low-income neighborhoods, about 40% of whom were receiving case welfare payments when they were first interviewed in 1999. It also includes an ethnographic study of 241 families residing in the same neighborhoods as the survey families. The survey data I will present are from the first wave, conducted between March and September 1999 with a response rate of 74%. Low- and moderate-income households with children in the specified age range who were living with female caregivers—mothers, in 90% of the cases—were sampled. We interviewed all the caregivers and the older children and their caregivers. We asked the caregivers whether they were currently receiving welfare (Temporary Assistance for Needy Families, or TANF). If not, we asked them whether they had received welfare in the previous two years—the period since most states had implemented the Personal Responsibility and Work Opportunity Reconciliation Act of 1996 (PRWORA). The ethnographers selected neighborhoods from among those incorporated in the survey. They then recruited families between June 1999 and December 2000 at formal childcare settings, such as Head Start, WIC, neighborhood community centers, local welfare offices, churches, and other public assistance agencies. Ethnographers met with each family an average of once or twice a month for 12–18 months and then twice at six-month intervals.[1]

A major feature of PRWORA is toughened penalties, or "sanctions," for noncompliance with program rules. According to one estimate, during the first few years of PRWORA, more families left the rolls because of sanctions than because they reached time limits (Goldberg & Schott, 2000). Prior to PRWORA, states had the authority to reduce a family's AFDC benefit—usually by withholding the adult's portion—if a mother did not comply with required work. This is known as a partial sanction. Under PRWORA, many more mothers are subject to work requirements; and states are allowed to withhold the entire grant—a full sanction—if the mother does not comply (U.S. Department of Health and Human Services, 2000). Thirty-four states have chosen to apply full sanctions. States may also impose full sanctions on recipients who do not cooperate with attempts to determine paternity or obtain child support payments. And states may impose partial sanctions on recipients who do not follow a variety of other rules, such as maintaining their children's attendance in school or keeping their children inoculated against certain illnesses. States have also long had the authority to close a recipient's case and terminate benefits if she did not follow administrative rules.

In our 1999 survey, we questioned the 1,262 caregivers who said they had received TANF at some point in the past two years about their experiences with sanctions and administrative case closings.[2] For those who had left, we asked whether it was because the welfare office said they were not following rules or for some other reason. Caregivers who said they had left for some other reason, or who had been receiving TANF continuously, were asked whether the welfare office

---

[1] See Winston et al. (1999).

[2] The survey results in this section and Figure 1 are drawn from Cherlin, Bogen, Quane, and Burton (2002).

had reduced their benefits at some point because the office said they were not following the rules. A full loss of benefits could have been due to a sanction or a case closing.[3] A partial loss of benefits could only have been due to a sanction. Four percent of the caregivers experienced a full loss of benefits and another 13% experienced a partial loss of benefits.

We asked everyone who had experienced a full or partial loss of benefits which rules they had not followed according to the welfare office. As Figure 16.1 shows, the most common reasons were missing an appointment or not filing paperwork. Together, these reasons accounted for more than half of the reductions and eliminations of benefits for not complying with rules. (The percentages in Figure 16.1 sum to slightly more than 100% because caregivers were allowed to give more than one reason, although less than one in ten did so.) In 11% of the cases, the caregivers reported either refusing to work or not showing up for work—the reasons that most people think of when they consider welfare sanctions. Yet penalties for work-related noncompliance were said by the caregivers to be far less common than penalties for meeting- or paperwork-related penalties.

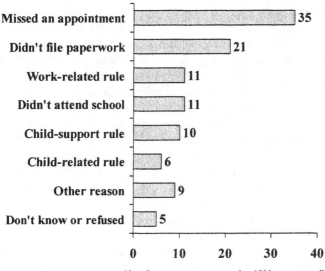

Note: Percentages sum to more than 100 because a small number of individuals gave more than one answer.

Figure 16.1.   Individuals' reports on which rules the welfare office said they were not following. (Source: Cherlin et al., 2002).

---

[3] We did not distinguish between full sanctions and administrative case closings because it was our impression that the respondents could not always make this distinction.

Our survey interviewers did not inquire further about what type of appointment was missed or what kind of paperwork was not filed. But the information from our ethnographic study suggests that few of the missed appointments involved job interviews or job-training activities. Rather, it would appear that the vast majority of the cases in these two categories involved failing to meet with caseworkers or failing to provide them with necessary documents.

Consider, for instance, Evelyn Santero (a pseudonym), a woman in our ethnographic sample who began working full-time in fall 1998 but still received reduced TANF benefits.[4] She was required to fill out a monthly form with information such as her income and work hours for the previous four weeks and who was living in her household. After she failed to submit the first form on time, the welfare office sent her a notification that she was in danger of losing her benefits. With the help of her daughters, she filled out the form and left it at the welfare office. The cycle of tardiness, warning, and just-in-time submission of the form continued for a few months. Finally, after apparently missing the filing deadline completely, she received a notice that her TANF and food stamp benefits had been suspended for "refusal to return the completed monthly report."[5]

Strictly speaking, Evelyn's loss of benefits was related to enforcing work: she failed to turn in a required form documenting her earnings and household composition on time. But Evelyn was not avoiding work; on the contrary, she was working full-time. There are several explanations for her noncompliance. Evelyn could not read well; her caseworker did not speak her native language, Spanish; and her phone had been disconnected for part of the time—all of which led to communication difficulties. She had never received pay stubs before, and she had difficulty completing the week-by-week income section. She also had other sources of stress that caused her to neglect the form: in addition to a holding a job that required a daily three-hour commute, she cared for six children and one grandchild and had a boyfriend threatening her with violence.

As Evelyn's case suggests, work requirements are drawing into the labor force mothers in families with limited education, daily lives filled with stress, and serious time constraints—the very families who find it most difficult to regularly perform the steps necessary to obtain and maintain benefits. In fact, we found, as have others (Pavetti & Bloom, 2001; U.S. General Accounting Office, 2000) that families who are sanctioned tend to be more disadvantaged in terms of health and education. Our sanctioned families were also less likely to have a telephone they could use or to own a car—two factors that could increase the difficulty of contacting caseworkers when procedural problems arise. We doubt that sanctions caused these limitations; rather, it appears that families with limitations such as these are less successful at filling out and sending in their forms and showing up at all required meetings. They then are sanctioned, which may increase their hardships.

---

[4] This description is drawn from Cherlin et al. (2001).

[5] The notice does not state whether Evelyn was sanctioned or whether her case was closed. It says only that the Department "will suspend" her "benefits" as of a certain date. However, the notice does provide numerical references to two articles of the Massachusetts welfare regulations, which indicate that her case was closed.

The Compliance Burden Today

The three-city study's information on sanctions and case closings suggests that the compliance burden is still with us today for TANF. The findings presented by Clampet-Lundquist et al. suggest as much for in-kind programs such as food stamps and childcare subsidies. But there are important differences between the caseloads of the 1970s and the 2000s that potentially make the problem even worse now. First, the requirement that more TANF recipients work, combined with more generous earnings disregards that keep people on the TANF rolls while they are working (until they either earn higher wages or reach a time limit), means that a larger share of the TANF caseload must now report on their earnings and employment. As the effort to move recipients into the workforce digs deeper into the caseload, it is reasonable to expect that a larger share of the new workers, like Evelyn, will have limited reading skills and little familiarity with the paperwork associated with earnings. They will be at high risk of failing to comply with administrative requirements.

Because more recipients are working, more of them face the time constraints any working parent must deal with. Moreover, employers in the low-wage market are probably less tolerant of tardiness and absences than are the employers of the middle-class. Low-wage employers have little invested in their workers, whom they can usually replace. They may be less understanding of the need to be late, leave early, or miss a day to remain in compliance. And low-wage workers can least afford to take an unpaid day off, even when employers will allow it. Indeed, our benefit system still takes the mid-twentieth-century AFDC as its model—a system in which relatively few recipients worked outside the home and in which food stamps and medical coverage were linked to the receipt of cash assistance. But just as the 1950s middle-class family no longer represents the norm, the 1950s welfare family does not either. It is a model in need of updating to fit twenty-first century realities.

In addition, as the caseload falls, the growing number of former recipients with modest earnings must apply for and maintain benefits separately for each program. As Clampet-Lundquist et al. note, food stamps, Medicaid, State Children's Health Insurance Program (SCHIP) benefits, childcare subsidies, and housing vouchers usually must be obtained separately, thus multiplying the compliance burden. Putting a post-TANF benefit package together requires great effort. It was not uncommon for non-TANF mothers in our ethnographic study to have multiple visits scheduled per month to obtain and maintain benefits. The difficulty was often compounded by the lack of an automobile or a telephone: one third of the respondents in the three-city study did not have a telephone they could regularly use at home.

Toward a New Social Contract?

Can this system be changed to better meet the needs of low-income employed mothers, whether receiving TANF or not? Perhaps the easiest fix would be to make benefit offices friendlier to working parents by opening early in the morning and remaining open into the evening. More difficult, but certainly possible, would be to provide clients not on TANF with a single caseworker who can help them obtain benefits from multiple programs—food stamps and childcare subsidies and SCHIP coverage for their children. Most difficult of all is to reduce the burden of compliance by simplifying forms, requiring verification less frequently, and minimizing meetings. It is possible on a modest scale: Clampet-Lundquist et al. point out that Philadelphia required monthly forms, whereas Cleveland required them quarterly. But to really accomplish this goal, we would have to modify the system so that it would place a higher priority on ensuring that working-poor parents get the support they need than on guarding against awarding benefits to ineligible families.

That change in priorities would require a political change because the compliance burden is rooted in the public's distaste for welfare. Survey after survey has shown that Americans think the U.S. spends too much on welfare but not enough on assisting the poor. Some observers have predicted that the emergence of work requirements and time limits may help change the public's views. If welfare recipients are willing to work, so this argument goes, then the public may be more receptive to expanding the public support available to them (Heclo, 2001). This would be a new social contract; or, as England and Folbre (2001) more aptly name it, a "contingent" social contract: if you work, we will be more generous in providing assistance.

If the contingent social contract were to emerge, it might ease public anxiety enough to move agencies' priorities away from preventing fraud and toward providing a reliable stream of benefits to all workers who qualify for them. And work supports *have* expanded over the past decade; for example, the government now spends more money on the EITC than on TANF. In fact, the EITC is the program most often mentioned as indicative of a contingent social contract. Essentially a wage supplement for low-income workers with children, the EITC has enjoyed bipartisan support in Congress. But despite the expansion of the EITC and the massive reduction in the welfare rolls, it is not clear that the much-vaunted new social contract has emerged. No studies suggest so far that the administrators of means-tested programs have shifted their emphasis from minimizing error to easing the compliance burden. Whether the political climate will allow for, even encourage, this shift is a key factor in whether the working poor and near-poor will be able amass the supports they need to truly make work pay.

References

Cherlin, A. J., Burton, L., Francis, J., Henrici, J., Lein, L., Quane, J., & Bogen, K. (2001). *Sanctions and case closings for noncompliance: Who is affected and why* (Policy Brief 01-1). Retrieved October 2, 2002, from Johns Hopkins University web site: http://www.jhu.edu/~welfare/18058_Welfare_Policy_Brief.pdf

Cherlin, A. J., Bogen, K., Quane, J. M., & Burton, L. (2002). Operating within the rules: Welfare recipients' experiences with sanctions and case closings. *Social Service Review, 76*, 387–405.

Danziger, S., Heflin, C. M., Corcoran, M. E., Oltmans, E., & Wang, H. (2002). Does it pay to move from welfare to work? *Journal of Policy Analysis and Management, 21*, 671–692.

Edin, K., & Lein, L. (1997.) *Making ends meet: How single mothers survive welfare and low-wage work.* New York: Russell Sage Foundation.

England, P., & Folbre, N. (2001). Reforming the social family contract: Public support for child rearing in the United States. In G. J. Duncan & P. L. Chase-Lansdale (Eds.), *For better or worse: Welfare reform and the well-being of children and families* (pp. 290–306). New York: Russell Sage Foundation.

Goldberg, H., & Schott, L. (2000). *A compliance-oriented approach to sanctions in state and county TANF programs.* Washington, DC: Center on Budget and Policy Priorities.

Handler, J. F. (1995). *The poverty of welfare reform.* New Haven: Yale University Press.

Heclo, H. (2001). The politics of welfare reform. In R. Blank & R. Haskins (Eds.), *The new world of welfare* (pp. 169–201). Washington, DC: Brookings Institution.

Lipsky, M. (1984). Bureaucratic disentitlement in social welfare programs. *Social Service Review, 58*, 3–27.

Pavetti, L., & Bloom, D. (2001). State sanctions and time limits. In R. Blank & R. Haskins (Eds.), *The new world of welfare* (pp. 245–269). Washington, DC: Brookings Institution.

U.S. Department of Health and Human Services. (2000). *Temporary Assistance for Needy Families (TANF) Program: Third annual report to Congress.* Washington, DC: U.S. Government Printing Office.

U.S. General Accounting Office. (2000). *Welfare reform: State sanctions policies and number of families affected.* Washington, DC: Author.

Winston, P., Angel, R. J., Burton, L. M., Chase-Lansdale, P. L., Cherlin, A .J., Moffitt, R. A., & Wilson, W. J. (1999). *Welfare, children, and families: Overview and design.* Retrieved March 18, 2003, from Johns Hopkins University web site: http://www.jhu.edu/~welfare/overviewanddesign.pdf

17

BALANCING WORK AND FAMILY: PROBLEMS AND SOLUTIONS FOR LOW-INCOME FAMILIES

Daniel N. Hawkins
Shawn D. Whiteman
The Pennsylvania State University

Over the last 50 years, the traditional mother-homemaker, father-breadwinner family has been increasingly replaced by two-parent, dual-earner families and single-parent, single-earner families. As a result of this shift in work-family arrangements, researchers and policy makers have directed greater attention toward the connections between work and family life. Historically, sociological and psychological research, dating back to classic work by Kohn (1969), has been concerned with the way work conditions and personality variables relate to mothers' and fathers' parenting and socialization behaviors. Likewise, economists have connected notions of human capital to the study of work and family (e.g., Becker, 1988). Today, however, as the proportion of families adhering to "traditional" work and family structures diminishes, researchers and policy makers are presented with a unique and challenging opportunity to critically examine and adjust work and family policies to better fit current work and family conditions.

The current volume brings together a diverse set of scholars who have taken on this challenge to examine the ways in which low-income families in particular negotiate work and family life. Specifically, the research covered within this volume examines how the availability and prevalence of low-income work has changed over the past 25 years, how aspects of work timing affect families, how low-income families manage work roles and childcare, and how the challenges of juggling jobs, childcare, and compliance with welfare rules are experienced by low-income mothers, especially as they move from welfare to work. We identify four major themes presented here that link these diverse topics. First, low-income work is here to stay as a permanent and growing part of the American economy (Bernstein, this volume). Second, much of this low-income work operates within a 24/7 economy that creates additional scheduling and logistical problems for families (Presser, this volume). Third, possibly the greatest challenge to low-income families in the current economy is finding affordable and available childcare (Huston, this volume). And fourth, the challenges that low-income families need to meet are especially obvious and pressing for those families who are moving from welfare to work, as difficulties in balancing work and family are heightened by the compliance regulations surrounding this process (Clampet-Lundquist et al., this volume). We begin by reviewing the current status of low-income work in the United

States and continue by examining how low-income work and current policies are linked to work timing, childcare arrangements, and welfare-to-work transitions. Finally, we conclude by presenting possible directions for future research.

Low-Wage Work Issues

Defining Low-Wage Work

Providing a comprehensive definition of low-wage work is a complex and somewhat arbitrary process. Although a complete description of low-wage work is beyond the scope of this chapter, research suggests that a definition should consider many different factors. First, following the theoretical framework of "segmented labor markets," Bernstein (this volume) asserts that the secondary labor market is primarily composed of low-wage work. Within this lower-wage market, Bernstein derives an hourly wage of $8.70 for full-time year-round employment as the threshold for poverty status in 2001. Nevertheless, this figure is based on the threshold level for a family of four, and thus does not consider either family size or income in its final analysis. This is unfortunate, since a broader perspective of low-wage work may be gained if factors such as family structure, family size, worker age, degree of attachment to the labor force, and cost of living were considered when calculating the "poverty level wage" statistics (Bernstein, this volume; Casper & King, this volume). Additionally, as noted by Jensen and Slack (this volume), in order to gain a more complete picture of the low-wage job market, it is important to consider extending the notions of low-wage work to groups such as the underemployed.

Low-Wage Work: Past, Present, and Future

Although low-wage work can be defined in different ways, researchers agree that low-wage work appears to be a permanent fixture of the United States economy. Despite an overall economic boom in recent years, the proportion of poor in the United States remains relatively constant (Bernstein, this volume). This implies that the growth in income has occurred disproportionately at the high end of the pay distribution, while individuals at the lower end of the pay spectrum have experienced static wages. In fact, from 1970 to 1995, wages at the bottom half of the pay distribution did not keep up with inflation rates. Although this pattern changed with a slight increase in wages at the bottom half of the pay distribution during the economic boom of the late 1990s, whether this will continue remains to be seen under the current administration (Bernstein, this volume). It is possible that families relying on low-wage jobs will have more financial difficulties than ever before. Furthermore, despite relative and projected growth over the last 20 years in high-wage, high-skilled jobs, mainly related to the technology industry, low-wage jobs such as those in the service industry have experienced and will likely continue to experience the greatest absolute growth. If these employment patterns continue, it is especially important for researchers and policy makers to continue to identify who primarily composes this segment of the economy and examine the ways in which low-wage work influences family dynamics and family functioning.

Who Are Low-Wage Workers?

Although current employment statistics suggest that the United States economy is moving towards a more egalitarian work force in terms of gender and racial composition, statistics presented by Bernstein in this volume reveal that low-wage workers are disproportionately female and minority. This is an interesting observation in the face of statistics that reveal that the gender gap in pay is diminishing (Bernstein, this volume). A closer inspection reveals that this erosion is the result of two separate factors. First, an examination of both the high- and low-wage labor markets indicates the high-wage labor market is largely influencing increases in women's wages. That is, the desegregation of the labor market is occurring at the high end, where women are increasingly moving into high-paying careers that require many years of education. In contrast, the erosion of the sex gap in pay in the low-wage labor market appears to be the result of the slow attrition of men's blue collar market jobs, as opposed to the increase in women's wages (England, this volume). This indicates that researchers and policy makers should attend to both between- and within-group differences when evaluating trends in the labor market.

In addition to focusing attention on sex differences within the low-wage labor market, another area in need of research and policy attention is how family and household structure are connected to the labor market. As families continue to move away from a traditional two-parent, single-earner structure (see Casper and King, this volume), it is important to examine how shifts in household composition can increase inequalities. Data show that in both absolute and relative levels, married, dual-earner families have enjoyed the highest per capita income and the greatest percentage income increases over time as compared to all other family types. Single-parent families, both mother- and father-headed, fare much worse, with up to 30% of families headed by single-parent mothers experiencing wages at or below poverty levels. These figures imply that single-headed families may be more reliant on their earnings; as such, these families should be the targets of political policy.

Work Timing Issues

Low-Wage Work and Work Timing

Over the past 30 years, the United States economy has undergone drastic transformations. In both absolute and relative terms, employment has risen, while rates of unemployment have decreased, at least over the last 10 years (Bernstein, this volume; Presser, this volume). There are several reasons for these changes in rates of employment and unemployment, but one of the most prominent explanations has to do with the shift towards a "24/7" economy. In the United States, many groceries, retail stores, restaurants, convenience stores, and even factories are open for business 24 hours a day, 7 days a week. As a society, we often expect that no matter the time of day, we should be able to find an open store to meet our needs. Yet, in order for businesses to remain open and operating at all hours of the day, employees will be required to work "non-standard" shifts, or shifts other than the 9–5 work day. As Presser notes (this volume), there have been dramatic increases in the percentage of workers who work non-standard shifts and fringe-time jobs that start before 9 in the morning or end after 6 at night. While health investigators have long explored the individual health consequences of non-standard shift work, only recently have researchers begun to consider the family consequences of such work. We now review the links between non-standard shift work and family life presented in this volume.

Non-Standard Shift Work and Family Relationships

In a thorough review of the empirical literature, Presser (this volume) notes that across a number of studies non-standard shift work is negatively related to marital happiness, marital quality, and marital stability. Importantly, Presser shows that many of the negative links between non-standard shift work and marital happiness, satisfaction, and daily contact are especially pronounced for couples with children. This point highlights the importance of studying family units as whole systems, instead of as a sum of individuals, when considering the links between work and family.

In contrast to marital relationships, a mixed pattern of findings has emerged concerning the parent-child relations of individuals who work non-standard shifts. This group of parents has been found to spend less time with their children eating dinner and participating in leisure activities (Presser, this volume), especially when non-standard shift work includes weekend work (Almeida, this volume). Non-standard shift work is also related to more transitions between parents between shifts. In other words, in families with at least one parent working a non-standard work schedule, parents only have a small period of time to communicate with each other about what needs to be done around the house, which child needs to be picked up where, and who needs help with their homework, before the other has to leave for work. In fact, Daly (this volume) has wryly termed parenting associated with many transitions as "tag-team parenting." That is, when one parent has to leave for work, he or she will tag the other parent to take over the parenting role. Although this type of transition between parents may create added difficulties in tagging in and out of the parenting role, it does allow for is less reliance on non-relative childcare. According to research on parents who work non-standard shifts, these parents are less likely to utilize childcare facilities, relying instead on familial resources (Perry-Jenkins, this volume; Presser, this volume). As such, non-standard shifts may be more attractive to those parents who do not want to rely on others for childcare or do not have the financial resources to afford quality care.

In discussing how non-standard shifts affect family life, Perry-Jenkins, Daly, and Almeida highlight the importance of studying how the transitions between parents are made. Daly suggests that these interactions between parents are a "third shift," or another area in which parents must invest time and energy in simply coordinating family life. Within this third shift, families in which at least one parent works a non-standard shift are likely to experience temporal friction between work and family schedules, and thus difficulty in coordinating family activities (Almeida, this volume). With limited time for face-to-face interaction, how are parents to manage such tasks? Daly (this volume) suggests investigating a variety of under-explored questions such as whether "to-do lists" are passed from one parent to another and whether parents take advantage of new technology such as cell phones, pagers, and e-mail. However, many of these strategies may be prohibitively expensive for many low-income parents.

Most importantly, in our view, the researchers within this volume identify the need to study the roles of all members of the family during these transitions. Children themselves may play important roles in managing them. How accurately and reliably children pass messages from one parent to another may have important consequences for family life. This consideration of children as managers and mediators of their mothers' and fathers' parenting transitions highlights the importance of moving research towards treating the family as the unit of analysis, allowing for the exploration of differences both between and within families. In doing so, topics such as how husbands compared to wives parent and carry out household tasks and how sons may be given more or less responsibility compared to daughters can be studied. Similarly, in addition to exploring how families may differ in terms of how they manage these transitions, Almeida highlights the importance of analyzing the temporal rhythms of family schedules, because, in combination with work schedules, they drive the coordination of family life.

Low-Wage Work and Non-Standard Shifts

Throughout this section we have reviewed the links between non-standard employment hours and family life without focusing on low-wage workers. As Perry-Jenkins notes, non-standard shift work is especially salient for low-income families with young children for a variety of reasons. First, low-wage jobs are often tied to service industries that require non-standard shift work. As such, these employers will demand that their employees work schedules that may or may not be congruent with their family agendas. Additionally, because in absolute terms these jobs are on the rise (Bernstein, this volume), we can expect that more families will experience greater temporal friction between their work and family lives. Second, due to the rising expense of childcare, low-wage workers may elect to work non-standard shifts in order to minimize the necessity for non-familial childcare. Moreover, low-wage workers may also elect to work more fringe times in order to gain greater overtime opportunities to help with other financial constraints. Yet, from this perspective, non-standard shift work can also make finding satisfactory childcare arrangements more difficult. Quality, non-familial childcare is often not available during non-traditional shifts, and this lack may deter parents from working extra hours. This also implies that single parents may have the most difficulty balancing non-standard shift work and childcare because services may not be available for their children when they are at work. Policy makers need to consider how policy affects non-standard shift workers and their families. Further implications for childcare will be discussed in the next section.

Childcare Issues

Childcare Challenges for Low-Income Families

One of the major challenges facing low-income families is obtaining adequate childcare. The availability of and access to childcare are pressing issues facing low-income families. The supply of childcare is especially limited for parents living in low-income and rural neighborhoods, and these parents often lack the ability to transport their children to more distant facilities (Huston, this volume). An even more relevant issue is that childcare is quite expensive, costing parents up to 25% of their total income (Huston, this volume). While childcare subsidies are available to low-income parents, only 15–20% of eligible children are receiving such aid, often only for a brief time (Huston, this volume; Thorne, this volume). Many factors cause such a small percentage of children to receive childcare through subsidies. First, childcare providers often do not receive full reimbursement from subsidies, especially when parents cannot afford required co-payments. As a result, providers limit the numbers of unsubsidized children they accept (Huston, this volume). Second, parents who do not receive welfare are actually at a disadvantage in obtaining subsidies, because priority is given to families receiving cash assistance and much of the information about subsidy availability is distributed through welfare caseworkers (Huston, this volume). Finally, administrative barriers such as multiple required office visits and caseworker misinformation add difficulties in acquiring and maintaining eligibility (Clampet-Lundquist et al., this volume). In addition, "notch effects," in which parents slightly increase their income but lose their eligibility, further disadvantage low-income families.

Ironically, low-income families who are able to obtain childcare may actually miss out on important opportunities to enhance their children's development. As Huston (this volume) details, childcare encompasses two main functions: support for maternal employment and developmental enrichment for children. Unfortunately for many low-income families, the policies that support these two goals are often in conflict. Women who utilize welfare-to-work programs increase their use of childcare, but are not able to take advantage of educational programs for children such as Head Start because their new work schedules are not conducive to participation (Huston, this volume). Zaslow (this volume) takes a somewhat different view, suggesting that there have been exciting developments in integrating the two policy streams. She points to new employment support policies that contain developmental enhancement components, early development programs that have attempted to increase the supply of childcare, and state-initiated policies that support both children's school readiness and parental employment. The question that remains to be answered is whether or not current trends in integration will lead to lasting and meaningful change that will simultaneously support childcare as a work support and as educational enrichment.

Another concern for low-income families utilizing childcare is the overall quality of that care. Low-income children are especially vulnerable to the detrimental effects of low-quality care on their cognitive development (Raver, this volume). In addition, low-quality preschool environments may contribute to the finding that high-risk, low-income children are more likely to exhibit behavioral problems than the general population of preschoolers (Raver, this volume). The quality of care is generally defined by structural features such as class size, and by caregiver qualities such as the extent to which they are cognitively stimulating, sensitive, and responsive in their interactions with children (Huston, this volume; Raver, this volume). Unfortunately, many care providers face major stressors in their attempts to provide quality care. There are great demands on their time and attention, they receive little emotional support in the classroom, they are often forced to work with inadequate material resources, and they are paid very little (Raver, this volume). In fact, many childcare workers are low-income parents themselves. These stressful working conditions can lead to emotional negativity at work with the children, thus reducing the quality of care (Raver, this volume).

How Do Low-Income Families Meet Childcare Needs?

Qualitative research shows that low-income parents turn to diverse and often complex strategies to acquire childcare when their needs are not being met through traditional avenues. Clampet-Lundquist et al. and Thorne relate several stories that reveal the multitude of ways that parents, especially single mothers, patch together childcare. These strategies required such activities as long bus rides for children or parents bringing their children into work for extended periods of time. Parents call on a combination of church services, kindly neighbors, unreliable relatives, and overwhelmed older siblings to provide childcare. They are often uncomfortable with these childcare arrangements, which put their children in potentially dangerous situations and can be especially prone to breaking down. Clearly, most parents would prefer more reliable childcare situations, but adopt these alternative strategies out of necessity. Helping low-income parents find and hang onto affordable, accessible, high-quality childcare remains an important challenge for federal, state, and local policy makers.

Policies to Improve Childcare for Low-Income Families

Suggestions in this volume for how to improve childcare for low-income families range from reconceptualizing our view of childcare down to specific policies that have been or could be implemented. In Thorne's alternative vision of childcare, a collective, rather than privatized, responsibility for care comes to the forefront. This vision also relies on childcare becoming more valued in our society and on men balancing work and family responsibilities to same extent that women do. While this task is both tall and noble, specific programs and policies may move this vision in the right direction. Huston discusses several programs that provide expanded childcare assistance to families and include the promotion of formal care, enhanced support services, efficient reimbursement of payments to providers, restriction of subsidies to regulated care, and reduction of bureaucratic hassles related to obtaining subsidies. Overall, these expanded programs increase the utilization of childcare and reduce the costs to parents (Huston, this volume). This also suggests that a consolidation of programs and benefits would clearly help low-income families gain and maintain eligibility for access to childcare. In terms of the quality of care for low-income children, grants to improve caregiver resources and training would go a long way toward addressing deficits (Raver, this volume). In addition, the policies that integrate educational goals with work supports may also improve the cognitive development of children in center care (Zaslow, this volume).

Welfare-to-Work Issues

Meeting Basic Needs

Clampet-Lundquist et al. provide a wealth of qualitative research that depicts the experiences of mothers struggling to meet basic needs during the welfare-to-work transition. The basic needs these families require most are childcare, food, and medical coverage. As childcare has been discussed in the previous section, this part of the review focuses more on the latter two basic needs. The overriding theme of women's experiences with the welfare system is generally one of frustration and confusion. Most women in the Clampet-Lundquist et al. study experienced serious barriers to obtaining adequate food and health care. The main assistance to welfare-to-work families in terms of food resources is food stamps, but many mothers do not receive this important form of aid. The most commonly cited problem is conflict with caseworkers; clients claim that these individuals them gave misinformation, purposely misfiled papers, and sometimes directly insulted them. Many clients resorted to delivering their paperwork to the various welfare offices in person – a tedious and time-consuming task. In terms of medical care, misinformation from caseworkers and administrative hassles again prevented many women with eligible families from securing health insurance. Obtaining adequate medical coverage is especially imperative for families with special needs children, as out-of-pocket medical expenses would be overwhelming without some form of insurance. When parents cannot procure adequate food and medical care from public sources, they often turn to other avenues. Many mothers borrow from or barter with relatives for food or receive items from food pantries. Others resort to selling plasma for food money or even stealing from local grocery stores. For medical care, some women rely on emergency room visits, where they feel they will not be refused service, but which result in expensive and often unpaid bills.

Overall, it seems the greatest problem faced by mothers in meeting basic needs is dealing with their caseworkers. The reasons for the antagonistic behavior of the welfare caseworkers are unclear. Certainly, welfare casework may often be a difficult and unrewarding job. Clampet-Lundquist et al. suggest that caseworkers often contend with inadequate resources, high rates of staff turnover, insufficient training, and frustration with clients. Their motivation may flag due to low pay and high demands. It is also possible that clients misinterpret the behavior of harried caseworkers as unfriendly when caseworkers are actually reacting to the demands and limitations of their jobs. Nonetheless, caseworkers seem especially insensitive to the compliance burden faced by many welfare-to-work mothers.

Cherlin makes very clear just how deep the burden of compliance is for mothers attempting to receive public benefits. He argues that the main problem is administrative practices that focus more on denying benefits to unqualified families than on supplying them to those in need. In addition, the outdated design of the system assumes that women who need assistance are not working, even though the employment requirements of the new welfare system place major time constraints on now-working mothers. The most striking statistics from Cherlin's analysis are that more families leave the welfare rolls due to sanctions than expired time limits and that the most common reasons for receiving these sanctions are missing appointments or not filing paperwork. The families who are sanctioned tend to be disadvantaged in terms of education and health and are not receiving help in maintaining eligibility. In addition, food stamps, insurance benefits, childcare subsidies, and housing vouchers usually need to be obtained at separate sites, thereby increasing the transportation and paper work burdens. Overall, it seems that many families are meeting the major goal and requirement of welfare reform, namely employment, but are not receiving the full benefits entitled to them due to administrative hassles.

What is Effective and Ineffective in Moving Families from Welfare to Work?

The major finding of the study by Clampet-Lundquist et al. is that work supports for low-income families, not work itself, is the key to leaving the welfare rolls. While work does increase families' net incomes, they still must rely on money from transitional cash benefits, food stamps, and medical insurance. This is especially true for families who lack private safety nets to fall back on in hard times. The implication is that work supports are especially helpful as families attempt to get on their feet and adjust to the new demands and schedules required by employment. Such supports are crucial in the tentative period when welfare mothers first begin work. In terms of obtaining these work supports, the compliance burden can be greatly reduced by small changes in procedure, such as having clients file for subsidies on a quarterly rather than monthly basis.

Bond and Carmola Hauf (this volume) highlight a strategy with potentially vast benefits for successful welfare-to-work transitions that revolves around engaging diverse stakeholders in a collaborative effort. This strategy also includes improving the ongoing monitoring, evaluation, and modification of the current system. In addition, multiple safety nets within multiple systems are required; a suggestion inspired by Clampet-Lundquist et al.'s account of women with little in the way of private resources to fall back on. Possibly most importantly, simply the process of involving parents and their children in the process of welfare evaluation and change may be highly beneficial. Acknowledging low-income families' own creative coping strategies and providing them with a voice in the process can encourage the development of women's abilities and confidence as they move from welfare to work.

In contrast, Karney and Springer (this volume) make a strong point that the current administration may be misguided in some of their current attempts to aid families in moving from welfare to work. Programs to promote marriage for low-income, single mothers are currently being funded with a substantial amount of welfare money with the view that marriage will both prevent families from slipping into welfare and allow families to rise out of poverty. Karney and Springer (this volume) point to several problems with this line of reasoning and its implementation. Their basic argument is that direction of causality does not run from being unmarried to being in poverty, but instead that poverty makes the negotiation of a successful and happy marriage a very difficult prospect. It is the state of being happily married, not simply being married, that provides benefits to parents and children in terms of mental and physical health. The chronic and acute stresses that low-income couples face as a result of their economic situation give rise to great difficulties in devoting enough energy and time to the relationship and in positively evaluating the actions of one's spouse (Karney & Springer, this volume). All of these stressors exacerbate the problems of negotiating the work-family issues that have been discussed in this volume. The unintended result of such a program is that marriage as an attempt to keep families out of poverty may have serious negative consequences for their health and well-being. As a final note of caution, the programs that promote relationship education have been tested only on middle-class couples, not the low-income, highly-stressed families at which the current policy is aimed. Overall, the evidence that Karney and Springer present indicates that welfare funds would be better spent attacking poverty directly and providing some of the aforementioned work supports, rather than by promoting marriage.

Directions for Future Research

There are still many unanswered questions regarding the challenges faced by low-income families. In general, research on low-income families must continue due to recent changes in the economy. There is general caution on the part of the authors (e.g., Clampet-Lundquist et al., this volume) that the picture of life for low-income families presented may not be as positive in the year 2003, given the weakening of the economy and its implications for the effect of work on family life. Research in other specific areas is also needed. The first broad area includes the relationships among low-wage work, work timing, and family functioning. The second focuses on how low-income families meet basic needs such as childcare, food, and medical care, and what can be done to aid them in this endeavor.

There are many ways in which the links among low-wage work, nonstandard shifts, and family life can be investigated and detailed. First, as Perry-Jenkins notes, it is important for researchers to clarify definitions of non-standard work schedules so that the links between work and family life for those individuals who work different types of non-standard shifts can be analyzed separately. Yet, it is also necessary for researchers to expand notions of work schedules to consider additional kinds of work arrangements that include seasonal work, contingent or temporary work, and even work in the underground economy in order to gain a more complete picture of the links between work timing and family life. Second, it is important for researchers to also move towards treating the family as the unit of analysis so that both between- and within-family differences relating to work and family life can be explored. Such work would allow for the exploration of main effects from both parents' and children's characteristics and schedules as well as the ability to analyze the interactive effects between those characteristics and schedules. Third, as life-span developmental theory (Lerner, 1998) and ecological theory (Bronfenbrenner & Crouter, 1983) suggest, both the personal characteristics of the individuals and the social context play important roles in development (e.g., how do adolescents' work schedules affect family time and family income?). Researchers should attend to possible mediating and moderating factors of the links between work and family such as family structure, family size, length of marriage, age of parents and children, education, and occupational flexibility and complexity. Finally, researchers need to further explore the processes by which non-standard work shifts affect family dynamics such as family time and parenting. Undoubtedly, the patterns of relationships are complex, and as such it is important for researchers to take advantage of new methodologies, such as diary methods (see Almeida, this volume; Larson & Almeida, 1999; McHale, Crouter, & Tucker, 2001) and natural experiments that arise when governmental agencies institute new policies or laws.

The successes and failures of low-income families in meeting basic needs, especially childcare, should receive greater attention in the future. The enhanced benefits that lead to greater use of childcare and reduced fees for parents need to be examined in detail (Huston, this volume). At present, it is not clear which benefits affect which outcomes – this question needs to be answered to help streamline policy and allow funds to be directed where they are most needed. Furthermore, it is unknown whether these care enhancements work only in the context of welfare-to-work or whether all low-income parents would benefit from such aid (Zaslow, this volume). Future research should focus attention on both the positive and negative effects of center care. While center care is associated with cognitive gains in children, it also may lead to greater behavioral problems (Huston, this volume). Research in this area may not only lead to higher quality center care, but may also relieve some of the distrust that many low-income parents have toward formalized care. In terms of welfare-to-work studies, future research could focus on the relative lack of male involvement in the transition. By finding ways to encourage men to aid their families in moving from welfare to work, some of the barriers faced by low-income working mothers could be alleviated. One of the major barriers that women receiving public benefits will continue to face is difficulty with caseworker relationships. We need to better understand how caseworkers experience their own jobs and what assumptions they might make about their clients, as suggested by Bond and Carmola Hauf, if we are to improve caseworker-client relations. In general, we need more research on the way in which such factors as working for low wages, struggling to find childcare, and moving away from welfare affect various family relationships. To what extent do the stresses of working for low pay affect parent-child and couple relationships? How do children feel about their childcare situations? Do the economic gains of moving from welfare to work offset the stresses and strains that balancing work and family schedules can cause?

Conclusion

It is clear that more needs to done to help low-income parents and their children meet current work-family challenges. The research presented here brings us closer to this goal by demonstrating that low-wage work is here to stay, that scheduling demands related to balancing work and family are prevalent for low-wage workers, and that government policies truly can and do have a positive effect on both aiding low-income families in meeting important needs such as childcare and in leaving the welfare rolls. Yet this research also reveals that the problems associated with helping low-income families find gainful employment, obtain quality childcare arrangements, and receive benefits and supports from society are significant, widespread, and hard to solve. Recognizing that low-wage workers have an important role in our economy deserving of a living wage, and realizing that we as a society are all responsible for helping each other meet the demands that are required by work and family, would go a long way towards addressing this distressing situation. However, we should not expect to see such radical changes in the near future due to current political and economic realities. As such, researchers and policy makers are faced with the challenge of finding ways to improve the quality of life for low-income families by critically examining and improving upon existing programs within the current socio-political climate.

Acknowledgments

The authors wish to thank Alan Booth, Ann C. Crouter, Susan M. McHale, and Juliana McGene Sobolewski for their helpful comments.

References

Becker, G. S. (1988). Family economics and macro behavior. *American Economic Review,* *78,* 1–13.

Bronfenbrenner, U., & Crouter, A. C. (1983). The evolution of environmental models in developmental research. In P. Mussen (Ed.), *Handbook of Child Psychology* (pp. 358–414). New York: Wiley.

Kohn, M. L. (1969). *Class and conformity: A study in values.* Oxford, England: Dorsey.

Larson, R. W., & Almeida, D. M. (1999). Emotional transmission in the daily lives of families: A new paradigm for studying family process. *Journal of Marriage and the Family, 61,* 5–20.

Lerner, R. M. (1998). Theories of human development: Contemporary perspectives. In W. Damon (Ed.), *Handbook of child psychology, 5th ed.* (pp. 1–24). New York: Wiley.

McHale, S. M., Crouter, A. C., & Tucker, C. J. (2001). Free-time activities in middle childhood: Links with adjustment in early adolescence. *Child Development, 72,* 1764–1778.

Author Index

287

Subject Index